From Civil to Human Rights

For Matthias Mann

From Civil to Human Rights

Dialogues on Law and Humanities in the United States and Europe

Helle Porsdam

Professor of American Studies, University of Copenhagen, Denmark

Edward Elgar

Cheltenham, UK • Northampton, MA, USA

Published by
Edward Elgar Publishing Limited
The Lypiatts
15 Lansdown Road
Cheltenham
Glos GL50 2JA
UK

Edward Elgar Publishing, Inc.
William Pratt House
9 Dewey Court
Northampton
Massachusetts 01060
USA

A catalogue record for this book
is available from the British Library

Library of Congress Control Number: 2009930436

Mixed Sources
Product group from well-managed forests and other controlled sources
www.fsc.org Cert no. SA-COC-1565
© 1996 Forest Stewardship Council
FSC

ISBN 978 1 84720 901 6

Typeset by Cambrian Typesetters, Camberley, Surrey
Printed and bound by MPG Books Group, UK

Contents

Acknowledgements

For this book, I have relied on and quoted from the works of numerous other scholars. Among these works should be mentioned Henry J. Steiner and Philip Alston (eds.), *International Human Rights in Context: Law, Politics, Morals* (Oxford University Press, 2000 – second edition); Philip Alston (ed.), *The EU and Human Rights* (Oxford University Press, 1999); Gráinne de Búrca (ed.), *EU Law and the Welfare State: In Search of Solidarity*, (Oxford University Press, 2005); Michael D. Goldhaber, *A People's History of the European Court of Human Rights* (Rutgers University Press, 2007); Michael Ignatieff (ed.), *American Exceptionalism and Human Rights* (Princeton University Press, 2005); John F. Murphy, *The United States and the Rule of Law in International Affairs* (Cambridge University Press, 2004/2005); Geir Lundestad, *The United States and Western Europe Since 1945: From 'Empire' by Invitation to Transatlantic Drift* (Oxford University Press, 2003); and Anthony Pagden (ed.), *The Idea of Europe: From Antiquity to the European Union* (Woodrow Wilson Center Press & Cambridge University Press, 2002).

Parts of Chapters 1, 2 and 7 have been excerpted from my articles, 'From *Pax Americana* to *Lex Americana*: American Legal and Cultural Hegemony', in Fiona Macmillan (ed.), *New Directions in Copyright Law, Volume 1*, (Cheltenham, UK: Edward Elgar, 2005) and 'On European Narratives of Human Rights and Their Possible Implications for Copyright', in Fiona Macmillan (ed.), *New Directions in Copyright Law, Volume 6* (Cheltenham, UK: Edward Elgar, 2007). I thank Fiona Macmillan for allowing me to use these excerpts in this context. Also, in Chapter 8, I use an excerpt from my introduction to *Folkways and Law Ways: Law in American Studies* which I edited for Odense University Press in 2001. I thank Editor Martin Lindø Westergaard for giving his permission for me to do so. Finally, the idea of pursuing a civil-law approach to law and humanities, which I outline in Chapter 8, first came up in connection with my review essay, in *Law and Humanities*, vol.1, issue 1 (Summer 2008) of Kieran Dolin, *A Critical Introduction to Law and Literature*. I thank Editor Gary Watt for permission to reuse that idea and a couple of my paragraphs from this review essay here.

I furthermore wish to thank the following colleagues and friends who have been kind enough to read through and offer comments on some of my chapters: Mark Gibney, Ida Elisabeth Koch, Stéphanie Lagoutte, Dorte Sindbjerg Martinsen, Morten Rosenmeier, Karen-Margrethe Simonsen, Stina Teilmann,

Manuela Thurner, Kim Treiger-Bar-Am. Needless to say, whatever mistakes might still remain are my own – and not their – responsibility.

Special thanks are due to the Council of Europe (Publishing Division) for granting me permission to use the photo of the copy of the Magna Carta – donated to the Council of Europe by Great Britain – as the cover illustration for this book.

And finally, special thanks are due to my husband Matthias Mann as well as to our son Sebastian Porsdam Mann. It is a wonder how they find the patience to deal with their wife and mother, respectively, when she is heavily into her research and writing!

Introduction

In a call for papers for the 'Women in German Annual Conference 2007', the organizers introduce the notion of Europe as 'contested terrain':

> The transatlantic tensions in the run-up to the Iraq invasion produced, for a while, the heady possibilities of imagining Europe as counterweight to American-style globalization. And while some believe that that utopian window has closed, we think it is still necessary to explore Europe as contested terrain – caught between colonial, imperialist, fascist, and totalitarian histories and their legacies (Pim Fortuyn's Europe, as Arjun Appadurai has called it), and the enlightened, post-Eurocentric, antifascist Europe that is committed to learning its lessons from the past (Bassam Tibi's Europe).[1]

In this book, I, too, wish to explore Europe as contested terrain. For me, as for the organizers of the 'Women in German Annual Conference 2007', the point of departure is transatlantic tensions. Transatlantic feelings are not as warm as they used to be, and if Timothy Garton Ash is correct in his assessment that the old Atlantic-centered West only has about twenty more years in which to play at least some part in setting the agenda of world politics and in seeking solutions to global problems such as global warming, the widening gap between rich and poor countries, and terrorism, then it really is 'stupid for Europeans and Americans to waste any more time squabbling with each other'.[2]

The run-up to the Iraq invasion may indeed have made Americans on the Left view Europe as a counterweight to American-style globalization for a while. Chances are, though, that these Americans would soon have gone back to a much less positive view of Europe – one that would tend to associate Europe with genocide, colonialism and aggression (Pim Fontuyn's Europe). Let me mention one small personal experience as an illustration: on the evening in July 2006 when it became clear that the last four teams to remain

---

1 'Contesting Europe: Feminist Critiques and Globalization' – call for papers for the 'Women in German Annual Conference (WiG)', to be held at Snowbird, Utah, 18–21 October 2007. This call for papers used to be available at www.womeningerman.org (last visited on 3 March 2007).

2 Timothy Garton Ash, *Free World: America, Europe, and the Surprising Future of the West* (New York: Vintage Books, 2004), 176.

in the 2006 Football World Cup – the four semi-finalists, that is – were all European teams, an American friend informed me that she was very disappointed about this turn of events, and that she could never ever support a European team. To my amazed question why this was the case, she rather emphatically answered: 'Because Europe colonized South America'.

This was by no means the first time that I had encountered such an anti-European attitude on the part of otherwise well-meaning and progressive Americans. Within American Studies circles it has led, for example, to a refusal by some to deal with the European past of what was to become the United States. Instead, it is the Asian-American, the African-American and other non-European pasts that receive scholarly treatment. Europe, it would seem, has simply become politically incorrect.

On the European side, unfortunately, things do not look much better. I regularly teach courses on human rights, both to students at my own university and to students from all over Europe in the European Master's Degree in Human Rights and Democratisation in Venice.[3] To these students, who are always very dedicated to the promotion of human rights worldwide, I speak of American and European perceptions of human rights. Most often, these young Europeans have a hard time accepting that there may be reasons why the US is acting as it is. It is quite clear that the US is the absolute enemy for them. They point – not unreasonably – to the way in which the US refuses to ratify international human rights treaties and to support the International Criminal Court, as well as to the role played by various US administrations in fostering hostilities around the world. What always surprises me, however, is the lack of knowledge, on their part, of the strong American rights tradition and belief in the rule of law.

I always wonder during such encounters what can be done to ease transatlantic intellectual tensions. On the American side, left-wing anti-European sentiments have played into the hands of the George W. Bush administration and the contempt shown by its neo-conservative supporters toward what former Secretary of Defense Donald Rumsfeld famously called, a few years ago, 'Old Europe'. And on the European side, anti-American feelings have at times been so strong that they have exerted a powerful influence on European politics. What motivates me to write about this issue is the feeling or hope that it may help to remind people on both sides of the Atlantic of the intellectual and cultural heritage that unites us. A useful first step toward initiating dialogue with one's 'adversary' is to understand where this adversary comes from. Many scholars and writers have focused on that which separates us. This is important – but it is no less important to stress whatever common ground there may still be.

---

3 For more information about the programme, please see www.emahumanrights. org.

Among the elements that make up our shared intellectual and cultural heritage, one of the most important is our rights tradition. Those same Americans who denounce Europeans as colonizers and aggressors only will be the first to use their courts to fight for equality and for the rights of minorities. And those same Europeans who scorn the US for failing to commit to international law and human rights are well on their way not only to supplanting their parliamentary democracies with constitutional democracies, American-style, but also to using solutions to current European problems with multi-ethnicity that look oddly familiar from an American context. Rights, in other words – or what Mary Ann Glendon once called 'rights talk'[4] – are central to who we are and to how we intend to solve problems on both sides of the Atlantic. They are a European 'invention', going back to Enlightenment philosophers such as Locke, Rousseau and Montesquieu, but it was in the US that they first came to play a major role in political, social and cultural life.

The main argument here will be that Europeans have attempted for some time to develop their own version of rights talk: a human rights talk. European intellectuals as well as European Union politicians and policy professionals are talking about the need to construct 'European narratives'. What they have in mind are narratives that will emphasize a political, but also a cultural, vision for a multi-ethnic and more cosmopolitan Europe. These narratives evolve around human rights, partly because their authors hope that they may function as a kind of cultural glue in an increasingly multi-ethnic Europe, and partly because they are intimately connected with that part of Enlightenment thinking that sought to promote democracy and the rule of law. In addition, modern Europe is 'self-reflexive', argues German sociologist Ulrich Beck; it is built on a conscious wish to learn from the terrible mistakes of the past, and this also makes human rights central.

Human rights, that is, is developing into a discourse of atonement as well as of hope for these Europeans. It is a discourse that speaks to Bassam Tibi's, and not Pim Fontuyn's, Europe – to the enlightened, post-Eurocentric, antifascist Europe that is committed to learning its lessons from the past. And it is a discourse which has the potential to become a shared, transatlantic discourse.

THE NINE CHAPTERS

This book is divided into nine chapters. Chapter 1, 'A soul for Europe? On European culture and narratives of human rights', opens with German film

---

[4] See Mary Ann Glendon, *Rights Talk: The Impoverishment of Political Discourse* (New York: Free Press, 1991).

maker Wim Wenders's argument, presented at the 2006 'A Soul for Europe' conference in Berlin, that Europe does indeed have a soul – a soul that is to be found not so much in its politics or in its economy, but in its culture. In order that Europeans may be 'won' over, may see the emotional potential of 'Europe', it is important that European artists commit themselves to creating European literature, art and films. Wenders's emphasis on culture is echoed by European Union (EU) politicians and policy makers who have lately turned to 'culture' as a possible instrument for popularizing Europe.

One of the most important current cultural discourses in the European context is arguably the discourse of human rights. Arguments are being circulated in favour of seeing human rights as a defining characteristic of European culture and identity. European narratives of human rights are presented by both European intellectuals such as Ulrich Beck and Edgar Grande and EU politicians and policy makers who focus on human rights as a kind of cultural glue. The Europe we meet in these narratives is a chastened and realistic Europe that has admitted to and worked through the many horrible mistakes in its past – a self-reflexive Europe. In the last two chapters of the book, we shall get (back) to those creative narratives of human rights that Wenders would like European artists to construct. The narratives presented in Chapter 1 are of a more intellectual and/or policy oriented kind. But this does not mean that they are any less preoccupied with cultural matters.

What it does mean, though, is that intellectuals and policy makers succeed in avoiding some of the problems that invariably present themselves to anyone attempting to deal in a more direct way with the concept of 'European culture'. We take a closer look at these problems in Chapter 2 which is entitled 'The problem(s) with European culture'. Both 'Europe' and 'culture' are entities that have been problematized over the past many years. What does 'Europe' mean – is it a geographical entity or a state of mind? And the concept of 'culture' – does it encompass the fine arts only, or do we think of an entire way of life when we refer to 'culture'? When the two concepts are put side by side, moreover, and we start to talk about 'European culture', even more problems turn up. This makes it hard to discuss Europe and its future without touching upon politically incorrect or sensitive ground.

As several of the intellectuals whose work we look at in Chapter 2 argue, though, this is necessary. In order to get to a fruitful discussion of the current and possible future state of transatlantic relations, we must get at least some idea of what 'Europe' and 'European culture' encompass. And interestingly enough, any discussion of these issues has as its subtext the United States; the differences or similarities of Europe to the US and the relationship, historical and present, between these two parts of the world are invariably touched upon by Europeans today who try to figure out what 'Europe' and 'European culture' might mean. For some, who may not formerly have believed in

'Project Europe', it is the need NOT to become like the US and to fight the enormous political and cultural power of the world's only remaining super power that today defines 'Europe'.

It should be clarified at this point that throughout the book, the transatlantic dialogues that interest me are both the dialogues conducted on the part of European and American intellectuals, policy makers and artists, and also the dialogues conducted between the EU and the US. This means that I do not get into the differences that exist between mainland Europe and Great Britain – for example in terms of the civil-law systems of the mainland European countries versus the British common-law system – or between the various traditions in mainland Europe itself. I mostly talk about Europe as one entity, and my focus is on intellectual responses that present themselves as 'European' or see themselves as coming out of a European tradition as well as on the official reaction of the EU toward the various issues dealt with in this book. Doing research for the book, I have been amazed at the many reports and books that are published by both the EU and the Council of Europe and that cover a lot of different issues – and I have been positively surprised at the quality, both of the reports and books written for a wider audience and of those written for a more scholarly audience.

I confess to finding the experiment in supranational governance that is the EU not only intriguing, but also promising. And I think that if transatlantic dialogues are going to improve, Europeans will have to work through the EU to be taken seriously by the US. Though bearing at times witness of window dressing, official reactions between the US and the EU are relevant – if only to give us a hint as to the direction in which things seem currently to be moving. 'If the union did not exist, it would not now be created', writes Professor Anand Menon in his conclusion to *Europe: The State of the Union* (2008). I am afraid that Menon is right, and what a shame this would be:

> War, material devastation, fear, and the unusual status and mindset of the continent's most powerful country combined in the 1940s to create a unique historical moment in which sovereign nation states consented to relinquish a part of their autonomy in order to accomplish something together. Yet it does exist, and the member states would be all the poorer – both literally and metaphorically – without their unlovable Union.[5]

Chapter 3 concerns 'Transatlantic dialogues, past and present'. In the first part of the chapter, we will look at transatlantic perceptions – at the way in which 'Europe' has always had a special place in the American imagination,

---

[5] Anand Menon, *Europe: The State of the Union* (London: Atlantic Books, 2008), 252.

just as 'America' has been an object of the European imagination from the very beginning. An understanding of this cultural dynamic, which has given rise over the years to much friendly curiosity but also to many prejudices, is crucial to an assessment of today's European anti-Americanism and American anti-Europeanism as well as of the consequences these have for transatlantic policy. What have developed into political problems on the world scene today, it will be argued, originate to a large extent as cultural problems.

We will then move on, in the second part of the chapter, to look at some of the official EU dialogues with the United States. Interestingly enough, these seem to be in somewhat better shape than the transatlantic perceptions would make us think. At the official level, the EU has pronounced its willingness to pursue, together with the US, issues of importance to people on both sides of the Atlantic (as these are revealed in various surveys), such as the need to do something about current environmental problems and to combat international terrorism. When we 'deduct' from the official rhetoric the inevitable element of window dressing, mentioned above, the fact remains that dialogues are taking place on issues on which the EU and the US do not agree – environmental problems and the fight against international terrorism being two of the very best examples – but on which their respective populations ironically enough *want* them to find a common solution. This is, in my opinion, a hopeful sign.

Among the official EU–US dialogues are twice-yearly meetings dedicated to human rights. These meetings are mostly focused on issues related to the fight against terror, though. They do not touch on broader human rights issues. From time to time, there have been informal attempts at starting a broader dialogue, but apart from such attempts and from the meetings focusing on the fight against terror, the closest we get to transatlantic dialogues on human rights are the dialogues the EU and the US are having with third world countries. These official EU–US dialogues will be the topic of Chapter 4, 'Institutionalized European human rights'.

We will furthermore look, in Chapter 4, at the two European courts: the European Court of Justice (ECJ) and the European Court of Human Rights (ECtHR). As some see it, the two European courts roughly divide the functions of the US Supreme Court between them: the ECJ resolves questions that concern the regulation and the division of power between EU Member States and between the EU and its Member States, whereas the ECtHR deals with questions concerning the fundamental rights of citizens of the member states of the Council of Europe, as these are laid down in the European Convention on Human Rights and the protocols supplementing it. By most criteria, these two courts have been very successful. Some critics have reacted to this very success by claiming that it has led to a prevalence of law over politics, which in turn has led to an impoverishment of the political sphere. In order to solve human rights violations in Europe, these critics furthermore argue, it will not do to focus exclusively on redress by the courts. The discussion of law versus politics is one we shall return to repeatedly in other chapters.

The interesting parallels between the American and the European high courts and their way of interpreting fundamental rights notwithstanding, a number of transatlantic tensions come together or are expressed in the area of human rights. In Chapters 5 and 6, on 'Divergent transatlantic views on human rights: economic, social and cultural rights' and 'Divergent transatlantic views on human rights: the role of international law', respectively, we shall analyse two human rights areas or issues on which there is disagreement. The first of these is the core of human rights, the *kinds* of (human) rights emphasized, and the second is the attitude toward international law and international human rights regimes. Whereas Americans tend to think that the core of human rights consists of first-generation rights only (the civil and political rights), many Europeans tend also to believe in second-generation rights as a foundation for their welfare states. And when it comes to the international situation, Europeans are, again generally speaking, more willing to promote international law and human rights institutions than are Americans – even at the 'cost' of subsuming national law and national concerns under those of supranational law.

Chapter 7 deals with 'Transatlantic dialogues on copyright: cultural rights and access to knowledge'. Copyright, it will be argued, will increasingly set the parameters for creativity by allowing or prohibiting the reproduction of vital cultural texts – texts that help define the cultural milieu in which we live. Holders of copyright are in some senses able to exert monopolies over public meaning, and the more people will engage actively with commodified cultural forms – the more our culture becomes one of consumption – the more power these holders will have. Issues of copyright have everything to do with the sort of cultural politics going on, not only within Europe, but also across the Atlantic Ocean, that have been the focus of attention throughout.

We shall look, first, at cultural rights as these relate to the formation of identity – local, European and global. We shall then zoom in on the movement for access to knowledge. The fight for access to knowledge has a lot to do with cultural pride. Ostensibly about who owns the right to knowledge – and thus about issues having to do with copyright protection – the underlying issue is cultural copyright: gaining respect and recognition for oneself and/or for one's culture. The discussion of access to knowledge will be followed by a discussion of other copyright-related issues. There has been a tendency in recent times for human rights discourses to trespass into areas in which they were previously unknown. Copyright (and intellectual property as a whole) is a prime example of such an area – a reflection, in our current knowledge societies or economies, of the importance of cultural issues, especially as these relate to identity and cultural pride. In the copyright area, no less than in other areas in which 'culture' has become an 'issue', there are certain interesting transatlantic angles that reflect back on several of the transatlantic themes we have looked at in previous chapters.

In Chapters 8 and 9 we shall stay within the realm of culture. As its title, 'Transatlantic dialogues on "law and literature": from "law and literature" to "law and humanities"', implies, Chapter 8 argues that the time has come for law and literature scholars to broaden their field somewhat. It is not only in literary works of fiction that law and order are constitutive of dramatic action; non-literary works are also full of fights between good and evil and of themes such as justice, revenge and crime and punishment. Negotiations on societal values are taking place in many different public spaces. And precisely because so many of these important discussions are carried out in a legalistic, rights-talk vernacular, scholars studying law and humanities may be able to help both the general public and their fellow academics understand what the underlying and really significant issues are.

Chapter 9, 'Transatlantic dialogues on film: the case of Lars von Trier', presents Lars von Trier's so-called 'America trilogy' as 'evidence' that films are a worthy study for law and humanities scholars. It will be argued that Trier is being anti-American in an all- or semi-American way and that his work touches upon many of the 'big' themes that are of relevance in a law and humanities context. We shall take a brief look at some of the early films in order then to concentrate on three of Trier's later films – *Dancer in the Dark*, *Dogville* and *Manderlay*. These are set in the United States and feature, at least to a certain extent, American themes and concepts. It is Trier's way, in these later movies, of being critical of the US while simultaneously making much use of American phenomena and themes that is of interest. He is one of those European film makers and artists currently constructing that soul for Europe of which Wim Wenders speaks with such warmth. With his love-hate relationship with the US Trier joins the ranks of European critics and commentators such as Zygmunt Bauman and Ulrich Beck, just to mention a couple whose works we will discuss throughout the book, for whom 'America' is much more than just a nation or a place.

WORKING ON LAW AND HUMANITIES AS A CULTURAL HISTORIAN

I see myself as a law-and-humanities scholar and the work that I do as belonging within the discipline or area of law and humanities. My approach is that of the cultural historian or the historian of ideas rather than that of the literary scholar or the lawyer. Indeed, this is one reason why I argue, in this book, that law and literature ought to be broadened into law and humanities. Discussing transatlantic dialogues on human rights from a cultural-historical point of view is, in my opinion, just as much 'doing' law and humanities as is undertaking a legal-rhetorical interpretation of a play by William Shakespeare or a legal decision.

Doing interdisciplinary work and bringing together various fields of inquiry, as Stanley Fish once famously remarked, 'is so very hard to do'.[6] Some attempts are obviously more successful than others. Not being a legal expert myself, I have tried, where I thought it appropriate and needed, to stay close to the writings of scholars who are. By quoting people in the know about legal areas that I do not myself master and by asking colleagues to read through various chapters to verify the factual assertions that are made, I hope to have avoided the worst mistakes. There may still be some left, of course, and for these I apologize in advance.

My way of 'doing' law and humanities means, furthermore, that I may not always be as empirical as 'real' historians might wish me to be. Where are concrete analyses of events in the Middle East and other places where the US and the EU see issues related to human rights differently and call for different solutions, such historians may ask? To this I can only answer that, as a cultural historian, I am interested in laying bare the underlying cultural issues – those issues that shape people's lives, make them think and act as they do. It is the 'why did they do this?' behind that 'what did they do?' that is my main concern. And when interpretations of concrete events have been called for that I have not felt competent to make myself, I have attempted to find expert historical writing to guide me.

Because I believe in 'Project Europe' and because I think that an improvement of transatlantic relations will have to go through the EU, it makes me frustrated to hear Americans say incorrect things about Europe, and to hear Europeans say prejudiced and stupid things about America. All that I can do perhaps to correct such wrong and dangerous impressions as an academic is to write a book which attempts to state matters fairly and to see things from both sides. If only people on either side of the Atlantic would make the effort to understand why these 'stupid Americans' or these 'stupid Europeans' react as they do – then the transatlantic relationship would be in much better shape.

---

6 Stanley Fish, *There's No Such Thing as Free Speech: And It's a Good Thing Too* (New York: Oxford University Press, 1994), 231.

1. A soul for Europe? On European culture and narratives of human rights

> Europe has a soul, indeed.
> No need to invent or create one for our continent.
> It's there in plain sight.
> It is not to be found in its politics or in its economy.
> It is first and foremost embedded in its culture.[1]

In a speech delivered in November 2006 during the conference 'A Soul for Europe' in Berlin, German filmmaker Wim Wenders points to a paradox: Whereas Europeans themselves 'have *had it up to here* with Europe', Europe 'is heaven on earth, the *promised land*, as soon as you look at it from the outside'. To the rest of the world, the word 'Europe' is associated with 'culture, history, style, "savoir vivre" ' – to the Americans, European culture is even

> the only thing they feel strangely inferior about.
> Even rather permanently.[2]

Why is it, then, that this heaven on earth does not appeal to its own people? Well, Europeans are bored with Europe, Winders claims, because the European cause is presented to them as a political and economic project rather than as a cultural one:

> . . . Europe continues to present itself first of all as an economic power, insisting on using political and financial arguments over cultural ones at any given time.
>
> Europe is not taking advantage of its *emotional potential*!
>
> Who loves his (or her) country on account of its politics or its economy? No one![3]

---

1 Wim Wenders, 'Giving Europe a Soul?', speech delivered on 18 November 2006 in Berlin at the conference 'A Soul for Europe' – can be downloaded at http://www.signandsight.com/features/1098.html (last visited on 5 January 2009).

2 Ibid.

3 Ibid.

For Europeans to (re)gain enthusiasm for the European cause or project, Wenders goes on, European artists must play a more active role and help put into words and pictures those European myths and dreams that are definitely out there, but that politicians have allowed themselves and everyone else to lose sight of by talking about only dull things such as markets and trade.

Not surprisingly, being a filmmaker himself, Wenders especially points to the role of cinema in furthering European dreams. We do, he says, 'live in the *age of the image*. Today, no other realm of culture displays so much power than that of the image.' Europeans have to make their own movies; as it is, when Europeans go to the cinema, chances are that they will end up watching a Hollywood production. Europeans have let slip away one of the most effective ways of broadcasting dreams and values, and this must change:

> Those images of European cinema,
> could help a whole new generation of Europeans to recognize themselves,
> they could define what Europe is all about
> in emotional, powerful and lasting terms.
> These films could convey European thinking to the world.
> We could communicate our most valuable asset,
> our CULTURE, in a contagious way,
> could spread the word of the 'Open Society',
> which was so urgently invoked here by *George Soros*, only yesterday,
> our civilization of dialogue, peace, and humanity ...[4]

Wim Wenders' insistance on the necessity of making Europeans believe in the power of their own imagery and of linking the area of culture with more political ideas of an 'Open Society' and dialogues on peace and humanity has not gone unheeded. At the first international conference on culture following the Balkan wars, held in Belgrade in March 2007, for example, calls were made for new paths of cooperation between civil society and the world of politics. Present at the conference were representatives from the world of culture, business and politics in South-eastern Europe together with leading political figures. These agreed on a declaration, 'The Forum Belgrade Declaration', which emphasizes that culture has a key role to play in the democratic development of South-eastern Europe:

> The conference provided examples of how cultural activities developed by non-institutional initiatives and organizations can have a strong and productive impact as part of European culture. The conference further demonstrated that such activities also can assume a key role in the process of democratic transition in the Balkan countries. Moreover, it became clear that these examples are significant in terms of

4 Ibid.

> sustainable regional development beyond their own local and regional context, indeed throughout Europe. Cultural activities foster the development of new social structures, provide impetus for economic consolidation and serve the cause of social reconciliation.[5]

We see these arguments for the importance of culture reflected in the attempts made over the past decade or so by the European Union (EU) and its policy professionals to find in the area of culture and cultural politics answers to some of Europe's most pressing problems. Realizing that neither economic nor political visions of a united Europe have been able to create a sense of common identity among the peoples of Europe, EU policy professionals have turned to 'culture' as a possible instrument for popularizing Europe.

In this chapter, we will take a closer look at this turn toward culture on behalf of both European intellectuals and artists and the official EU and its policy professionals. We will furthermore zoom in on one of the arguably most important of current cultural discourses in the EU: the discourse of human rights. Arguments are presently being circulated in favour of seeing human rights as a defining characteristic of European culture and identity. Though mostly being presented as political, economic or legal, such arguments are every bit as much about 'culture' as are those presented by Wenders. Participating in discourses that are only indirectly about 'culture', intellectuals and policy makers succeed in avoiding some of the problems that invariably present themselves to anyone attempting to deal with the concept of 'European culture', moreover. We will take a closer look at these problems in Chapter 2.

Europeans generally have a hard time talking about, let alone agreeing on, common European values and norms. Take the issue of Christianity and the importance for European history of the Christian tradition, for example. Europeans cannot agree on what role to assign to Christianity in defining who they are and who they wish to be. This became very clear during the discussion of the Preamble to the Constitutional Treaty. Whether or not to include in this Preamble a passage on the importance of the Christian tradition for the new Europe turned out to be one of the most divisive questions during the Constitutional Convention. In the end, there was such widespread disagreement that nothing ever came of the attempt to declare European culture a fundamentally Christian one.

What most Europeans can agree on and even be proud of, however, are human rights. As listed in the European Convention on Human Rights, human

---

5 'The Forum Belgrade Declaration', Belgrade, 31 March 2007 – available at http://www.forumbelgrade.net/doc/FB%20declaration.pdf (last visited on 5 January 2009).

rights form for many Europeans a core of values that it is worth their while to defend, even fight for. It will be argued here that human rights act like a kind of cultural glue, and that Europeans are currently engaged in (re)constructing a 'Europe' of which the core is made up of human rights. This core shows a certain similarity to the political version of the American dream: the right to have rights. Indeed, as we shall see in Chapter 2, the American dream serves as a constant subtext to European discourses of human rights. To the extent, therefore, that the European soul has a lot to do with human rights, it will ultimately be argued, it shows an unmistakable similarity to its American cousin.

WHY THE NEED TO CONSTRUCT EUROPEAN NARRATIVES?

In 2005, in national referenda, first the French and then the Dutch voted 'no' to the proposed European Constitutional Treaty. And in 2008, the Irish voted 'no' to its successor, the Lisbon Treaty. This put on display – for the whole world to see – the scepticism with which the peoples of Europe still view the idea of forming an ever-stronger political union. That it was issues of a domestic nature that ultimately made people vote the way they did furthermore made it quite clear how marred European politics have been over the years by the pursuit of narrow, national interests. When we add to this the expansion of the EU toward the east and the ever-present question of Turkey's possibly joining the EU, we have, I think, one part of the answer to why the need for the construction of a European consciousness or identity arose during the past few years. The steady immigration, legal as well as non-legal, from Muslim and African countries has furthermore made identity politics – and the need to formulate a set of common rules – more noticeable and pressing.

A human rights framework, moreover, is by and large a secular one. It is not secular in the sense that it seeks to prevent people from being or becoming religious, freedom of religion being one of the most important of political and cultural rights, after all. It is secular, rather, in the sense that it encourages the separation of church and state and wants to turn religion into a private matter. With religion presently (re)surfacing in Europe as an important, but highly divisive cultural factor, it has become important for some European intellectuals and policy makers to insist on a secular human rights framework for Europe. The discussion about whether or not the Christian tradition ought to be mentioned in the Preamble to the European Constitutional Treaty was a good example of this. A born-again Christian president in the US (George W. Bush) and the insistence on a religious view of the world in many other parts of the world may give us one more part of the answer to why European narratives of human rights are presently being constructed.

But there is something else going on, too, as I hope to show. There is a feeling of recovery that is beginning to make itself felt. Europe may slowly be healing, and this healing brings with it a feeling of hope for the future. Europe is like a patient in therapy for whom there is hope when she is finally able to put into words what has happened to her, and how she feels about it. Nothing can ever undo the terrible deeds of the past, and Europeans will always be burdened with the guilt that goes with their past. And indeed, if they should forget they would soon be reminded and be brought to their senses by non-Europeans. Intellectual currents or movements such as post-modernity and post-colonialism have done exactly that: they have reminded Europeans of the effects on others of their arrogant behaviour in the past and thereby humbled any European attempt to suggest that European values are unique and absolute.

Allow me a brief digression. Being commissioned in 2005 to write a hymn on human rights, Italian composer Francesco Cali and Danish poet Jeppe Marsling suggested that the International Declaration of Human Rights may be compared to a tree growing on a grave. The roots of the tree will forever be tied to the grave – but the tree has found a way to grow all the same. 'Finding inspiration for an art work on justice', wrote Marsling, who was responsible for the lyrics of the hymn,

> is not easy. It is not possible to search one's heart for the glory of human rights without having to feel the dark inhuman background out of which the declaration emerged 60 years ago. The declaration is a tree on a grave. And therefore: the most beautiful of trees. Its bitter-sweet fruits are to be handled with care.

The 'Human Rights Hymn', which consists of four parts and a chorus, opens with a reminder of the war and the 'loss of humanity'. It then goes on to celebrate peace as 'both an end and a new beginning' and ends on the suggestion that 'out of remembrance and darkness the inspiration now surfaces and unfolds into a celebration of how we – the human race(s) – can avoid injustice' now and in the future.[6]

The very naïveté of both the hymn's lyrics and its creator's way of talking about it is embarrassing yet at the same time endearing. And this takes me to a point made by the Danish writer Jens Christian Grøndahl in the anthology *Europa schreibt. Was ist das europäische an den Literaturen Europas?*, put together by Ursula Keller and Ilma Rakusa in 2003. Grøndahl points to that major European paradox: much as European history is full of cruelty and lack of respect for human dignity, it is also characterized by the idea that each human being is special and that we are all equal. And then he continues:

---

6 Jeppe Marsling, 'On the Human Rights Hymn', Institute for Human Rights, Copenhagen, 2005.

> Since democracy has been instituted all over the continent, it is no longer the remote dream that is was fifty or even ten years ago; only, now all talk of universalism and European individualism may sound somewhat arrogant, even naïve – except when we talk about literature.[7]

From the troubadours of the Middle Ages to the dissident-writers in Eastern Europe – for all of them, literature and literary endeavour have been about finding and expressing an autonomous voice that would forever object to tyrannical attempts of imposing particular norms and values on other people:

> Much like the idea of having a private life and of having a right not to have one's personal sphere violated, the novel is a European invention, and we need not be afraid of being called Eurocentric on that score . . . If the history of democracy is also the history of the individual, and if it shows how the idea of individuality has grown out of the warm, secure, but also highly suffocating embrace of cultural identity, then the novel presents the possibility of telling this history.[8]

What Grøndahl is getting at here is central to my argument. After post-modernity and post-colonialism, putting into words, discussing and updating the values that derive, to a large extent, from the European Enlightenment is tricky business. What looks naïve and embarrassing in a political science treatise may, however, look much more palatable in a piece of literature, a piece of art or a movie. Among the most self-reflexive of art forms, literature, art and movies can do what other media cannot do. For the discussion of what Europe is, can and perhaps also ought to be, Europeans need not only their politicians and intellectuals, but also their writers and artists. This is true in the well-known sense that literary and artistic narratives can create empathy, make their readers feel and thereby come to a better understanding of that which is important for others. But it is true in another sense, too. These narratives turn 'Project Europe' into an open project – a project which makes accessible to everyone the still unresolved tensions between local, regional, national and European identities. The future of Europe depends on the way in which such tensions are dealt with.

In the laying bare of and the exploration, in a non-essentialist way, of issues relating to European identity/identities lies hope. The process is a very slow and sometimes also very painful one, and there are writers and artists who strongly doubt that it will lead anywhere. 'What is Europe then?', asks Irish writer Colm Toíbín, for example. 'It is not a culture and not an identity. It is a

---

7 Ursula Keller and Ilma Rakusa (eds), *Europa schreibt. Was ist das europäische an den Literaturen Europas?* (*Europe writes. What is European about European Literature?*) (Hamburg: edition Körber-Stiftung, 2003), 136. My translation from the German.

8 Grøndahl, in ibid., 137. My translation from the German.

word we should set about undermining further as time goes by.' Yet, when it comes to Ireland's membership of the EU, Toíbín is very positive. If not for this membership, Irish women would still earn less than Irish men, and homosexuality would be a punishable offence, he admits.[9] Even for a Euro-sceptic such as Toíbín, it would thus seem, 'Europe' is associated with human rights gains and with respect for individual autonomy.

For European intellectuals such as Ulrich Beck and Edgar Grande – just to mention a couple of scholars whose work touches upon issues concerning European identity – the time has come to move on. They call their vision of the new Europe a 'cosmopolitan Europe'. It is a Europe which has admitted to and worked through the many mistakes of the past – a self-reflexive Europe. And it is a Europe which has come to see that there are elements of European intellectual thinking that are worth preserving. Again, these evolve around individual rights and cultural diversity.[10]

In *Das kosmopolitische Europa* (Cosmopolitan Europe), published in 2004, the point of departure for Beck and his co-author Edgar Grande is that 'Europe has to be thought anew'.[11] Europe is presently going through a crisis. Not only did the attempt to make the peoples of Europe approve of a common Constitutional Treaty fail; European Member States also keep pursuing their own, narrow nation-state agendas and have utterly failed to integrate all the new immigrants coming to their countries. Institutional reforms will no longer do the trick; they cannot create the feeling of belonging and solidarity that is needed for Europeans to take a more positive attitude toward the European project. What might help foster such a sense of solidarity, however, is a 'European narrative'. It is a narrative that has to be constructed – 'Europe cannot be found, it must be invented'.[12]

---

9 Colm Toíbín, in ibid., 323–329.

10 The following pages concerning the work of Ulrich Beck and Edgar Grande, and the 'Official EU European Narratives' are taken from my article, 'On European Narratives of Human Rights and Their Possible Implications for Copyright', which was published in Fiona Macmillan (ed.), *New Directions in Copyright Law, Volume 6* (Cheltenham, UK and Northampton, MA, USA: Edward Elgar, 2007).

11 Ulrich Beck and Edgar Grande, *Das kosmopolitische Europa. Gesellschaft und Politik in der Zweiten Moderne* (Frankfurt am Main: Suhrkamp, 2004), 7: 'Europa muβ neu gedacht werden.' – I thank translator and scholar Manuela Thurner who has translated this and the following passages from Beck and Grande from the German. The book is the last in a trilogy of books which marks an attempt on Beck's part to develop a 'cosmopolitan realism'. The first two books are *Macht und Gegenmacht im globalen Zeitalter* and *Der kosmopolitische Blick* (both Frankfurt am Main: Suhrkamp, 2002 and 2004, respectively).

12 Ibid., 18: 'Europa kann nicht *ge*funden werden, es muss *er*funden werden.'

The new European narrative is a supra-national or 'cosmopolitan narrative'. The concept of cosmopolitanism, Beck and Grande tell us, is both pre- and post-national. Its roots go all the way back to ancient Greece, and it later came into play whenever European societies were confronted with profound changes. As examples they mention the philosophies of the Enlightenment and those of the nation-state oriented cultural critics of the late 19th century.

Today, in debates about globalization, cosmopolitanism has come to play a vital role for critics and activists who wish to refute market- and/or nation state-oriented values. At the core of the contemporary, post-national and future-directed cosmopolitanism is a combination of two things: a positive view of multiethnic diversity and a wish to work toward a form of political democracy which no longer revolves around the nation-state. The key words are tolerance, democratic legitimacy, and efficiency.

The European project and its narrative is a 'reflexive' one. Europeans are currently, Beck and Grande argue, in 'the second' and 'reflexive modern'.[13] The nation-state was the basis of 'the first modern', but at the moment Europeans are being forced into new and more international relations with others. They experience different actors at work in society from nation-states – actors like for example networks, experts and NGOs. Europe is both a product of and a driving force behind this whole process. In a post-colonial acknowledgement of all that was negative in European history, Europeans have self-critically or reflexively made the choice to break away from their militant past.

As Beck and Grande see it, modern Europe has developed out of a conscious attempt to come to terms with and never forget the past. In this, the realization of the importance of self-criticism, Beck and Grande hint, Europe may well be different from both the United States and Islamic societies: 'Is it perhaps this radical, self-critical confrontation with its own history that makes Europe different from, for example, the United States or the Islamic societies?'[14] If there is much *not* to be proud of, this is one kind of 'European exceptionalism' that Europeans *can* be proud of, they suggest.

Human rights form a very important component of Beck's and Grande's vision for a better Europe. Indeed, it could hardly be otherwise, their vision resulting from a self-critical reflection on the crimes of European history. It was during the Nuremberg trials that the world first heard of 'crimes against humanity', the Nuremberg court being the first truly international court to

---

[13] Cf. the subtitle of the book: 'Gesellschaft und Politik in der Zweiten Moderne' (Society and Politics in the Second Modern).

[14] Beck and Grande, supra n. 11, 21: 'Ist es vielleicht diese radikale selbstkritische Konfrontation mit der eigener Geschichte, die Europa beispielsweise von den USA oder den islamischen Gesellschaften unterscheidet?'

prosecute such crimes and the first to create international categories of law that went beyond the sovereignty of the nation-state – 'here was invented a political-legal practice to come up with, after all, legal concepts and legal procedures for this "break in civilization" (*Zivilisationsbruch*), the monstrous, state-organized destruction of the Jews.'[15]

The transnationalization of human rights in opposition to the legal sovereignty of the individual nation-states is thus the key, for Beck and Grande, to the creation of a European civil society. The universal or cosmopolitan quality of human rights serves a further purpose, too. Human rights guarantee diversity, but they also form a set of common rules according to which that very diversity can be regulated and integrated. This point about a cosmopolitan Europe being both one of difference/diversity *and* integration is an important one for Beck and Grande. Without this integrative perspective, we would slide into a post-modern particularism:

> Cosmopolitanism accepts difference; however, it does not make it absolute, but searches for ways to make it universally agreeable. To this end, it relies on a framework of common and binding norms that are to prevent a lapse into postmodern particularism.[16]

Europe must be lived on a day-to-day basis. At best, this will be a grass-roots endeavour. While we are waiting for this to happen, certain supra-national European institutions are doing their best to make the dream of cosmopolitan Europe come true. Chief among these, argue Beck and Grande, is the European Court of Justice (ECJ). Much like the US Supreme Court, the ECJ has created a supra-national law that trumps that of the individual states. It has thus become a 'cosmopolitan entrepreneur who, by virtue of the law, succeeds in gaining some ground for a cosmopolitan Europe against a nationalist Europe'.[17]

On the role that the law and the courts have played in the integration of Europe, Beck and Grande are in agreement with other scholars. 'It was the Romans who elevated the law to the place it still holds today as the sole guar-

---

15 Ibid, 204: 'Hier wurde eine politisch-rechtliche Praxis erfunden, den Zivilisationsbruch der monströsen, staatlich organisierten Judenvernichtung dennoch in rechtliche Begriffe und rechtliche Verfahren zu giessen.'

16 Ibid., 28–29: 'Der Kosmopolitismus akzeptiert Andersartigkeit, er verabsolutiert sie aber nicht, sondern sucht zugleich nach Wegen, um sie universell verträglich zu machen. Dabei stützt er sich auf ein Gerüst von verbindenden und für alle verbindliche Normen, mit deren Hilfe ein Abgleiten in einen postmodernen Partikularismus verhindert werden soll.'

17 Ibid., 19: 'kosmopolitischen Unternehmer, der mit der Macht des Rechts ein Stück kosmopolitisches Europa gegen das nationale Europa durchsetzt.'

antor of the continuity of civilization . . . that law remained, and remains, the single most unifying feature of the continent', writes Anthony Pagden, for example.[18] And on a more popular note Mark Leonhard rhetorically asks in *Why Europe Will Run the 21st Century*: 'What was it that transformed Europe from being an incubator for world wars into a transmission belt for peace and democracy?' The simple answer, he continues, 'is: international law. The law is Europe's weapon of choice . . .'[19]

Like most other Europeans who set out to discuss Europe and the European project, Beck and Grande contrast and compare it to the United States. The transatlantic relationship forms an important subtext throughout, and while the two authors are careful to emphasize the importance of cooperating with the US, they cannot quite hide their wish to promote Europe as an alternative to the US. Characteristically, the very last words of the book concern the transatlantic relationship:

> Then there will be, all over the world, an alternative to the *American way*, a *European way* which will focus on the rule of law, political equality, social justice, cosmopolitan integration and solidarity.[20]

OFFICIAL EUROPEAN UNION NARRATIVES

We see these arguments and analyses reflected in the attempts made over the past decade or so by the EU and its policy professionals to find in the area of culture and cultural politics answers to some of Europe's most pressing problems. Realizing that neither economic nor political visions of a united Europe have been able to create a sense of common identity among the peoples of Europe, EU policy professionals have turned to 'culture' as a possible instrument for popularizing Europe.

The official EU European narrative is very much a human rights narrative. 'The formation of Europe – and of the European Communities and the Union that lie at the heart of the continent's political life – has largely been expressed in legal terms', writes Philip Ruttley. On 'the long road' toward European

---

[18] Anthony Pagden, 'Europe: Conceptualizing a Continent', in Anthony Pagden (ed.), *The Idea of Europe: From Antiquity to the European Union* (Washington, DC: Woodrow Wilson Center & Cambridge University Press, 2002), 42–43.

[19] Mark Leonhard, *Why Europe Will Run the 21st Century* (London: Fourth Estate, 2005), 36.

[20] Beck and Grande, supra n. 11, 393: 'Dann gibt es welt-weit eine Alternative zum *American way*, einen *European way*, der die Herrschaft des Rechts, politische Gleichheit, soziale Gerechtigkeit, kosmopolitische Integration und Solidarität ins Zentrum stellt.'

unity and integration, the law has made a large contribution.[21] In a 2007 publication by the European Commission, 'The European Union: Furthering Human Rights and Democracy Across the Globe', it is stated in the Introduction that 'liberty, democracy, respect for human rights and fundamental freedoms, and the rule of law, are founding principles of the European Union and an indispensable prerequisite for the Union's legitimacy'. A bit further on, the importance of 'mainstreaming human rights and democratization' is explained: '[m]ainstreaming is the process of integrating human rights and democratization issues into all aspects of EU policy decision-making and implementation, including external assistance. European institutions are deeply committed to intensify the mainstreaming of human rights.'[22]

It was the Treaty of Amsterdam of 1997 amending the Maastricht Treaty on European Union from 1992 that truly made explicit the human rights foundation of the Union:

> In addition, the Treaty [of Amsterdam] declares that the Union is founded on respect for human rights, democracy, and the rule of law. Respect for human rights, particularly those enshrined in the European Convention on Human Rights (ECHR) are made central to the Union.[23]

New applicant states must honour and observe the rights outlined in the ECHR; if they do not, they become liable to legal action. Indeed, should a state be in 'serious and persistent breach' of its human rights obligations, the European Council has the power to suspend its voting rights. An earlier proposal went so far as to talk about the possible expulsion of infringing states, but this met with too much resistance ever to receive serious consideration.[24]

The role played by the European Court of Justice has been remarkable. 'One of the most adventurous – some would say interventionist – courts of any regional system . . . the European Court of Justice has behaved very much like the US Supreme Court.'[25] With one important ruling after another, it has furthered Community integration and has helped shape the emerging European Union:

---

21 Philip Ruttley, 'The Long Road to Unity: The Contribution of Law to the Process of European Integration since 1945', in Pagden, supra n. 18, 228.

22 European Commission, External Relations, 'The European Union: Furthering Human Rights and Democracy Across the Globe' (Luxembourg: Office for Official Publications of the European Communities, 2007).

23 Ruttley, supra n. 21, 246.

24 Ibid.

25 Ibid., 250–251.

> Nearly fifty years after the first European Community was created in 1951, one can discern a unique and distinct European political and legal framework. It will, in turn, create a European identity. In retrospect, EC law and the European Court of Justice were fundamental in shaping the new political consensus.[26]

Underlying the judicial activity of the ECJ, Ruttley claims, is a federalist vision of European unification and a belief in a common European culture – a vision and a belief that are shared by other agents of the official EU system:

> What is undeniable, and should not be underestimated, is the strength of the European ideal. A wide spectrum of political forces – socialist, democratic, liberal – can support this ideal. Yet it is the consciousness that Europeans have a common heritage and a common culture, that there exists a 'European' way, that inspires the various intergovernmental conferences where the . . . Member States . . . meet.[27]

The vision of the law as a kind of European cultural glue is not a new one. It was the Romans who gave Europe its legislative habits, and the creation of a common system of law throughout Europe 'remained an ambition of the most powerful of Europe's rulers from the Emperor Justinian in the sixth century, through Philip II of Spain and Louis XIV to Napoleon'. In a somewhat muted form, 'this ambition is held by the European Court of Justice today'.[28]

As for allowing for diversity while also emphasizing that which is shared, the idea of *e pluribus unum* has been as hard a nut to crack for the EU as it has been for the United States. In the first few years of the Union's existence, the idea of a European common culture did not seem too problematic. But when people started becoming more interested in social, cultural and ethnic issues in the 1960s, claims about 'common European ideals' were attacked as being Eurocentric. This made the official EU system emphasize that such claims of a common European culture were based on the notion of a common cultural history or heritage.

The Declaration on European Identity issued by the European Community, as it was then called, in 1973 is a good example of this. While recognizing the fact that there are many different cultures in Europe, the Declaration spoke of a 'basic necessity to ensure the survival of the civilization which [the Nine] have in common'.[29] The core of this common heritage upon which a European identity could be based was the belief in representative democracy, the rule of

---

26 Ibid., 259.

27 Ibid., 250.

28 Pagden, supra n. 18, 43.

29 Declaration on European Identity (1973), quoted in Luisa Passerini, 'From the Ironies of Identity to the Identities of Irony', in Pagden, supra n. 18, 194.

law, human rights and social justice. At this point, of course, as Luisa Passerini dryly points out, 'an essential part of Europe's supposed identity was represented by a common market based on a customs union, established institutions, as well as policies and machinery for cooperation'.[30]

The Declaration does, however, make a first significant step toward defining a *cultural* – as opposed to an economic and/or political – basis for European integration. Until 1973, little attention had been paid to the cultural dimensions of European integration. For the architects of European unification, building a united Europe primarily had to do with removing obstacles to the free movement of capital and services – something that could best be left to lawyers and economists.

> The emphasis on 'culture' as an integrative mechanism and possible solution to the riddle of European unification marks a fundamental shift in official EU discourses on integration away from old assumptions that socio-political integration would proceed as a by-product of economic integration and technical harmonization.[31]

As Chris Shore sees it, this shift in official EU discourses on integration has been driven largely by political imperatives. Chief among these is the need to give to the whole supra-national EU system a political legitimacy. As election after election has shown, the citizens of Europe do not feel close to what goes on in Brussels at all. They perceive EU politicians and policy professionals as bureaucrats who are far removed from the concerns of the average European, and who communicate in a political lingo that only they themselves understand. Until the 1980s, public support was not on the list of priorities of the EU policy professionals. They simply took for granted that loyalty to the Union and a sense of belonging to Europe would follow automatically from economic and legal integration. As it became increasingly clear that this was not the case, they started looking at 'culture' as a political instrument for fostering a European consciousness or identity.[32]

The attempt to popularize Europe through 'culture', Shore furthermore claims, was and is essentially an elitist project. He identifies various ways in which EU policy professionals have sought to use 'culture' as a possible solution to the EU's problem of legitimacy. Among these are the creation of new symbols to represent Europe – the EC emblem and flag, a European 'anthem' (the fourth movement of Beethoven's Ninth Symphony), the harmonized European passport, driver's licence and car number-plates, and the Euro, for

---

30 Ibid., 194.

31 Chris Shore, *Building Europe: The Cultural Politics of European Integration* (London: Routledge, 2000), 42.

32 Ibid., introduction.

example – and the attempt to 'Europeanize' higher education – providing funding for the ERASMUS and SOCRATES programmes, for the rewriting of national histories also to include European history, for museums and other places interested in preserving the European heritage, for example.[33]

Until 1992, when the Maastricht Treaty brought the area of culture within the jurisdiction of the Community, purely economic reasons were used for achieving cultural ends. Jacques Delors openly acknowledged as much when he said in a speech in 1985 that:

> the culture industry will tomorrow be one of the biggest industries, a creator of wealth and jobs. Under the terms of the Treaty we do not have the resource [sic] to implement a cultural policy; but we are going to try to tackle it along economic lines . . . We have to build a powerful European culture industry that will enable us to be in control of both the medium and its content, maintaining our standards of civilization, and encouraging the creative people amongst us.[34]

Title IX, Article 128 of the Maastricht Treaty outlines the cultural goals of the Community: '[t]he Community shall contribute to the flowering of the cultures of the Member States, while respecting their national and regional diversity and at the same time bringing the common cultural heritage to the fore'. It ends by demanding that 'the Community shall take cultural aspects into account in its actions under other provisions of this Treaty' – thus assigning to 'culture' a very high priority.[35] Article 128 (later to become Article 151 of the Treaty of Amsterdam) does not explicitly say how the difficult task of promoting at one and the same time diversity and unity is to be carried out, however.

CONCLUDING REMARKS

Europe's record is not exactly great when it comes to human rights. In fact, European history may be viewed as one long story of colonial, imperialist, fascist and totalitarian histories and their legacies. 'Why should we believe you this time around when you talk of human rights?', an American colleague recently asked me. Why indeed would the rest of the world want to believe that Europeans are serious about human rights at this point in time? In an essay on 'European Hypocrisies' in the September 2007 issue of the *London Review of Books*, the well-known British-American historian Perry Anderson gives voice

---

33 Ibid., chapter 2.
34 Jacques Delors, quoted in ibid., 45–46.
35 Quoted in ibid., 53.

to a different kind of scepticism. The title, of course, says it all. Reviewing a number of recent books on Europe, Anderson writes how 'self-satisfaction is scarcely unfamiliar in Europe'. But the contemporary mood 'is something different: an apparently illimitable narcissism . . .'[36]

Not only have rumours concerning the bureaucratic nature of the European Union been totally understated, continues Anderson; 'constitutionally, the EU is [also] a caricature of a democratic federation, since its Parliament lacks powers of initiative, contains no parties with any existence at European level, and wants even a modicum of popular credibility'.[37] What is worse, though, there is little left of the social Europe intended by either Monet or Delors – all talk of welfare and second-generation human rights (the economic and social rights) has been relegated to the level of the various European nation-states. With its pinched spending and absence of independent taxation, today's EU may be characterized neither by its democracy nor its welfare, but by its capital. The EU is basically about business, Anderson claims, and though the EU contrasts itself to the US, the sad truth is that 'Europe surrendered to the United States. This rendition is the most taboo of all to mention.' And as for human rights, forget it. Not a single European government has 'conceded any guilt' in relation to the war in Iraq and the war on terror in general; instead, 'all continue to hold forth on human rights. We are', Anderson concludes, 'in the world of Ibsen – Consul Bernick, Judge Brack and their like – updated for post-moderns. Pillars of society, pimping for torture.'[38]

One possible answer to the critical question asked by my American colleague and the points of criticism raised by Anderson is to argue, with Yale historian Jay Winter, that human rights have become a 'minor utopia' – a 'minor utopia' that developed out of one of the darkest moments of European history, World War Two. In his book, *Dreams of Peace and Freedom* of 2006, Winter tells 'the story of what may be termed "minor utopias", imaginings of liberation usually on a smaller scale, without the grandiose pretensions or the almost unimaginable hubris and cruelties of the 'major' utopian projects' of the 20th century.[39] He identifies six such minor utopias and argues that 'from the 1940s, and increasingly after 1968, minor utopians have focused less on nation and social class and more on civil society and human rights'.[40] The modern human rights movement started with the Universal Declaration of

---

[36] Perry Anderson, 'European Hypocrisies', in 30 *London Review of Books*, 20 September 2007, 13.

[37] Ibid., 17.

[38] Ibid., 21.

[39] Jay Winter, *Dreams of Peace and Freedom: Utopian Moments in the 20th Century* (New Haven, CT, & London: Yale University Press, 2006), 4–5.

[40] Ibid., 5–6.

Human Rights in 1948. We normally focus on the importance of Eleanor Roosevelt (and through her of her husband, Franklin Delano Roosevelt) when we talk about the origin of the Universal Declaration; in fact, says Winter, we ought, also, to focus on the importance of another player, the French jurist René Cassin. A disabled French veteran of World War One and hero of the French Resistance, Cassin made his career in law as practitioner, professor, scholar and administrator. He received the Nobel Peace Prize in 1986 (at the age of 81) for his legal as well as moral work for the recognition of the rights of man.

What Cassin did, according to Winter, was to 'put human rights on the agenda of the future world order'.[41] He did so as early as 1941 (as a member of de Gaulle's Free France movement), at two conferences in London of Britain's occupied Allies in exile, during which he 'made the point that a future peace could be secure only if it were based on a set of international commitments on human rights'.[42] The two St. James conferences became the foundation for the whole United Nations project. However, the UN is not where the human rights project would end up in the end. On five occasions between 1946 and 1968 Cassin was a French delegate to the Assembly of the United Nations, and for many years between 1945 and 1960 also a delegate to the UNESCO conferences. Disappointed at the slow progress made in terms of human rights within the UN framework that he was witnessing first-hand, Cassin eventually turned his attention toward Europe. He helped write the European Convention on Human Rights in 1950 and even served as president of the European Court of Human Rights at Strasbourg between 1965 and 1968.

Cassin's major achievement, according to Jay Winter, is to have helped *institutionalize* human rights. The European regional system of human rights, to which we shall come back in Chapter 4, is the only one of the world's three regional systems (the other two being the Inter American and the African) that really works in practice. What started as a utopian dream at the St. James conferences in 1941 is beginning to work in practice. The Europe we see today is very different from the Europe of before World War Two in no small part *because* of human rights. First and foremost, this has to do with the assault on sovereignty launched by Cassin and others. Cassin wanted to 'desacralize' claims of state sovereignty, to create something *beyond* the nation state. Furthermore, by privileging the concept of domicile over nationality – that is, founding the rights of each human being not in civil rights and citizenship, but in a right of domicile independent of nationality – he pointed the way toward establishing the standing of the individual within international law itself.[43]

---

41 Ibid., 113.
42 Ibid., 115.
43 Ibid., 109–110.

Well, pimping for torture or minor utopian dream, that is the question? Maybe what at least some of it boils down to is a question of temperament. Modern history is almost always written as the story of a series of catastrophes. 'Over the past four decades', writes Jay Winter in his introduction to *Dreams of Peace and Freedom*, 'I too have contributed to this apocalyptic vision of the recent past. Yet for many years I have felt that this dominant historical narrative is incomplete. This book is an attempt to fill in some of what has been left out. In particular, I want to tell the story of moments in the 20th century when a very disparate group of people tried in their separate ways to imagine a radically better world. I term these people minor utopians . . .'[44] Is the cup half empty or is it half full? René Cassin would say half full.

[44] Ibid., 1.

2. The problem(s) with European culture

Talking about 'European culture' is not easy. The first problem that one runs into is defining what 'Europe' and 'European' mean. Once such a definition, however tentative, is obtained, a second problem immediately presents itself: is this 'Europe' an entity that we should do our very best to promote, or is it an entity we should set about undermining as quickly as possible? Regardless of whether one sees 'Europe' today as a geographical destination only, encompassing the 27 countries that form the membership of the European Union, the 47 countries that make up the European Council, or whether one perceives 'Europe' as referring to a state of mind or way of life and therefore as open to anyone and any country that considers him/herself or itself European, it is hardly possible to be neutral when discussing what Europe is, has been and should be.

'Thus, the name of Europe – derived from distant antiquity and first designating a little region of Asia or Asia Minor', – as Etienne Balabar ably sums it up:

> has been connected to cosmopolitan projects, to claims of imperial hegemony or to the resistance that they provoked, to programs dividing up the world and expanding 'civilization' that the colonial powers believed themselves the guardians of, to the rivalry of 'blocs' that disputed legitimate possession of it, to the creation of a 'zone of prosperity' north of the Mediterranean, of a 'great power in the twenty-first century'.[1]

'Europe', in other words, is a construction which may refer both to a continent and to a civilization – a source of pride for some and very much the opposite for others.

In addition, there is the problem of defining that word, 'culture'. And when these two problematical entities – 'Europe' and 'culture' – are brought together, things get even tougher. Most scholars would subscribe, today, to the broad anthropological definition of 'culture' as simply a way of life, but the odd thing is that precisely when European culture is the topic of analysis and conversation, old-fashioned 'highbrow' views of 'culture' as being closer to the fine arts refuse to be defeated.

---

[1] Etienne Balabar, *We, the People of Europe? Reflections on Transnational Citizenship* (Princeton, NJ, and Oxford: Princeton University Press, 2004), 10.

Creating the imagery that will speak to what Wim Wenders calls, as we saw in Chapter 1, Europe's *emotional potential* and that will help foster a feeling of European identity is not entirely unproblematic, in other words. In this chapter, we will look into why this seems to be the case by analysing discourses relating to, first, 'Europe' and, secondly, 'culture'. Unless we succeed in breaking through some of the biases and pre-conceived notions connected to these two concepts, it will be argued, we will not be able successfully to enter into a discussion of what Europe is and should be – a discussion, moreover, which is a precondition for any further analysis of transatlantic relations.

THE CONCEPT OF 'EUROPE'

Historically, Europe's borders have shifted quite a bit. The representation of those borders is, as Talal Asad points out, in and of itself 'symbolic'. The signs and symbols of Europe 'have a history', and today it is simply 'not possible for Europe to be represented without evoking this history'.[2] The history that is evoked is, of course, Europe's colonial past, and if we add to this the atrocities of the twentieth century, then it is no wonder that the word 'Europe' is associated, for some, chiefly with genocide, colonialism and aggression. In his book, *Europe in the Global Age* (2007), Anthony Giddens talks about 'euro-hypocricy':

> The Europeans were the aggressors in world society for a long time. Talk of European values can ring hollow to those in less developed parts of the world still struggling with the long-term residue of colonialism. When Democracy was developing in Europe, and lasting right up to the 1960s, it was specifically denied to colonial subjects.[3]

In addition to the failure of the former European colonial powers to acknowledge and examine their colonial past, Giddens mentions as examples of this 'euro-hypocrisy' the way in which Europeans have often hidden behind US military power only in order then later to scold the Americans for their use of force, and Europe's tendency toward protectionism when it comes to the agricultural sector – a tendency which often has catastrophic consequences for

---

2 Talal Asad, 'Muslims and European Identity: Can Europe Represent Islam?', in Anthony Pagden (ed.), *The Idea of Europe: From Antiquity to the European Union* (Cambridge: Woodrow Wilson Center Press and Cambridge University Press, 2002), 220, 218.

3 Anthony Giddens, *Europe in the Global Age* (Cambridge: Polity Press, 2007), 228.

the very parts of the world which the EU officially wishes to help.[4] If Europeans can own up to this hypocrisy and can attempt to minimize it as far as possible, however, Giddens is of the opinion that Europe can still be, if not '*the* major force' then at least 'a major force in the world'.[5]

In proposing as the way forward an attitude of 'Eurorealism', a cautiously optimistic ambition for what Europe can achieve, Giddens places himself in line with those who think it is still worthwhile to explore Europe as 'contested terrain – caught between colonial, imperialist, fascist, and totalitarian histories and their legacies . . ., and the enlightened, post-Eurocentric, antifascist Europe that is committed to learning its lessons from the past . . .'[6] He is on a par, here, with certain contemporary European thinkers, such as Ulrich Beck and Edgar Grande, whose views we looked at in the previous chapter, who are again beginning to talk about the need to redeem certain parts of that European philosophical, political and cultural heritage which has been under attack for the past many years – those parts that sought to promote representative democracy, the rule of law and human rights.

Another such thinker is David Held. In *Global Covenant* (2004), he calls for a 'Social Democratic Alternative to the Washington Consensus'. I shall come back to both Held's and Giddens' interesting thoughts on the so-called European social model later; what I want to focus on in this context is Held's rebuttal of the view that the language of liberty and democracy does not work because it is the discourse of European/Western dominance. 'There are', he says,

> many good historical reasons why such language invokes skepticism. Understandable as they are, however, these reasons are insufficient to provide a well-justified critique: it is a mistake to throw out the language of equal worth and self-determination because of its contingent association with the historical configurations of Western power. The origins of principles should not be confused with their validity.[7]

Both Giddens and Held point to the importance of our recognizing as valid the framework of democratic principles, human rights and cosmopolitan values. To refrain from committing to such a framework simply because it originates in Europe/the West is a major mistake – one that prevents us from actively

---

4 Ibid., 228–229.

5 Ibid., 29.

6 'Contesting Europe: Feminist Critiques and Globalization' – call for papers for the 'Women in German Annual Conference (WiG)', to be held at Snowbird, Utah, 18–21 October 2007, which used to be available at www.womeningerman.org (last visited on 3 March 2007).

7 David Held, *Global Covenant: The Social Democratic Alternative to the Washington Consensus* (Cambridge: Polity Press, 2004), 156.

pursuing answers and cures to some of the worst problems in the world of today.

Certain 'crucial facts of history', Zygmunt Bauman agrees, 'tend to be shamefacedly concealed nowadays, and recalling them is often attacked point blank in the name of the current version of "political correctness" '. Among the crucial facts of history that he refers to is the way in which 'Europe was the first to proclaim that the "world is made by culture". . .' In its European version, ' "civilization" (or "culture", a concept difficult to separate from that of "civilization" . . .) [has been] a continuing process – forever imperfect yet obstinately struggling for perfection – of *remaking the world*.'[8] It was Europeans who discovered culture as something human-made, and who turned themselves and their world into objects to be critically and creatively examined: '[i]t was not just culture that happened to be Europe's discovery/intention. Europe also invented the need and the task of *culturing culture*.' Engaging in cultural became 'a human *job/destiny/vocation/task*' – one that would always look critically at anything that seemed to be settled and certain.[9]

Most talk of the unique historical role played by Europe is immediately met with a charge of 'Europocentrism', though, and this prevents a sober and fair assessment of 'Europe's function as a yeast and moving spirit in the long, tortuous and still far from finished unification of planet-wide humanity'. Not that there isn't much to be critical of. Like Giddens and Held, Bauman is careful to point out how Europe's 'globalizing mission', its wish to remake the rest of the world in its own image has had terrible consequences. These are consequences that no European can be proud of, and this may be one of the reasons why certain Europeans refuse to acknowledge their duty to help create a better life for people elsewhere in the world – 'a still outstanding duty', Bauman writes, 'and a moral imperative more acute and compelling than ever in the past'.[10]

To the question whether or not 'historic time [has] run out for the European adventure? For Europe *as* adventure?' – a question around which the entire book is organized – Bauman therefore offers an emphatic 'no'. Europe has lost much of its power and prestige; it has had to learn the hard way that its voice is no longer the leading one. 'But singed fingers may yet prove an asset', he argues, 'they would be reluctant to play with fire – and averse to piling up powder kegs.' It was Europe who invented the nation. Now the time has come to transcend nationhood and invent *humanity*, and when it comes to reaching that Kantian world of perpetual peace in which law and cooperation take the place of brute force, Europe has already taken the first crucial steps:

---

[8] Zygmunt Bauman, *Europe: An Unfinished Adventure* (Cambridge: Polity Press, 2004), 10, 11, 7–8.

[9] Ibid., 11, 12.

[10] Ibid., 10.

> Europe is well prepared if not to *lead*, then most certainly to *show* the way from the Hobbesian planet to the Kantian 'universal unification of the human species'. It has traversed that road itself, at least the initial part of it, up to the station of 'peaceful neighbourly cohabitation', and knows only too well the human costs of deviations and delays. And for the last half-century it has put in practice, even if with only mixed success, the measures that need to be taken if any further advance on that road is to be achieved.'[11]

The European Union is viewed by some as a protective shield against the 'have-nots' of this world – as a way of creating a 'Fortress Europe'. For Bauman, however, it provides a promising framework for living up to 'that still outstanding European duty' and for gathering the 'resources, force and will' that are 'necessary to tackle the tasks of supracontinental, planetary dimensions'. Having acquired as a result of its long involvement with the rest of the world an awareness of the realities of colonialism along with a sense of cultural hybridization and multi-ethnicity, Europeans now know that 'the other is a necessary component' of their own identity. What this means is that 'this time the interests of Europe and of the peoples outside its borders will not just coincide, but overlap', Bauman argues.[12]

For Bauman as for most other Europeans who set out to discuss Europe and the European project – we saw this to be the case with Ulrich Beck and Edgar Grande in Chapter 1 – the transatlantic relationship forms an important subtext. The longest of *Europe: An Unfinished Adventure*'s four chapters is devoted to Europe 'In the Empire's Shadow', and Bauman's ultimate concern is whether Europe is strong enough to offer an alternative to 'the Hobbesian world of the planetary frontier land brought into being, serviced and perpetuated by the new empire.' He ends up arguing, interestingly enough, that when all is said and done, it will be the US with its Hobbesian frontier-land mentality that will have created for European ways of thinking a new and more vital role to play:

> The salutary alternative which Europe – and only Europe – can offer, is based on the European – and only European – tradition. At a time when America, which relegated Europe to the second division of power games, has (in Will Hutton's words) 'disqualified itself from the fight for security, prosperity, and justice', Europe, as Inozemtsev and Kuznetsova point out, having learned the truth the hard way, stoutly refuses 'to regard force as a source of justice', and even more so to confuse the two, and it is well placed to 'oppose the United States as *justice* opposes *force* rather than as *weakness* opposes *power*'.[13]

---

11 Ibid., 34, 39, 40.
12 Ibid., 37, 41, 35.
13 Ibid., 88, 39.

Here, as throughout the chapter, Bauman is taking on Robert Kagan and his controversial theories about American strength and European weakness in *Of Paradise and Power: America and Europe in the New World Order* (2003). Thanks to its unique history, the unfinished adventure called Europe, Bauman counters, is the only viable or plausible alternative in an increasingly interconnected world. Europe's primary weapon of choice is that most 'socializing' of values: justice – 'the one value that guards the common good (that is, from everyone's point of view, the good of others) against the inroads of egotistic self-promotion. "Justice" primes the human habitat for peaceful and friendly togetherness.'[14]

THE CONCEPT OF 'CULTURE'

Browsing through the comparatively large section on books about Europe and the European Union recently at a major London bookshop, I was struck by the fact that with one or two exceptions all the books presented in this section had to do with political and/or economic aspects. The more cultural aspects were not represented. For most academics, it would seem, European projects and visions are still overwhelmingly concerned with politics.

Creating the imagery that will speak to what Wim Wenders calls Europe's *emotional potential* and that will help foster a feeling of European identity is, however, not entirely unproblematic, and this may be one reason why so few cultural European dreams or visions find their way into intellectual discourses. When attempting to discuss the notion of 'European culture' one does, in fact, run into a second cluster of problems – a cluster that has to do with the word 'culture'. There is no need to reiterate the discussions we have witnessed over the past many years concerning the view of culture as 'fine arts' versus the more anthropological view of culture as a way of life. These are well known. Suffice it to say that when it comes to European culture, older notions of culture as something refined or more highbrow still hover in the background – however much one would have thought they had been abolished by now.

Take the trouble Bassam Tibi ran into with his notion of a European '*Leitkultur*' (core culture), for example. Born in Damascus and raised in the Middle East before coming to Germany to study with members of the Frankfurt school, Tibi later became a professor of international relations at the University of Göttingen and the author of several books on modern Arab history and politics. He argues that Europeans have been too slow to acknowledge the need for a '*Leitkultur*', a set of common rules for the behaviour of

---

[14] Ibid., 127.

Europeans, new as well as old. In their eagerness not to appear intolerant and bigoted, Europeans have lost touch with the best part of Enlightenment thinking: respect for individual rights and freedoms. As a result,

> Europeans [now] seem to need a second Enlightenment, an inter-cultural dialogue during which they decide on their relationship with the rest of the non-European world. As part of the assignment, they need to de-romanticize their ethnically exclusive way of thinking. However, this should not lead to a false sense of self-denial . . . As the core of the European cultural modern, they need to insist on a catalogue of norms and values for others as well as for themselves. I call such a catalogue a 'Leitkultur'.[15]

Tibi sees Islamic fundamentalism as a modern totalitarian political movement that misuses popular religious devotion. In the global fragmentation that has emerged from the end of the Cold War, such Islamic fundamentalism threatens to provoke a new world disorder.[16] Brought up in the Islamic faith himself, Tibi has nothing against Islamic spiritual faith. It is Islamic fundamentalism and its political response to Western dominance that are the problem. Beyond targeting Western political power, he explains, the fundamentalist revolt also targets Western culture and values – hence the need for a '*Leitkultur*'.

The term, '*Leitkultur*', created quite a stir when it was first introduced. For European intellectuals, it had unfortunate echoes of a Europe that used to consider itself better, more refined than everybody else. Furthermore, it suggested that 'culture' can be talked about in the singular – something that is deeply problematic for intellectuals who value diversity and pluralism. For a while, the very term effectively blocked a discussion of Tibi's arguments, and he could probably have saved himself a lot of trouble by choosing a different one. The term was, Tibi claims, misused during the German general election of 2005 and thus ended up having mostly negative connotations – connotations that were never intended on his part. What he did intend the word to

---

[15] Bassam Tibi, *Europa ohne Identität? Leitkultur oder Wertebeliebigkeit* (Munich: Siedler, 2004), 183 – my translation from the German: 'Die Europäer scheinen einer zweiten Aufklärung zu bedürfen, in deren Rahmen sie ihr Verhältnis zum nicht-europäischen Rest der Welt im inter-kulturellen Dialog bestimmen. Zu den Aufgaben gehört, ihr ethnisch-exklusives Denkens zu entromantisieren. Allerdings dürfen sie damit nicht fälschlich eine Selbstverleugnung verbinden . . . Auf dem Boden der europäischen kulturellen Moderne müssen sie einen Normen- und Werte-Katalog verbindlich für sich und andere verlangen. Ich nenne diesen Katalog Leitkultur.' Several of Tibi's books have been translated into English.

[16] This is an argument that Tibi makes in *The Challenge of Fundamentalism: Political Islam and the New World Disorder* (Berkeley, CA: University of California Press, 2002), for example.

connote, he writes in the introduction to *Europa ohne Identität*, is 'nothing else but an orientation, a kind of red thread in the form of a value consensus concerning civilizational European values such as secular democracy, individual (*not* collective) human rights, civil society, tolerance as well as religious and cultural pluralism'.[17]

Precisely how problematic an issue 'culture' can be also becomes clear if we look at the attempts made through the 1990s by the European Union and its policy makers to popularize Europe through culture. According to Chris Shore, as we saw in Chapter 1, the Declaration on European Identity issued by the European Community, as it was then called, in 1973 marks the first significant step toward defining a *cultural* – as opposed to an economic and/or political – basis for European integration. And it was only with the Maastricht Treaty of 1992 (and its Title IX, Art. 128) that the area of culture was brought within the jurisdiction of the Community. Until then, purely economic reasons were used for achieving cultural ends.

In the mid-1990s, the Council of Europe took the initiative to form a Task Force on Culture and Development which issued the report *In from the margins* in 1997. The subtitle of the report is 'A contribution to the debate on Culture and Development in Europe', and as a part of this contribution the report suggests 'the addition of a protocol on the recognition of cultural rights to the European Convention for the Protection of Human Rights and Fundamental Freedoms'. However, 'recognising the difficulties some governments have in agreeing [to] standard-setting instruments in this sector', the Task Force 'commend[s] the work being undertaken on preparing a European Declaration on Cultural Rights'.[18] Such a declaration has not yet come to be, but it is interesting to see how very seriously the Task Force takes the cultural goals of Title IX, Article 128 of the Maastricht Treaty.

The central themes of *In from the margins* are two interlocking priorities – 'to bring the millions of dispossessed and disadvantaged Europeans in from the margins of society and cultural policy in from the margins of governance'. The latter priority is a precondition for the former. Unless more resources are

---

[17] Tibi, supra n. 15, p. xvi – my translation from the German: 'Dabei meint der Begriff "Leitkultur" . . . nichts anderes als eine Orientierung, eine Art Leitfaden in Form eines Wertekonsenses über zivilisatorische europäische Werte wie sakuläre Demokratie, individuelle (*nicht* kollektive) Menschenrechte, Zivilgesellschaft, Toleranz sowie religiösen und kulturellen Pluralismus.'

[18] The European Task Force on Culture and Development, *In from the margins: A contribution to the debate on Culture and Development in Europe* (Strasbourg: Council of Europe, 1997), 276. The following pages concerning *In from the margins* are taken from my article, 'On European Narratives of Human Rights and Their Possible Implications for Copyright', in Fiona Macmillan (ed.), *New Directions in Copyright Law, Volume 6* (Cheltenham, UK and Northampton, MA, USA: Edward Elgar, 2007).

made available to the area of culture and unless the status of those ministers, ministries and civil servants who are in charge of it is increased, policy makers will be unable to do their job properly. Culture, it should be acknowledged, is more than a 'soft' entity which has contributed to the economy and added to the quality of life in some loose way; 'culture is also "hard" – being both an objective factor of production and an asset for, and an indicator of, positive human growth defined in qualitative, but measurable terms (for example access to opportunities, positive self-definition, the ability to participate in social activity and intellectual and cognitive capacities)'.[19]

In today's knowledge society, our most valuable raw material is human intelligence: '[c]reativity, innovation, research and education – these are the motors of development. That is why to invest in culture is to invest in the economy.' The report lists three pre-conditions for promoting *creativity*: freedom of expression, access for artists and cultural workers to the appropriate means of production and distribution, and public support for creativity. Creative freedom is relatively widespread throughout Europe today. The problem lies elsewhere; 'there is a more subtle censorship at work which limits [creative] freedom, if not in law then in fact – namely, economic censorship. Lack of resources, the pressure for instant profitability and a general obsession with money tends to constrain the unrestricted exercise of creative expression.'[20] The more market-oriented European societies become, the more difficult it becomes to argue for state funding or subsidy of artists and the arts.

This market-orientation and its effects on the cultural domain are in some ways due to what the report calls 'the transatlantic challenge'. The fear that 'Americanisation', supported by the energy of US culture and its commercial power, affects most aspects of European life and puts the multicultural richness of our lives at risk runs like a red thread through the report. With the rise of neo-liberal economic policies in Europe, support for the arts has declined and a more commercial approach to fund-raising along American lines has been encouraged.

In the absence of a general agreement on the economic justification for subsidy, one possible way out, the report interestingly enough suggests, is to argue that certain kinds of artistic works may be looked upon as a collective common good, and as such deserve public support:

> If a distinction can be drawn between art which is valued according to consumer demand and that which acquires a significance through critical appraisal, intellectual property rights, and the interests of collectors, 'real' highly priced works of art become a collective good unconstrained by consumers' subjective likings or

---

19 *In from the margins*, supra n. 18, 9, 31.
20 Ibid., 49, 48.

> preferences. Such arguments can help to justify public support for maintaining the 'collective' cultural heritage and for seeing the arts as reservoir for exploitation (educationally, say, or commercially) by future generations.[21]

The distinction made here between art that is valued by general consumer demand (i.e. popular art) and that which is valued 'through critical appraisal', 'intellectual property rights' and 'the interests of collectors' is an interesting one. Throughout the report, the two notions of culture – culture as 'fine arts' versus the more anthropological view of culture as a way of life – are constantly being juggled. Right at the beginning, we are told how the very definition of culture provides 'a difficult terminological problem'. While opting for 'a definition which encompasses the arts in the widest possible sense', 'we' have not always been able to 'adhere strictly to the definition of culture we have chosen' and 'we' only hope that 'the context makes the sense clear.'[22]

Well, what the context does make clear to the reader is that the report is highly ambivalent – while regretting the bad American popular culture influence and wishing to counter it with some sort of state regulation and/or subsidy of highbrow culture, the report feels obliged, in its priority to bring the millions of dispossessed and disadvantaged Europeans in from the margins, to promote cultural rights in their totality. Except for the distinction made between 'art which is valued according to consumer demand and that which acquires a significance through critical appraisal' mentioned above, highbrow culture is never mentioned as such, though. What the report ostensibly wants to support is the diversity of European culture(s) – a somewhat more politically correct way of talking about culture.

In its focus on the issue of fund-raising as this relates to the organization of culture, *In from the margins* touches upon a problem that is of increasing interest to European scholars. Debating the Americanization of German culture, for example, Professor Winfried Fluck suggests that the most important thing to consider today is whether European countries are taking over American models of financing culture:

> The major issue at stake in the relationship of, and comparison between, American and German culture today is the question of how, or on what principles, culture should be organized and financed. In the US, the organizing principle is mainly commercial . . . In Germany, on the other hand, there still exists a public consensus that such cultural forms should be supported by direct or indirect forms of taxation . . .

21 Ibid., 64.
22 Ibid., 21.

The most important issue in the challenge of Americanization today is therefore, Fluck concludes, 'no longer whether we get the wrong kind of culture but rather whether we are drifting toward an American model of organizing and financing culture'.[23]

THE TRANSATLANTIC RELATIONSHIP AND EUROPEAN NARRATIVES OF HUMAN RIGHTS

The Transatlantic Relationship as Subtext

The European Union celebrated its fiftieth anniversary in March 2007. This is probably one reason why we have seen a number of books being published recently on Europe – on European history and identity and on the relationship of Europe with other parts of the world. As the titles of books such as T.R. Reid's *The United States of Europe: The New Superpower and the End of American Supremacy*, Jeremy Rifkin's *The European Dream: How Europe's Vision of the Future Is Quietly Eclipsing the American Dream*, Stephen Haseler's *Super-State: The New Europe and Its Challenge to America*, and Timothy Garton Ash's *Free World: America, Europe, and the Surprising Future of the West* indicate, it is especially the transatlantic relationship that preoccupies scholars and journalists interested in the future of Europe.[24]

As an American studies scholar, I have been intrigued to discover the extent to which fears of American political and cultural hegemony underlie, even drive, European discussions of the future. The US is ever present at the table – in much the same way that earlier Europe would invariably figure in American discussions about identity. Down through American history, the question 'What does it mean to be American?' would most often equal the question 'To what extent is America different from Europe?'. All the classic American texts centre around what later came to be known as 'American exceptionalism', and until fairly recently the wish was to appear 'exceptional' by comparison to Europe. Today, as other parts of the world are becoming

---

[23] Winfried Fluck, 'The Americanization of German Culture? The Strange, Paradoxical Ways of Modernity', in Agnes C. Mueller (ed.), *German Pop Culture: How 'American' Is It?* (Ann Arbor, MI: University of Michigan Press, 2004), 30–31.

[24] T.R. Reid, *The United States of Europe: The New Superpower and the End of American Supremacy* (New York: Penguin Books, 2004); J. Rifkin, *The European Dream: How Europe's Vision of the Future is Quietly Eclipsing the American Dream* (Cambridge: Polity Press, 2004); Stephen Haseler, *Super-State: The New Europe and Its Challenge to America* (London & New York: I.B. Tauris & Co. Ltd, 2004); T. Garton Ash, *Free World: America, Europe, and the Surprising Future of the West* (New York: Vintage Books, 2004).

increasingly relevant to the US and as demographic patterns underscore the interest in Asia and South America, Europe no longer occupies the space in American thinking that it used to. President George W. Bush's first visit outside the US was not to Europe but to Mexico, for example.

Needless to say, the suggestion often made by American neo-conservative thinkers and Bush supporters that Europe no longer counts politically and intellectually does not sit well with Europeans. Who likes to think that they are 'have-beens,' after all? Recent political events have likewise served to drive a wedge into transatlantic relations. With the notable exception of Great Britain, most European countries do not agree with current American politics in the Middle East, for example. Recent European opinion polls even suggest that a majority of Europeans (the British included) think that the US is itself a 'rogue state'.

The reaction on the part of European intellectuals and writers is one of mixed fear and contempt – fear that American culture and values, helped along by American economic and political power, will have so much of an impact worldwide that local European cultures will have no chance of surviving, and contempt at the very contents of this culture. They insist on their right to be critical and to ask questions. In its representation of life as uncomplicated and sunny, popular culture – especially that originating in the US – offers a surface treatment only of issues that deserve much more careful treatment. It is the self-reflexive quality of a Europe that has lost its naiveté and its feeling of superiority which is pointed out by those intellectuals and writers. As far as they are concerned, a Europe that reflects, remembers, and hesitates before it acts is to be preferred to a US that considers fast response to world matters a virtue in and of itself. Stefan Chwin puts it this way:

> The most European about us is that we are still capable of asking these questions, and that we do so over and over again. And that European literature is capable of asking them . . . What is European about us is an awareness of the complexity of the human world – an awareness that protects us from reducing things to a black-and-white perspective. An awareness of the conflicts between knowing and acting, between ethics and politics, between justice and mercy, individual fate and collective responsibility, between punishment and revenge, efficiency and truth. A difficult awareness that we inherited from Shakespeare, Goethe, Thomas Mann, Mickiewicz and the culture of the wise, old Greeks. For even the *unnecessary complications* that may arise from reflecting on what happens in the world as well as in the hearts of human beings make us European, even though European [and American] mass culture does whatever it can to make us forget such *complications*.[25]

[25] Stefan Chwin, 'Die Kindergärtnerin aus der Twerskaja-straβe', in Ursula Keller and Ilma Rakusa (eds), *Europa schreibt. Was ist das europäische an den Literaturen Europas?* (Hamburg: edition Körber-Stiftung, 2003), 91. My translation from the German.

Josef Joffe, the editor of the German newspaper *Die Zeit*, has argued that while the most vicious and direct expressions of anti-Americanism are to be found in the Arab and Islamic world, the essential features of such anti-Americanism may also be found in European discourses on the US. These features include 'stereotypization, denigration, demonization, obsession and elimination', and 'on the level of stereotypization and denigration, three basic themes obey a single common denominator: Yahoo America vs. Superior Europe'.[26]

As far as many Europeans are concerned, Americans are not only morally deficient (basic theme number one) in that they still have the death penalty, for example; Americans are also socially as well as culturally retrograde (basic themes two and three, respectively). And while thus denigrating the US, Joffe argues, Europeans are posing Europe as a refined counter-example. Deep down, Europeans are talking less about America than about themselves, elevating Europe as an 'Un-America':

> Some anti-Americanism will surely be muted by wiser American policies that reduce the (rational) fear of American power unbound. But *au fond*, anti-Americanism is not about America. At heart, any anti-ism is a crisis of collective self-esteem that cries out for compensation, be it by extolling one's own culture or by denigrating the Other's.[27]

The constant presence of transatlantic tension in European intellectual discourses may thus be seen as yet another way of negotiating Europe, its past and possible future.

Figuring out what 'Europe' is is hard enough. Things become really tough, though, when it is 'European culture' that is under discussion. These two words come with so much historical and symbolic baggage that it is no wonder most visions of a united and strong Europe centre around politics and economics. What this means in practice is that it has become extremely difficult to talk about quality – as opposed to quantity – in connection with the arts. This seems to be especially clear when it comes to issues of funding and arguments concerning which kinds of cultural products are deemed worthy of being subsidized by the state. One way of making it easier is to say what European culture is NOT – it is NOT American popular culture!

---

[26] Josef Joffe, 'Dissecting Anti-isms', *The American Interest Online*, Summernote 2006 – available at http://www.the-american-interest.com/ai2/article.cfm?Id=83&MId=4 (last visited on 5 January 2009), 5.

[27] Ibid., 10.

Law's Promise and European Human Rights Narratives

Considering this deep and abiding mistrust of all things American voiced in much European writing, it is interesting that Europeans seem currently to be taking over one of the most American of all discourses: rights talk. The social role of US law was already distinctive in the 1830s, when Alexis de Tocqueville wrote *Democracy in America*, and in 1983, historian Jerold S. Auerbach argued for the centrality of law in American history and culture in this way:

> By now the predominance of law as a cultural force is beyond dispute. It might be measured by the assertive role of the Supreme Court (whether heroic or villainous is beyond the point); by the hypnotic allure of the courtroom trial as a staple of national melodrama: by the astonishing attractiveness of the legal profession as a career choice. No longer is it possible to reflect seriously about American culture without accounting for the centrality of law in American history and society, and in the mythology of American uniqueness and grandeur.[28]

In my own *Legally Speaking*,[29] I talked about these American commitments to the ideal of law, or to what Kenneth Karst once called 'law's promise'.[30] One of the cultural texts that I discussed was Patricia Williams' *The Alchemy of Race and Rights* of 1991. Williams' was one of the texts later claimed by Derrick Bell to be one of the founding texts of Critical Race Theory.[31]

Williams' book is one long defence of rights talk. For blacks, she writes, but also for other Americans, the prospect of attaining full rights under the law has always been a highly motivational, semi-religious source of hope, and some of the worst moments in American history occurred, not because people asserted their rights, but because they failed to commit themselves to a fight for rights:

> 'Rights' feels new in the mouths of most black people. It is still deliciously empowering to say. It is the magic wand of visibility and invisibility, of inclusion and exclusion, of power and no power. The concept of rights, both positive and nega-

28 Jerold S. Auerbach, *Justice Without Law? Resolving Disputes Without Lawyers* (New York and Oxford: Oxford University Press, 1983), 115.

29 Helle Porsdam, *Legally Speaking: Contemporary American Culture and the Law* (Amherst, MA: University of Massachusetts Press, 1999).

30 See Kenneth L. Karst, *Law's Promise, Law's Expression: Visions of Power in the Politics of Race, Gender, and Religion* (New Haven, CT, and London: Yale University Press, 1993).

31 See Derrick Bell, 'Who's Afraid of Critical Race Theory?' *University of Illinois Law Review* 1995.4, (1995): 893–910.

tive, is the marker of our citizenship, our relation to others . . . In discarding rights altogether, one discards a symbol too deeply enmeshed in the psyche of the oppressed to lose without trauma and much resistance.[32]

In a dream toward the end of *The Alchemy of Race and Rights*, Williams speaks of the law and her relationship with it in this almost poetic way:

> The Law. The law says, the law is. My life, my tissue, my membrane. Connection, suspicion, privacy, the secret wedged in the void. The corrupt entrenchment of my thirst and loneliness. I am a tiny fragment, a gear and linchpin to the law.[33]

It is quite clear that, for Williams, in modern America the law has come to constitute one of the most important ways in which people define themselves and their relationship to each other.

I bring up Patricia Williams here because I hear echoes of her belief in law's promise in current discourses on Europe and human rights. At times oddly out of tune, in their insistence on universalism and colour blindness, with current intellectual tendencies toward cultural relativism, such discourses reflect a wish to use the law to do good, as it were. As already mentioned in Chaper 1, the role played by the European Court of Justice has been remarkable, for example. With one important ruling after another, it has furthered Community integration and has helped shape the emerging European Union. In addition, there is the role played by that other European court, the European Court of Human Rights (ECtHR). We shall come back, in Chapter 4, to the ECtHR and some of its important decisions. For now, we shall merely note, with Michael D. Goldhaber, that:

> over the past thirty years, the European Court of Human Rights has developed an American-style body of constitutional law, comparable in its level of ambition, and in many ways more progressive. Unheralded by the mass press, this obscure tribunal in Strasbourg, France, has become, in many ways the Supreme Court of Europe . . .The European court routinely confronts nations over their most culturally sensitive, hot-button issues. And – what is most extraordinary – the nations comply.[34]

The official EU European narrative is very much a legal narrative. In a somewhat polemical defence of what he calls 'the European Dream', Jeremy

---

[32] Patricia J. Williams, *The Alchemy of Race and Rights: Diary of a Law Professor* (Cambridge, MA: Harvard University Press, 1991), 164–165.

[33] Ibid., 208.

[34] Michael D. Goldhaber, *A People's History of the European Court of Human Rights* (New Brunswick, NJ, and London: Rutgers University Press, 2007), 1–2.

Rifkin[35] argues that 'the EU citizen is the first in the world to be fully guaranteed universal human rights enforceable by law'. Whereas the American Dream was based on property rights, markets and nation-state governance, the new European Dream – which, as the book's subtitle announces, is currently 'quietly eclipsing the American Dream' – is centred around human rights, networks, and multilevel governance. Human rights are 'the norms that govern network activity'; indeed:

> human rights are the legal articulation of the new European Dream. The European Dream and universal human rights come together as a single package. The Dream is the aspiration; the rights are the behavioral norms for fulfilling Europeans' hopes for the future.

More cosmopolitan and less focused on the brute force of power, the European Dream is better suited, argues Rifkin, to an increasingly interconnected and interdependent world in which norms of behaviour will be rewarded that further inclusion, instead of exclusion. Universal human rights are all about empathy and inclusion, narrowing 'the divide between the connected and the unconnected, the included and the excluded'.[36]

The belief in law's empowerment is perhaps nowhere more clearly expressed than in the discussions concerning that 'neglected' or 'underdeveloped' category of human rights: cultural rights. Even though cultural rights are routinely mentioned together with economic and social rights, they have always been treated as 'poor relations' of these other rights. But this may well be changing as human rights activists and social scientists have started arguing that cultural rights can be used as a means to protect cultural integrity and heritage.

An underlying claim made for cultural rights is that they are in fact fundamental to the protection of all other rights. The experience of the 1990s clearly shows how many internal conflicts, especially in the European context, are linked to the issue of cultural identity, argues Janusz Symonides. By the end of the 20th century:

> cultural rights formulated by the Universal Declaration of Human Rights, developed by the International Covenants and other human rights instruments, are obtaining new importance. They are today '*empowering rights*' . . . Without the

---

[35] Jeremy Rifkin is, of course, an American and not a European. I include him here, however, because he served as an adviser to Romano Prodi while the latter was the president of the European Commission (1999–2004), and because he has been a keen observer of European trends for many years.

[36] Jeremy Rifkin, *The European Dream: How Europe's Vision of the Future is Quietly Eclipsing the American Dream* (Cambridge: Polity Press, 2004), 278, 279, 280.

> recognition of cultural rights, cultural plurality and diversity, fully democratic societies cannot function properly [my emphasis].[37]

The scope of cultural rights, Symonides continues, depends on how one defines 'culture'. UNESCO has proposed, for example, that 'culture is not merely an accumulation of works and knowledge which an elite produces . . . is not limited to access to works of art and the humanities, but is at one and the same time the acquisition of knowledge, the demand for a way of life and the need to communicate.' And as far as the Council of Europe is concerned, '[c]ulture, as experienced by the majority of the population today, means much more than traditional arts and the humanities. Nowadays, culture embraces the education system, the mass media, the *cultural* industries . . .'[38]

This takes us right back to the attempt to come to terms with the word 'culture' undertaken in the European Council report, *In from the margins*, discussed above. It is interesting to note in this context that neither Symonides nor the Task Force behind *In from the margins* quite likes the tendency toward cultural relativism that is implicit in some scholars' arguments in favour of cultural rights. As Symonides puts it:

> The acceptance of the right of everyone to have different *cultural* identities, the recognition of *cultural* specificities and differences is viewed sometimes as 'justification' of *cultural* relativism. This approach is not only wrong but is also dangerous. The acceptance of the very idea that persons belonging to one culture should not judge the policies and values of other cultures, that any system of common values cannot and does not exist, indeed undermines the very basis of the international community and the '*human* family'. They cannot function without the existence of standards allowing them to determine what is right or wrong, what is good or bad.[39]

As for how to help strengthen this category of rights, Symonides argues, the best way is to see them as part of the whole or larger category of economic, social and cultural rights.[40]

When it comes to the first part of this category, economic and social rights, Symonides is on much more solid ground. The support for the so-called second-generation of human rights is very strong in Europe. In this, as we shall

---

37 Janusz Symonides, 'Cultural Rights: A Neglected Category of Human Rights', *International Social Science Journal*, Dec. 1998, Issue 158, also available at http://www.iupui.edu/%7Eanthkb/a104/humanrights/cultrights.htm (last visited on 5 January 2009). References are from this website. This quotation may be found at the end of 'Introduction'.

38 Ibid., quotations to be found in the middle of 2.1.

39 Ibid., at the beginning of 5.1.

40 Ibid., toward the very end.

see in Chapter 5, Europeans differ from Americans who tend to be mostly interested in first-generation human rights (civil and political rights). Europeans increasingly talk about the 'indivisibility' of human rights and do not agree with American arguments that the core of human rights is made up of first-generation rights only. The US only ratified the International Covenant on Civil and Political Rights in 1992 and to this day has not yet ratified the other major convention which, together with the International Declaration of Human Rights, makes up the so-called International Bill of Rights, the International Covenant on Economic, Social, and Cultural Rights.

It is not that the US has never acknowledged the tradition of economic and social rights. As Cass Sunstein has reminded us, Franklin D. Roosevelt's State of the Union Address of 1944 did introduce the idea that human beings have inherent economic and social rights. In this speech – echoing his famous Four Freedoms speech of 1941 in which he proposed the four freedoms: freedom of speech and of religion, freedom from want and from fear – Roosevelt called for a Second Bill of Rights. This new, modern Bill of Rights would consist of eight relevant rights – rights which would together 'spell security'. These rights were:

- The right to a useful and remunerative job in the industries or shops or farms or mines of the nation;
- The right to earn enough to provide adequate food and clothing and recreation;
- The right of farmers to raise and sell their products at a return which will give them and their families a decent living;
- The right of every businessman, large or small, to trade in an atmosphere of freedom from unfair competition and domination by monopolies at home or abroad;
- The right of every family to a decent home;
- The right to adequate medical care and the opportunity to achieve and enjoy good health;
- The right to adequate protection from the economic fears of old age, sickness, accident, and unemployment;
- The right to a good education.[41]

One of the rights in Roosevelt's proposed 'GI Bill of Rights', which was signed into law in June 1944, was the right of every returning World War Two veteran to receive a college degree or other training at the government's

[41] See Cass R. Sunstein, *The Second Bill of Rights: FDR's Unfinished Revolution and Why We Need It More Than Ever* (New York: Basic Books, 2004), 13.

expense. But other than that, argues Sunstein, these rights were never taken as seriously as Roosevelt had hoped. They were never enacted and were by and large forgotten by the public, although some of them actually were adopted thanks to the judicial activism of the Warren Court (1953–1969). The narrow election of Richard Nixon to the presidency in 1968 and the conservative Supreme Court appointments that resulted are partly to blame, according to Sunstein. To this we may add that the Cold War 'happened', and that economic and social rights, which were heavily supported by the Eastern Bloc headed by the USSR, came to be viewed by the Americans as a first dangerous step toward communism. We shall come back to this in Chapters 5 and 6.

CONCLUDING REMARKS: THE EUROPEAN 'SOCIAL MODEL'

While European thoughts of a European soul come in many shapes and variations, there seem to be two things that many European intellectuals share: a wish to promote tolerance for a multi-ethnic Europe and a wish to either preserve or create a new version of the European welfare state. The two go together, the argument most often voiced being that tolerance is best promoted in a welfare state framework of sorts.

According to Anthony Giddens, 'Europe's welfare system is often regarded as the jewel in the crown – perhaps the main feature that gives the European societies their special quality'.[42] Many different definitions of the so-called European Social Model (EMS) have circulated over the years, but the one Giddens offers includes an interventionist state funded through taxation; a welfare system with high social protection, especially for its weaker members; and the containment of inequality, especially in the economic area.[43] Underlying Giddens' version of the EMS is a set of values which he summarizes in this way:

> Sharing both risk and opportunity widely across society, cultivating social solidarity or cohesion, protecting the most vulnerable members of society through active social intervention, encouraging consultation rather than confrontation in industry, and *providing a rich framework of social and economic citizenship rights for the population as a whole* [my emphasis].[44]

---

42 Giddens, supra n. 3, 1.
43 Ibid., 2.
44 Ibid.

David Held shares Giddens' interest in and focus on economic and social rights. The guiding ethical basis for the sort of global social democracy he sets out to promote in *Global Covenant* is a set of cosmopolitan principles of equal respect, equal concern and the priority of the vital needs of all human beings. These, he says in his Preface, are not merely principles 'for some remote utopia; they are at the centre of significant post-Second World War legal and political developments'[45] – developments that were framed against Nazism, fascism and the Holocaust. For Held, moreover, the story of globalization is not just an economic one. True, we have witnessed an expansion of global markets which has put new questions about the regulation not just of national economies, but also of big international companies on the political agenda everywhere. But this does not change the fact that the story of globalization is

> also one of the growing aspirations for international law and justice. From the United Nations system to the European Union, from changes to the laws of war to the entrenchment of human rights, from the emergence of international environmental regimes to the foundation of the International Criminal Court, there is also another narrative being told – *a narrative which seeks to reframe human activity and entrench it in law, rights and responsibilities* [my emphasis].[46]

For Jürgen Habermas, too, equal social rights are the core of democratic citizenship. The social welfare state, as we have known it in the 20th century, is threatened by a global economy that increasingly escapes the control of the regulatory state as well as by proponents of neo-liberalism who seek to minimize that state's core function of redistribution and in general show a lack of concern with social justice. There is, he argues, one – and probably only one – hope left for the welfare state, and that is the construction of supranational institutions such as the EU. It will take such a supranational entity to keep pace with an increasingly transnational, globalizing economy. The question is, however, whether it will be possible to nurture a postnational sense of solidarity – a sense of solidarity beyond the nation state – in a Europe that remains integrated only through markets and a unified currency.

At the moment, such a cosmopolitan solidarity is still lacking, but Habermas is of the opinion that widening the sense of a collective identity *is* possible:

> But precisely the artificial conditions in which national consciousness arose argue against the defeatist assumption that a form of civic solidarity among strangers can only be generated within the confines of the nation. If this form of collective identity was due to a highly abstractive leap from the local and dynastic to national and

45 Held, supra n. 7, p. xi.
46 Ibid, pp. x–xi.

> then to democratic consciousness, why shouldn't this learning process be able to continue?[47]

Taking on, in the interesting essay 'Remarks on Legitimation through Human Rights', 'the apologetic role of a Western participant in a cross-cultural discussion of human rights', Habermas offers a 'working hypothesis': 'that the standards of human rights stem less from the particular cultural background of Western civilization than from the attempt to answer specific challenges posed by a social modernity that has in the meantime covered the globe'.[48] Among these challenges is the question of legitimacy – how to argue for the legitimacy of legal rules in a pluralistic society in which it is no longer possible to fall back on a religiously or metaphysically grounded natural law or some other eternally valid moral law. Today, our laws, even constitutional laws, can be and are changed regularly according to the political will of the legislator. How, then, in the midst of such temporality can we make people uphold their respect for the laws – such respect being a prerequisite for their actual compliance with these laws?

Political theory has, Habermas argues, offered 'a twofold answer to the question of legitimacy: popular sovereignty and human rights'. To the principle of popular sovereignty we owe democratic features such as the rights of communication and participation in the political process that 'secure the public autonomy of politically enfranchised citizens'. By contrast, classical human rights give to citizens the means to secure their *private* autonomy – or 'scope for the pursuit of personal life-plans'.[49] Between them, that is, popular sovereignty and human rights provide the legitimacy for ensuring both the civic/public and private autonomy of the individual. Until now, political philosophy has not been able to work out the correct balance between the two. This is a challenge for the EU, and only time will show whether it is able successfully to meet such a challenge.

Whether grounded in the challenges posed by a universal social modernity or the wish to uphold the norms and underlying values of the welfare state, human rights for these European intellectuals are what Europeans are good at, what they believe in – and European human rights narratives serve the important purpose of creating a kind of European cultural glue, something around which Europeans can rally and in which they believe. Europe could, says Held, play an important role in promoting the cause of global social democracy: '[a]s the home of both social democracy and a historic experiment in

---

47 Jürgen Habermas, *The Postnational Constellation: Political Essays* (Cambridge, MA: MIT Press, 2001), 102.

48 Ibid., 121.

49 Ibid, 115–116.

governance beyond the state, Europe has accumulated a wealth of experience in considering institutional designs for suprastate governance'.[50]

There are hints throughout both *Europe in the Global Age* and *Global Covenant* – as there are in Baumann, as we saw – to the effect that this makes Europe 'un-America', to borrow Joffe's phrase. For Held, especially, the weakening of international law that we have seen since 9/11 is directly related to the new American security doctrine of unilateral and pre-emptive war which 'contradicts most of the core tenets of international politics and international agreements since 1945'.[51] But he and his colleagues move beyond Europe as 'un-America'. Their idea of a European cosmopolitan narrative of human rights is not just a negative, anti- and un-American one. It is an affirmative idea – one that, perhaps somewhat ironically, shows a certain similarity to American dreams of the right to have rights. Some Americans may well wish to repudiate the contents of such an affirmative European narrative – both on the grounds that it places too much emphasis either on economic and social rights or on international or supranational law (or both) – but they would recognize the belief in law's promise. They would furthermore recognize the move from politics to law involved here, the way in which a legal or rights discourse is used to create identity and a set of common values.

Ostensibly about politics and economics, these books are in the end also about culture. They may not broadcast directly and concretely those images that speak to what Wim Wenders calls Europe's *emotional potential*, but they do link the area of culture with more political ideas of an 'Open Society' and dialogues on peace and humanity, and they do recognize – as have the European Union and its policy professionals – the potential of culture to popularize Europe. And in so doing, they manage to convey a strong interest in European culture without actually touching upon all the problems connected to the mine field of 'European culture'. The books of Ulrich Beck, Anthony Giddens, David Held and Zygmunt Baumann may be found in the section of the European Union and European Studies at major bookshops, but they could just as easily be placed in the sections of 'cultural studies' or, were there such a section, 'law and humanities'.

---

50 Held, supra n. 7, 167.

51 Ibid., p. xii.

3. Transatlantic dialogues, past and present

It was not until shortly before he died in 1916 that the American writer Henry James became a British citizen. And if it had not been for the refusal of the United States to enter World War One until late in the game, he most probably would have remained an American citizen. James had been a traveller all his life and had written extensively about it. In his travel writing, as in his novels, the theme that critics came to refer to in a rather Euro-centric manner as 'the international theme' – that is a comparison between Europe and the United States – is all-pervasive.

'Europe', as a physical entity but also a concept, had been very important in the Jamesian household, Henry James tells us in his *Autobiography*. Brought up by 'parents homesick, as I conceived, for the ancient order', whose 'theory of our better living was from an early time that we should renew the quest of the ancient', he was aware from a very early age of the existence of two different worlds, the Old and the New.[1] During his childhood and adolescence, the James family travelled extensively in Europe, and going back and forth between Europe and the US became for young Henry a very natural thing to do. Constant exposure to two different sets of values and lifestyles helped create in him an awareness of 'otherness'.

James's attitude toward Europe – the ancient – was by no means unambiguous, however. As a concept of the ancient, Europe possessed a 'positively pleasant "tone"' due to the fact that 'it has had in its past some strange phases and misadventure' – possessed a rich past, that is, compared to which the American scene looked a mere blank. At the same time, James saw this rich European past as a burden, 'the consequence of too much history', in contrast to which the very blankness of the US held up a promise of newness and freshness.[2] In this way, the European past betrayed a sense of narrowness and rigidity that could be downright suffocating.

[1] Henry James, *Autobiography* (Princeton, NJ: Princeton University Press, 1983), 22, 50.

[2] Ibid., 175.

In James's lifetime, the 'other' against which the US and its culture were always measured was Europe. Today, of course, this is no longer the case. The 'other' in the American context is rarely Europe, but rather South America, Asia or Africa. Or if it is Europe, it is Eastern Europe – or the New Europe, as former Secretary of Defense Donald Rumsfeld famously put it a few years ago – rather than Western Europe. Interestingly enough, though, as we saw in Chapter 2, the US has increasingly become over the past few years, and especially since the end of the cold war, a very important 'other' in European thinking. As Europe's role in the American world view becomes smaller, the US looms larger and larger in that of Europeans. And just as Henry James turned the 'international theme' into a fundamental search for identity, national as well as personal, the constant presence of transatlantic tension in European intellectual discourses may be seen as yet another way of negotiating Europe, its past and possible future.

There are many reasons for this, some of which have already been touched upon in previous chapters. In this chapter, the focus will be on transatlantic relations – as they have developed since 'America' was imagined as a 'City upon the Hill' by the first European settlers and as they are today. We will take a look, first, at transatlantic perceptions – at the way in which 'Europe' has always been an object of the American imagination, just as 'America' has been an object of the European imagination. We will then move on to look at some of the official European Union dialogues with the United States. These latter seem to be in better shape than the transatlantic perceptions would make us think. At the official level, the EU has pronounced its willingness to pursue, together with the US, issues of importance such as the need to do something about current environmental problems and to combat international terrorism.

There are real differences of opinion at stake in transatlantic dialogues, official as well as non-official. In terms of the former, some of the most crucial conflicts between the US and the EU concern the unwillingness on the part of the US to cede sovereignty to the structures of international governance. This conflict plays itself out in, among other forums, the international human rights forum, and we shall take a closer look at some of the practical as well as theoretical problems that follow from this conflict in the following chapters. In this chapter, we will take a historical look at European views of the US and vice versa.

The underlying argument will be that although European anti-Americanism and American anti-Europeanism have enormous consequences for policy, they may best be understood as cultural problems. Or, to put it in a different way, what have developed into political problems on the world scene today originate as cultural problems. This means that 'the tools of cultural analysis are necessary to understand [them]'.[3] We will argue, furthermore, that this carries some hope for the future of the transatlantic dialogue. If people can be made to understand, on both sides of the Atlantic, some of the underlying cultural (mis)perceptions vis-à-vis each other, then perhaps they may be able to distinguish between the real problems – the ones that we must discuss and analyse carefully – and the differences of opinion that are merely due to misunderstandings and/or lack of knowledge.

The relationship between the US and Europe has always been crucial. The 'international theme' is still with us. And so is the ambivalence toward that 'other' within the West that is so noticeable in Henry James's writing. It has been a while since Europe and the US were able to conduct world affairs between them. There are other players on the world scene today, and this is as it should be. More agreement and willingness to work together within the West, however, would be to the advantage of everyone. There are enough problems to deal with right now. Increasingly, the most severe of these are of a global kind and might stand a better chance of being resolved if Europe and the US were to stop fighting each other and instead put to good use their combined financial, political and cultural strengths.

TRANSATLANTIC PERCEPTIONS

American Attitudes Towards Europe

In a certain sense, Europe and the US have always used each other to define who or what they were *not* and who or what they would definitely never want to be. 'The United States was born in rebellion against one European power, Great Britain, in cooperation with another, France, whose assistance was crucial in the winning of America's independence', as Norwegian historian Geir Lundestad once reminded us.[4] No wonder, therefore, that the relationship with Europe has always been somewhat ambivalent.

For many of the early settlers, the Europe they had fled in search of new opportunities in the New World did not have much to offer. Politically and socially, this Europe was characterized by a rigid, hierarchical system in which it was very hard to move up the social ladder unless one was born into wealth and status. Only male members of the aristocracy, gentry and merchant classes

[3] Russell A. Berman, *Anti-Americanism in Europe: A Cultural Problem* (Stanford, CA: Hoover Institution Press, 2004), p. xiv.

[4] Geir Lundestad, *The United States and Western Europe since 1945: From 'Empire' by Invitation to Transatlantic Drift* (Oxford: Oxford University Press, 2003), 22. The next few paragraphs build on Lundestad's book.

had anything to say politically, and one's religion was also pretty much decided by one's social superiors. If one believed, as did the Pilgrims who eventually settled in Plymouth, Massachusetts, for example, that the Church of England was inherently corrupt and beyond redemption, one would be harassed and prosecuted. As opposed to this old and cynical, tired, decadent and corrupt Europe, the New World looked innocent and youthful, optimistic and full of promise. Neither religious nor class backgrounds mattered; instead, the task was to make of this new place an exceptional nation – to show the rest of the world, especially old Europe, how things ought to be done.

The most famous of the early utopian visions of America as a better place, a new world full of promise is John Winthrop's sermon, delivered aboard the *Arbella* in 1629, 'A Model of Christian Charity'. In this sermon, Winthrop suggested a social compact, or covenant, which would unite all members of society. 'Thus stands the cause between God and us', said Winthrop,

> we are entered into covenant with Him for this work . . . For we must consider that we shall be as a city upon the hill, the eyes of all people are upon us. So that if we shall deal falsely with our God in this work we have undertaken, and so cause Him to withdraw His present help from us, we shall be made a story and a by-word through the world.[5]

It was this vision of a 'city upon the hill' and the notion of the eyes of the whole world being upon America that would later translate into the notion of the US as an 'exceptional' nation – a nation that was different from and inherently also better than other nations, a nation that had a special role to play on the world stage. This notion has since been deconstructed by many critics, but it – and the original 'city-upon-a-hill' vision – keeps cropping up, not only in American literature and culture, but also in American politics. What was President Woodrow Wilson's idea of America's mission of 'making the world safe for democracy' in the early twentieth century – or the somewhat similar idea of his successor, George W. Bush, for that matter – other than a version of American exceptionalism, for example?

Key to preserving that special sense of innocence, it was felt, was not to get involved in European politics. In his farewell address, George Washington warned against 'foreign entanglements'. 'Why', he asked, 'by interweaving our destiny with that of any part of Europe, entangle our peace and prosperity in the toils of European ambition, rivalship, interest, humor, or caprice?'[6]

---

5 John Winthrop, 'A Model of Christian Charity', 1629, quoted in Kermit L. Hall, Paul Finkelman and James W. Ely, Jr. (eds.), *American Legal History: Cases and Materials* (New York & Oxford: Oxford University Press, 2005, 3rd edition), 15.

6 George Washington, 'Farewell Address', 1796, quoted in Lundestad, supra n. 4, 22.

Most of Washington's fellow Americans as well as their descendants failed to come up with a good answer to this question. Later, in the nineteenth century, some of the most important tasks for the new nation were to expand its territory, to get through the Civil War without falling apart, and to find its own feet in the Western hemisphere as well as in the Pacific. The isolation toward Europe lasted pretty much until April 1917 when the US declared war on Germany and joined World War One on the side of Britain and France.

In January 1918, President Woodrow Wilson presented his famous Fourteen Points to prevent future wars and to institute a League of Nations. Like so many later international treaties and conventions, Wilson's idea was voted down by the Senate. According to the Constitution, the Senate must approve of treaties for them to become the law of the land and, as we shall see in Chapter 6, this power has made the US Senate one of the most important stumbling blocks for the US joining international treaties and conventions. 'In the interwar years', writes Lundestad, 'America's intervention in the First World War came to be seen as a mistake.' World War One did not solve any of the major problems, and America did not succeed in 'making the world safe for democracy', as Wilson had hoped. Once again, the general opinion was that the US ought to stay out of European political and military matters.

This feeling lasted until Pearl Harbor and Hitler's declaration of war on the US in 1941. This time around, the American engagement was more wholehearted than it had been during World War One. When engaged in making plans for the postwar world, President Franklin D. Roosevelt sensed that his fate might be similar to that of his predecessor Wilson, however, and that his hopes for American 'isolationism' to come to an end would be defeated by the Senate and/or by American public sentiment. But 'FDR's fears were to prove groundless. America was finally prepared to play the role that its economic power had for so long and its military power now so clearly indicated.'[7]

On the cultural side, America's rise to military and political power notwithstanding, a feeling of cultural inferiority remained right through the nineteenth century. As the country matured as a nation, the vision of the US as an 'exceptional' nation resurfaced in the theory of the importance of the frontier. In a paper entitled 'The Significance of the Frontier in American History', delivered to the American Historical Association in 1892, Frederic Jackson Turner maintained that the wellsprings of American exceptionalism were the American frontier – that region in between urbanized, civilized society and the untamed wilderness. As Turner saw it, it was out there on the frontier that the American shed his or her European background and became truly an American.

---

7 Ibid., 26.

American culture, that is, was not merely a bad copy of European culture, but something completely new. It had been formed by the landscape and by the toughness acquired by settlers living on the frontier. Part of this toughness and the challenges of the frontier for Turner were the American Indians, those original 'settlers' on the land. With his Frontier Thesis, Turner may be said to have contributed to what political scientist Bonnie Honig has called 'the myth of an immigrant America'. In *Democracy and the Foreigner* (2003), Honig devotes a chapter to a discussion of the foreigner or immigrant as a prospective American citizen. American exceptionalists, she writes,

> treat immigrants as the agents of founding and renewal for a regime in which membership is supposed to be uniquely consent based, individualist, rational, and voluntarist rather than inherited and organic. For these and many other thinkers, the future of American democracy depends not on the native born but on the recent arrival, not on someone with a past to build on but rather on someone who left his past behind. In short, exceptionalist accounts of American democracy are inextricably intertwined with the myth of an immigrant America . . . [which] depicts the foreigner as a supplement to the nation, an agent of national reenchantment that might rescue the regime from corruption and return it to its first principles.[8]

While capturing something important about American democracy, this account also misrepresents certain things about or in the American past, Honig argues. We should not forget that American democracy is not only founded on immigration, 'but also on conquest, slavery, expansion and annexation'.[9]

The Frontier Thesis was nonetheless to form an important element in the formation of American national identity. The best way to shape such an identity, it increasingly came to be felt, was to repudiate the European cultural heritage – or at least certain parts of it. European intellectuals, needless to say, looked upon these attempts at cultural nation building – from the construction of cities upon a hill to the construction of frontier theses, all of which had 'Europe' as their negative subtext – with the greatest scepticism. What were these Americans doing, they wondered, other than destroying all respect for culture, tradition and social privileges? The problem was, though, that such scepticism was not always shared by the European masses. An early testament to American cultural influences was the British journalist William Stead's 1901 book with the telling title, *The Americanization of the World*. More famous is Henry Luce's article in *Life* in February 1941 on 'The American Century' in which 'American jazz, Hollywood movies, American slang, American machines and patented products' were presented as 'in fact the only

---

8 Bonnie Honig, *Democracy and the Foreigner* (Princeton, NJ, and Oxford: Princeton University Press, 2003), 73–74.

9 Ibid., 75.

things that every community in the world, from Zanzibar to Hamburg, recognizes in common'.[10]

And what about the more contemporary picture? It was not hard to hear contempt for 'Europe' in much of what the Bush Administration did and said. 'The "cowboys" in the White House', as Todd Gitlin wrote in *The Guardian* in 2003, 'were raised in an anti-European culture'.[11] When then Secretary of Defense Donald Rumsfeld dismissed the anti-war climate of 'Old Europe' after the terrorist attacks on New York City and Washington, DC on 11 September 2001, he was, of course, talking about Germany and France – and by 'Old' he meant 'loser: not virile, not vigorous, incapable of defending itself against marauders'. When Robert Kagan wrote about Americans being from Mars and Europeans from Venus,[12] he was echoing this kind of thinking.

Rumsfeld's and Kagan's disdain – and that of their president for that matter – is as old as the US, which, as Gitlin aptly sums up, 'in a certain sense founded itself as the anti-Europe – democratic and neither royal nor aristocratic, vigorous and not effete, pragmatic and not committed to hidebound tradition. In one long strand of American opinion, Europe meant culture, while America meant either nature or God or a combination.' For most of its history, though, the US needed Europe – its culture and ideas, its investment and its markets. But this changed in the twentieth century; from now on, it was agreed in Washington, it was Europe that needed the US.

> The interrupted Thirty-one Year War of 1914–1945 shattered European claims to an exalted place at the heights of western civilization. In the eyes of America's Atlanticists, Yankee indispensability in World War Two extended into the cold war. The proof of America's leadership of the 'free world' would lie in its ability to bring Europe along . . . If Europe had proved not only decadent but dependent, a rejuvenated America had as one of its central missions the revival of Europe. The problem was to make sure that Europe was up to its new role as willing but subordinate partner.[13]

On the front page of its issue of 14 and 21 October 2002, *The New Yorker* featured a drawing by Bruce McCall. What we see in this drawing are three lines of people in an airport, possibly waiting to go through US Immigration: US citizens, non-US citizens and Eurotrash, respectively. In the first two lines,

---

[10] Henry Luce, 'The American Century', *Life*, February 1941, quoted in Lundestad, supra n. 4, 24.

[11] Todd Gitlin, 'Europe? Frankly, America doesn't give a damn', *The Guardian*, 3 February 2003 (http://www.guardian.co.uk/world/2003/feb/03/usa.comment1 – last visited on 5 January 2009).

[12] Robert Kagan, *Of Paradise and Power: America and Europe in the New World Order* (New York: Knopf, 2003).

[13] Gitlin, supra n. 11.

people are dressed and look normal. In the last line, the Eurotrash line, however, everyone is dressed (up) in black. Some are sitting in big armchairs, some are dancing and socializing – but all are sipping champagne served by an elegantly dressed waiter standing behind a table with a white table cloth. While all of this is going on, the other passengers are looking on, supposedly wondering what on earth is happening in that third line. The implication is clear: what is left of the formerly so grandiose European culture is nothing but a degenerate and effeminate attempt at being 'high-brow'.

European Attitudes Towards the US

On the European side, too, matters do not look too good. European attitudes regarding the US have declined considerably since 11 September 2001. According to the Pew Global Attitudes Project, positive opinions of the US dropped in France from 62 per cent in 1999/2000 to 43 per cent in June 2003. In Germany the decline was even more noticeable, from 78 per cent to 45 per cent, and in Spain, from 50 per cent to 38. From this, writes Russell A. Berman, 'one can clearly conclude that large majorities in key Western European countries have ceased to be positively predisposed to the United States'.[14]

It seems only to get worse, moreover. European views have hardened over the past five years. A British Council survey published in March 2008 shows, for example, that 46 per cent of the Europeans asked thought the overall influence of the US in the world was negative. The survey was conducted in January 2008 in six European countries (Britain, Poland, Germany, France, Spain and Ireland), the US, Canada and Turkey, and more than 500 people were questioned in each country.[15] No wonder that *The Economist*, in a special report on America and the world of March 2008, had one of its journalists write a column called 'Wooing the world: America badly needs to improve its global image'.[16]

From a cultural-historical perspective, in much the same way that 'Europe' has always been an object of the American imagination 'America' has been an object of the European imagination. Taking his cue from Edward Said's famous discussion of orientalism as a repertoire of European representations concerning 'the Orient', Rob Kroes has argued, for example, that:

---

14 Berman, supra n. 3, p. xi.

15 More can be read about the survey at http://www.worldpublicopinion.org/pipa/articles/breuropera/458.php?lb=breu&pnt=458&nid=&id= (last visited on 5 January 2009).

16 'A special report on America and the world', *The Economist*, 29 March–4 April 2008, 12.

> much like the Orient, the Occident was a European invention devised long before the historical discovery of the Americas. It has served as the screen for the projection of a wide range of European dreams, utopian as well as dystopian. Among the many repertoires in which 'America' figured as the quintessential counterpoint to Europe, representing everything that Europe was not or had not yet become, would never be or want to be, modernity was one important point of reference.[17]

From the very beginning, it was especially the US as the site of the politically and culturally modern that interested European observers. In *Them and Us* (2000), Kroes outlines three different early European constructions of the US. The first of these is the 'humanist' construction which focuses on 'the American' as a 'new man'. To Michel-Guillaume Jean de Crèvecoeur, who wrote as Hector St. John (*Letters from an American Farmer*, 1782), the American – this 'New Man' – does not simply represent yet another different nationality, adding to a European pattern of national differences. He is new in the sense that he transcends the European pattern altogether; he overcomes European differences of religion, of nationality, and perhaps most importantly of social standing. The US tends not only to level all these European differences, but it also elevates everyone in the process. It is conceived in a spirit of openness, as a land where people can build new identities, grounded in the present and the future, not the past.

Crèvecoeur's is an early statement of the US being modern in the sense of fulfilling the promise of the European Renaissance: the humanist dream of individuals as their own free agents, moulding their private and collective destinies as they see fit.

The second early European construction of 'America' is political, Kroes claims, and it focuses on the US as a successful republican experiment. For Alexis de Tocqueville, for instance, 'America' was an ideal type of democracy – a type that showed what was in store for Europe. 'I admit that I saw in America more than America', he wrote in his introduction to *Democracy in America*, 'it was the shape of democracy itself which I sought, its inclinations, character, prejudices, and passions; I wanted to understand it so as at least to know what we have to fear or hope therefrom'.[18] The third and last construction is existential. It focuses on 'America' as empty space, as a place in a constant state of transition. This means on the one hand that American culture is perceived as banal and vulgar – that nothing seems worthy of the name of culture. It also means on the other, however, that America offers a regenerative

---

17 Rob Kroes, *Them and Us: Questions of Citizenship in a Globalizing World* (Urbana and Chicago, IL: University of Illinois Press, 2000), 147.

18 Alexis de Tocqueville, 'Author's Introduction', *Democracy in America*, translated by George Lawrence and edited by J. P. Mayer (New York: Anchor Books, 1969), 19.

potential, an endless number of possibilities of taking apart other cultures, e.g. European culture, in order then to put them back together again in exciting new ways.

This last construction had to do with the US as empty space, sometimes – but not always – being associated with such modern technologies of communication as the railway and the telegraph. Completely ignoring the fact that the North American continent had been settled thousands of years before the arrival of the European settlers, this construction bought into Honig's 'myth of an immigrant America'. These early European constructions were accordingly by and large positive and optimistic, concentrating on the promise of the US for 'the huddled masses yearning to break free'.[19] By the mid-19th century, the US had assumed the features of a technical civilization – that is, modern American dreams of individual transfiguration and regeneration had been linked to technical prowess. Not everyone thought of this as positive; there were Europeans for whom this provided the ingredients for a discourse of cultural anti-Americanism.

Toward the end of the nineteenth century, we find two additional images of the US cropping up in European thinking: the socialist idea of the US as a working-class paradise and the (corresponding) conservative idea of the US as democratic chaos. Later still, when the US began transmitting to Europe tempting images of a mass-consumption society (a democracy of goods), various calls to arms began to be heard in defence of European cultural values, as we saw.

At this point – and we're talking the mid-1900s now – many Europeans were of two minds about the impact of American modernity.

> In search of cultural renewal, [some] could enthusiastically endorse the freedom they found in American mass culture or envy the informality and mobility of American social life while at the same time begrudging America's political dominance. Others could welcome American leadership in political and economic life while deploring the impact that American mass culture had on European societies.[20]

No one disliked American dominance more than the Vietnam generation. However, while loudly protesting both US imperial aggressiveness in Southeast Asia and social, racial, and political inequality within the US itself, European Vietnam War radicals also put to good use, in their own revolutionary fights, American music as well as the tactics, styles, and vocabulary of protest movements in the US. With these children of Marx and Coca-Cola, as the saying went, we find a different kind of creative relationship with the US

---

19 Kroes, supra n. 17, 148–154.

20 Ibid., 156.

developing – one which made it possible simultaneously to criticize and to feed upon American politics and culture.

True, there were still European intellectuals such as Jean-Paul Sartre who declined an invitation to give a series of lectures at Cornell University in 1965 as a protest against the war in Vietnam. '[The US] is the greatest power in the world?', he explained, 'Granted. But note. It is far from being the center of it. When one is European, one has the duty not even to consider America as the world's center.'[21] More and more, though, this sort of refusal to deal with the US came to be seen as a futile struggle against the inevitable. Instead, some European intellectuals adopted a kind of double nationality. The Danish writer and poet Dan Turèll is an interesting case in point. He referred to himself as an 'American-Dane': '[i]n one way or another I always did feel Danish, but as if Danish meant Mom and Dad, and I was American, as if that was the extended family, the common denominator that included everybody you knew', he explained about his own experience in an essay from 1976. Denmark was in a position of cultural dependency toward the US, but Turèll never saw this colonial relationship as repressive. 'I like Denmark, and I like the United States, but all things considered I think that the United States has given me more.'[22]

In Chapter 9, we shall look at another Dane, film maker Lars von Trier, who has succeeded in being critical of the US while simultaneously making much use of American phenomena and themes. Trier is anti-American in that all- or semi-American way that contemporary European commentators often are – or, to borrow a phrase from Berndt Ostendorf, his 'cultural Americanophilia . . . co-exist[s beautifully] with [his] political Americanophobia'.[23] Trier's way of being anti-American corresponds very well, as we shall see, with the conclusion drawn by Peter J. Katzenstein and Robert O. Keohane after having looked at *Anti-Americanisms in World Politics* (2007).[24] Thinking about the varieties of anti-Americanism in politics, they write in their conclusion that two questions come to mind. 'First, why does such a rich variety of anti-American views persist? Second, why do persistent and adaptable anti-American views have so little direct impact on policy and political practice?' The answer to both questions, they then suggest, involves the *polyvalent* symbolism generated by America – a symbolism that:

---

21 Jean-Paul Sartre, quoted in Ole Bech-Petersen, *Encounters: Danish Literary Travel in the United States* (unpublished dissertation, the University of Southern Denmark, March 2000), 255.

22 Dan Turèll, quoted in ibid., 256.

23 Berndt Ostendorf, 'Why is American popular culture so popular? A view from Europe', in *American Studies in Scandinavia*, 34:1 (2002), 2.

24 Peter J. Katzenstein and Robert O. Keohane (eds.), *Anti-Americanisms in World Politics* (Ithaca, NY, and London: Cornell University Press, 2007).

> continually creates a diversity of material on which to construct anti-Americanism. The polyvalence of America embodies a rich variety of values . . .[which] resonate differently with the various cognitive schemas held by individuals and reinforced by groups – schemas that vary greatly cross-nationally . . . When polyvalent American symbols connect with varied, shifting, and complex cognitive schemas, the resulting reactions refract like a prism in sunlight. Many colors appear in the prism, just as America elicits many different reactions around the world. Often, different components of what is refracted will simultaneously attract and repel . . .[25]

Americanization and anti-Americanism interact, in other words. In Europe, as throughout the rest of the world, people play with, use and abuse American culture in various ways, most of which do not have any direct and/or practical consequences for 'serious' politics.

OFFICIAL EUROPEAN UNION–UNITED STATES DIALOGUES

In a provocative book entitled *Uncouth Nation: Why Europe Dislikes America*, Andrei S. Markovits takes issue with Katzenstein and Keohane's assessment of the current situation. What the latter do not take into consideration, Markovits argues, is that whereas anti-Americanism used to be a core element among Europe's elites only, it now also seems to have entered the European mainstream. That 'ambivalence, antipathy, and resentment toward and about the United States [that] have comprised an important component of European culture since the American Revolution at the latest', has spread from the leftist literati not only to the political elites, but also to the man/woman in the street.[26] Popular support for the withdrawal of American troops from Iraq is widespread and opposition to American foreign policy has 'become a mainstay of popular culture'.[27]

As Markovits sees it, Katzenstein and Keohane are therefore not correct when they claim that anti-Americanism(s) have no direct impact on politics. In fact, mainstream European anti-Americanism is fast becoming a very handy tool in the hands of European policy makers and professionals. It serves to create a common European identity: Europe is emphatically *not* America, but something altogether different. Ironically enough, since 9/11 and the Bush administration's failure – in the eyes of many Europeans – to conduct a fair and sane foreign policy, the same European leftist elite that would speak out

---

25 Ibid., 306.

26 Andrei S. Markovits, *Uncouth Nation: Why Europe Dislikes America* (Princeton, NJ, and Oxford: Princeton University Press, 2007), 4.

27 'A special report on America and the world', supra n. 16, 12.

against a united Europe now seems to be in favour of an ideology that may help 'substantiate an identity for Europe as a growing power bloc'.[28] Anti-Americanism, harboured by élites for centuries and now fast becoming part of popular sentiment, seems to be translating, in some curious way, into pro-Europeanism.

Markovits is thinking here of some of the European intellectuals whose work has been discussed in previous chapters, and his views that 'fundamentally, the European views about America have little to do with the real America but much to do with Europe', are shared by critics such as Josef Joffe, as we saw.[29] Whether such anti-Americanism will in the end succeed in jump-starting a European identity – and whether such identity formation will become Euro-centric and exclusionary or instead lead to 'a positive and universalistic ideology building on the commonalities of Western values' – is, Markovits admits, anyone's guess. But, he argues,

> outfitted with a mass base and the already mentioned congruence between elite and mass opinion, anti-Americanism could, for the first time in its long European history, become a powerful political force going well beyond those ambivalences, antipathies, and resentments that have continuously shaped the intellectual life of Europe since July 5, 1776.[30]

So, is anti-Americanism in Europe a cultural phenomenon mostly or has it also taken on a political quality by now? Katzenstein/Keohane and Markovits may actually both be on to something. Culture being as much of a money maker as it is in our knowledge society, and cultural matters being as politicized as they currently are, cultural criticism inevitably also becomes a political statement. This is something we shall come back to in future chapters. If we return to the recent British Council survey once more, it is interesting to note that even after 9/11 there seems to be widespread support for closer relations between Europe and the United States among the countries polled. On average, 62 per cent of all European countries polled in favour of closer European–American relations; in the US, the number favouring such relations is somewhat higher (91 per cent). As for the *current* cooperation between Europe and North America, as we noted above, it is seen as not being very effective, and overall transatlantic feelings are fairly cool, especially on the European side.

There does indeed not seem to be much love lost between Americans and Europeans at the moment; yet, the sense that it is still important to carry on

---

[28] Markovits, supra n. 26, 149.
[29] Ibid., 201.
[30] Ibid., 221.

those transatlantic dialogues is very much there. That is a hopeful sign. To Steven Kull, who as the director of the Program on International Policy Attitudes helped develop and analyse the survey, what it suggests is that:

> clearly Europeans and Americans are looking for a thaw in what has been a wintry period in transatlantic relations. On both sides of the Atlantic there seems to be a view that the US and the EU – the powers with the greatest resources in the world – need to work together to address global problems.[31]

The thing is, moreover, that Americans, Canadians and Europeans seem to agree on which issues are the most important for their countries to work on together. Thus, the British Council survey indicates that 'large numbers agree about the importance of environmental issues, including climate change, pollution and natural disasters. This was the most widely cited issue in the United States, Canada and five of the seven European countries. The only exceptions were the French and Turks who rated it third most important.' The second most frequently mentioned issue of importance was war and conflict. It received the second highest rating, not only in the US and Canada but also in the UK, Germany, Turkey and Ireland.[32]

These two issues are, interestingly enough, precisely the issues chosen for special EU–US consideration and cooperation. For all the criticism of their being too far removed from and having no clue about the wishes of the ordinary European, on these two issues EU politicians do seem to be on a par with the people who have elected them. Ever since EU–US summit meetings were initiated in 1990, the leaders of the European Union and the United States have in fact reaffirmed the historic partnership between the EU and the US. When they met in Göteborg, Sweden, on 14 June 2001, for example, they said in a joint statement after the summit meeting that they were determined to strengthen the transatlantic bond – a bond that is founded on 'strong and enduring ties between our peoples and shared fundamental values, including respect for human rights and individual liberty, democratic government and economic freedoms. What unites us far outweighs that which divides us'.[33]

---

[31] Steven Kull, director of the Program on International Policy Attitudes, quoted in 'Nine-Country Poll Finds Europeans and Americans Desire Closer Relations', World Public Opinion.Org – available at http://www.worldpublicopinion.org/pipa/articles/breuropera/458.php?lb=breu&pnt=458&nid=&id=.

[32] More can be read about the survey at http://www.worldpublicopinion.org/pipa/articles/breuropera/458.php?lb=breu&pnt=458&nid=&id= (last visited on 5 January 2009).

[33] Göteborg Statement, 14 June 2001. It can be read in its entirety at http://www.consilium.europa.eu/ueDocs/cms_Data/docs/pressdata/en/er/09934.en1.html (last visited on 7 January 2009).

The Göteborg summit meeting was one of the regular presidential summits held by the EU and the US in order to assess and develop transatlantic cooperation. They had come about as a result of the November 1990 'Transatlantic Declaration on EC–US Relations' according to which 'both sides agree that a framework is required for regular and intensive consultation'.[34] The Transatlantic Declaration constitutes the first formalized US contact with what was then the European Community. When the European Union subsequently succeeded in developing a European common foreign and security policy and a European security and defence policy, the EU became a more and more important international partner for the US in many areas, beyond trade matters. A need was eventually felt on both sides of the Atlantic to go beyond the regular consultations that had been introduced by the Transatlantic Declaration and to come up with a joint response to external challenges such as the threat of proliferation of weapons of mass destruction, and of international terrorism, as well as to the fragile peace process in the Middle East.

The result was the New Transatlantic Agenda (NTA) which was signed in December 1995, at the EU–US summit in Madrid. The NTA provided for joint action in four major fields: promoting peace and stability, democracy and development around the world; responding to global challenges; contributing to the expansion of world trade and closer economic relations; and building bridges across the Atlantic.[35] In terms of building bridges, it was recognized that the Agenda should be shaped and driven not only by government officials, as had hitherto been the case, but by people from many different professions. A number of Transatlantic Dialogues were accordingly started to bring together business people, parliamentarians, scientists, academics, trade unionists and a broad range of citizens' groups from both sides of the Atlantic to discuss transatlantic policy questions.

These dialogues include the Transatlantic Legislators Dialogue, which constitutes the formal response of the European Parliament and the US Congress to the commitment in the New Transatlantic Agenda; the Transatlantic Business Dialogue, which was also launched in 1995; the Transatlantic Consumer Dialogue, launched in 1998; the Environment Dialogue, inaugurated in 1999; and finally, the Transatlantic Labour Dialogue Project, launched in 2001 between the European Trade Union College and its training agency, and the training agency of the American Federation of Labor

---

34 More information on the Transatlantic Declaration on EC–US Relations, 1990 can be found at http://ec.europa.eu/external_relations/us/docs/trans_declaration_90_en.pdf (last visited on 7 January 2009).

35 The New Transatlantic Agenda can be read at http://eurunion.org/eu/index.php?option=com_content&task=view&id=2602&Itemid=9#IV (last visited on 7 January 2009).

and Congress of Industrial Organizations (AFL–CIO). Within the framework of the NTA, moreover, a new initiative, creating the Transatlantic Economic Partnership, was launched at the EU–US summit on 18 May 1998 in London, and more recently, the June 2005 EU–US economic summit launched the EU-US Initiative to Enhance Transatlantic Economic Integration and Growth. This initiative is intended to promote further economic integration across the Atlantic and to cover cooperation in a broad spectrum of areas.

The Göteborg summit took place in June 2001 – only three months before that transatlantic bond would be tested by the terrorist acts in New York City and Washington, DC. The first European reaction, as we all remember, was an outpouring of solidarity with the victims of 9/11 and with the US in general. On 13 September, Jean-Marie Columbani famously commented in *Le Monde* that '*nous sommes tous Américains*' (we are all Americans). And on the following day, the official European Union reaction came in the shape of a Joint Declaration by the Heads of State and Government of the European Union, the President of the European Parliament, the President of the European Commission, and the High Representative for the Common Foreign and Security Policy. The Declaration opened in this way:

> In Europe, and around the world, the horrific terrorist attacks on the United States have shocked our citizens. As an expression of solidarity with the American people, Europe has declared 14 September a day of mourning. We invite all European citizens to observe, at noon, a three-minute silence to express our sincere and deepest sympathy for the victims and their families.[36]

It was followed up a few days later, on 20 September, by a Joint EU–US Ministerial Statement on Combating Terrorism which promised that 'in the coming days, weeks and months, the European Union and the United States will work in partnership in a broad coalition to combat the evil of terrorism'.[37] The following day, an Extraordinary Informal Meeting of the European Council was called in Brussels. In the Presidency Conclusions that followed this extraordinary session, the European Council declared its total support for the American people 'in the face of the deadly terrorist attacks'. It furthermore proclaimed its decision 'that the fight against terrorism will, more than ever, be a priority objective of the European Union'.[38]

---

36 The Joint Declaration of 14 September 2001 can be read at http://www.consilium.europa.eu/ueDocs/cms_Data/docs/pressdata/en/er/Declaration.en1.pdf (last visited on 7 January 2009).

37 Joint EU–US Ministerial Statement on Combating Terrorism, 20 September 2001, can be read at http://www.consilium.europa.eu/ueDocs/cms_Data/docs/pressdata/en/er/12109.en1.html (last visited on 20 March 2008).

38 Conclusions and Plan of Action of the Presidency, 21 September 2001, can be

There have since been other efforts by the EU and the US to boost cooperation on combating international terrorism. Under the umbrella of the NTA, a specific vehicle for justice, freedom and security cooperation was created in the form of twice yearly 'informal' Justice and Home Affairs meetings between EU and US policy makers. Concrete results include the signature of two Europol–US agreements in December 2001 and December 2002, respectively (the latter allowing for the sharing of personal data); of two criminal judicial cooperation agreements in June 2003 on Mutual Legal Assistance and Extradition; of a May 2004 agreement on the Transfer of Passenger Data as well as of a comprehensive joint declaration on combating terrorism including financing, preventive measures and transport security, adopted at the EU–US summit of June 2004. In addition, contacts have been established between the EU body for judicial cooperation in criminal matters EUROJUST and US law enforcement authorities.[39]

There have furthermore been efforts to cooperate on combating climate change. In April 2005, two days of meetings took place between key decision-makers of the EU (among them EU Environment Commissioner Stavros Dimas) and of the US Congress. Both sides agreed that climate change presented a major challenge for policy makers now and in the future. More concretely, agreement was reached to bring together EU–US representatives to discuss policies combating climate change, and a broader environmental agenda. 'The results of these talks could well mark the beginning of a new phase of US–EU co-operation on climate change. We are ready to seriously discuss with our American partners the future of an international climate change regime after 2012', said Commissioner Dimas in a press release after the Washington meeting.[40]

At the official level, it would thus seem, things seem to be working reasonably well. There are obviously differences of opinion – and we shall come back to some of these in later chapters – but regular EU–US meetings do take place on various issues, and these meetings do seem to result in concrete

read at http://ue.eu.int/ueDocs/cms_Data/docs/pressData/en/ec/140.en.pdf (last visited on 7 January 2009).

[39] Please see 'Justice, Freedom and Security high on US–EU Transatlantic agenda' (http://ec.europa.eu/justice_home/fsj/external/usa/fsj_external_usa_en.htm (last visited on 7 January 2009) and 'US–European Union Cooperating on Combating Terrorism', Fact sheet reviewing implementation of 2004 US–EU declaration (http://www.america.gov/st/washfile-english/2005/June/ 20050617163853xlrenne F0.7303583.html (last visited on 7 January 2009) for more information.

[40] Press release, 'Commissioner Dimas hopeful about new phase in EU–US relations on climate change' can be read at: http://europa.eu/rapid/pressReleases Action.do?reference=IP/05/463&format=HTML&aged=0&language=EN&guiLanguage=en (last visited on 7 January 2009).

efforts from time to time. The issues chosen for special EU–US consideration and cooperation, such as the environment and combating terrorism, moreover, seem to be precisely the ones that are also the most important to people on both sides of the Atlantic.

CONCLUDING REMARKS

Since 11 September 2001, more and more the talk on both sides of the Atlantic has been about differences and about drifting apart. 'No one can predict the future', wrote Geir Lundestad in 2003, 'were I to hazard a guess, I would certainly not be predicting any direct confrontation between the United States and Western Europe as such, but rather a conflict with some European countries and a general continued slow drifting apart between the two continents'.[41]

While the history of European–American relations since World War Two seems to be characterized by one conflict after another – from the Korean War and the rearmament of West Germany in the early 1950s, via the Suez crisis in 1956, to disputes over Bosnia and NATO enlargement during the Clinton administration and growing American unilateralism under George W. Bush – transatlantic relations, with NATO as one of their most significant manifestation, may actually be said to have been quite close. The Europeans quickly realized that they had interests in common with the US, keeping Germany under control or 'down' being one of the most important. They needed the Americans, and so what Lundestad has called 'empire by invitation' was born:

> The Europeans had such a strong interest in keeping the Americans in that they actually 'invited' them in . . .Most Europeans evidently thought it much better to have one clearly superior leader who was far away than two or more smaller European leaders very close at hand. Thus, the imbalance between the United States and the leading European powers, Britain, France, and West Germany, and the rivalry among the three, facilitated Atlantic cooperation. Even after the Cold War was over, European governments issued new invitations to the Americans to stay involved; in moderate form, but still clear enough from the Western Europeans; much more explicitly from the liberated Central and Eastern Europeans.[42]

Today, the question is whether the future will be a continuation of the past, or whether conflict will replace cooperation in the relationship between Europe and the US. Lundestad lists various reasons for concern. Among these are the facts that unilateralism is growing in the US and that the EU is 'slowly

---

41 Lundestad, supra n. 4, 292.

42 Ibid., 11.

but steadily taking on an ever stronger role'.[43] As far as the Europeans are concerned, they no longer need the Americans in quite the same way as before, and in the US demographic changes are taking place that would seem to diminish the interest in the fate of Europe.

In addition, there is the fact that increasingly conflicts no longer occur within the traditional NATO area. Most conflicts today are out-of-area, with the Middle East being the most difficult and most consistent issue in European–American relations. And when it comes to these out-of-area conflicts, writes Lundestad,

> the United States will generally be more activist than the Europeans . . . the American definition of security is much more absolutist than the European one. Washington wants to eradicate threats many European capitals are prepared to live with, and its vast military arsenal gives Washington options the Europeans quite simply do not have. Most Europeans emphasize the options they do have: diplomatic negotiation and economic instruments.[44]

The thing is, though, Lundestad notes, that there is a good deal of ambiguity connected with many of these points of concern. European leadership seems to be drifting away from Britain and France and toward Germany, and American–German relations may well improve again. Under Chancellor Gerhard Schröder, those relations cooled considerably, but Chancellor Angela Merkel has seemed intent on doing something about this. Under the headline, 'Merkel's pact with America', the German magazine *Der Spiegel* wrote an article shortly before Angela Merkel was to pay a visit to Washington in April 2007 which claimed that the German Chancellor 'has reoriented Germany away from Russia and toward the United States'. As a former East German, Merkel feels closer to the US than to Russia, according to *Der Spiegel*, and she is convinced that no progress can be made anywhere in the world without the US. The way forward is thus for her to take over from Tony Blair, as it were, and to act as a mediator of sorts between the US and Europe.[45]

Merkel seems to have the backing of not only her own countrymen and -women, but also of other Europeans. As we saw, the recent British Council survey shows widespread support for closer relations between Europe and the United States among the countries polled – even after 9/11. Both Europeans

---

[43] Ibid., 281.

[44] Ibid., 287.

[45] Ralf Beste, Jan Fleischhauer, Georg Mascolo, Christian Reiermann, Matthias Schepp and Gabor Steingart, 'Merkel's Pact with America: Germany Rediscovers the United States as a Partner', *Spiegel* Online International, 30 April 2007 – available at http://www.spiegel.de/international/germany/0,1518,480221,00.html (last visited on 7 January 2009).

and Americans overwhelmingly favour closer relations, and they agree on which issues are the most important to address together. This is the case even though current cooperation between Europe and North America is perceived as largely ineffective and overall transatlantic feelings are fairly cool, especially on the European side.

Americans and Europeans may not necessarily like each other, in other words, but this does not seem to prevent them from seeing the need for further cooperation on a number of important issues. I hope that Steven Kull is right, and that both Europeans and Americans are indeed looking for a thaw in transatlantic relations. The British Council survey is not that comprehensive a survey – after all, only about 500 people from each country were polled. We should be careful not to read too much into it. But maybe, just maybe, there is that beginning willingness to (re)negotiate on which so much depends for/in the future. We shall turn, now, to what might at first look like a very problematic area with much disagreement between Europe and the US, but which might – after the main issues have been analysed and discussed – conceivably turn into a common transatlantic discourse and course of action that could potentially help thaw those cool transatlantic feelings: human rights.

4. Institutionalized European human rights

'The case law of the European Court of Human Rights', writes Michael D. Goldhaber in his conclusion to *A People's History of the European Court of Human Rights*, 'is an unmined source of self-understanding in a region that seemingly craves self-understanding. It's a system of myth in search of an audience.' There are symbols that may help create a modern European mythology of the sort that is needed for Europeans to feel a common identity, but 'outside of human rights law, the list of Europe-wide rituals is short – and not very serious'.[1] Just think of the Eurovision Song Contest or the Ryder Cup golf tournament; they do not seem to be doing the trick, and neither does the Euro for that matter.

Goldhaber could have mentioned some of the more serious attempts made by the European Union to create new symbols to represent Europe – the EC emblem and flag, a European 'anthem' (the fourth movement of Beethoven's Ninth Symphony), the harmonized European passport, driver's licence and car number-plates, for example. Yet, he does have a point. Reading his six chapters on cases that came before the European Court of Human Rights concerning 'the expanding ambit of personal life', followed by his three chapters on cases concerning 'the rights to expression' and his four chapters on 'state violence' (the headings of parts 1, 2, and 3, respectively), one does indeed get the impression that here is plenty of stuff for European myths and symbols.

I regularly teach courses on American legal history – not to law students, but to students of History and American studies. With the right textbook, such a course, in my opinion, is an excellent introduction to American history and civic culture. Approaching American culture and history through law can teach something very useful about American norms and views. What Goldhaber suggests is that something similar ought to happen in the European context. Human rights law would be, he argues,

---

[1] Michael D. Goldhaber, *A People's History of the European Court of Human Rights* (New Brunswick, NJ, and London: Rutgers University Press, 2007), 180, 175.

> the most satisfying basis for a communal identity. Americans are raised to revere cases like *Brown v. Board of Education* and *New York Times v. Sullivan* as central pieces of the civic culture. Clarence Gideon, who established the indigent right to counsel in the case of *Gideon v. Wainwright*, has become an American folk hero, thanks to the book *Gideon's Trumpet* by journalist Anthony Lewis, and the movie version starring Henry Fonda. By all rights, *Lingens v. Austria* ought to be as famous in Europe as *New York Times v. Sullivan* is in America. Inspiring figures like Zeki Aksoy and P.J. McClean ought to become rallying symbols for European sentiment. The case law of the European Court of Human Rights is a veritable mythology in waiting.[2]

In this chapter, we shall start by looking at the workings of the two European courts, the European Court of Justice (ECJ), which as the high court of the European Union covers the twenty-seven Member States of the EU, ensures compliance with EU law in its interpretation and application of the European Treaties of the European Union and meets in Luxembourg; and the European Court of Human Rights (ECtHR), which is the judicial arm of the Council of Europe and therefore covers the forty-seven member states of the Council, interprets the European Convention on Human Rights and is based in Strasbourg, France. In some ways, these two courts divide the functions of the US Supreme Court between them: generally speaking, the ECJ resolves questions concerning the regulation and the division of power between EU Member States and between the EU and its Member States, whereas the ECtHR deals with questions concerning the fundamental rights of citizens of the member states of the Council of Europe, as these are laid down in the European Convention on Human Rights and the protocols supplementing it.[3] In its desire to protect the competences of the European Community, the ECJ has, however, over the years also evolved its own doctrine of human rights.

There are thus a number of interesting parallels between the American and the European high courts and their ways of interpreting fundamental rights. Policy professionals from the EU and the US do meet on a twice-yearly basis to discuss human rights. These meetings are mostly focused around issues that have to do with the fight against terror, though. They do not touch on the broader human rights issues. From time to time, there have been informal attempts at starting such a broader dialogue – and we shall take a look at one such attempt – but other than that and the meetings concerning the fight against terror, the closest we get to transatlantic dialogues on human rights are those other dialogues we mentioned in the previous chapter, which do touch on human rights issues, if only indirectly. Human rights do play a part in some of the dialogues the EU and the US are having with third world countries, too.

---

2 Ibid., 176–177.

3 Ibid., 2–3.

This may be due to complacency – along the lines of 'were're alike and don't need to talk about human rights'. But then again, it may also be due to the fact that it is precisely in the area of human rights, broadly speaking, that so many of the present transatlantic tensions come together or are expressed. In Chapters 5 and 6, we shall look at two human rights areas or issues that radically divide the waters. The first of these is the core of human rights; the second is the role of international law and international institutions. We will end this chapter by looking at the two European courts in the larger context of the European Union, the Council of Europe and their political systems. While the story of the workings of the two courts – and especially the ECtHR – has in many ways been an undisputed success story, there are critics who would claim that this success has led to a prevalence of law over politics, which in turn has led to an impoverishment of the political sphere. In order to solve ongoing human rights violations in Europe, these critics furthermore argue, it will not do to focus exclusively on redress by the courts. The other branches of the system will have to be involved too.

THE TWO EUROPEAN COURTS

The European Court of Justice (ECJ)

The origins of the European Union (EU) lie, first, in the Treaty of Paris of 1952, which established the European Coal and Steel Community, and subsequently also in the Treaty of Rome of 1957 which created the European Economic Community (EEC), or 'common market'.[4] The idea was for people, goods and services to move freely across borders. In 1993, with the Treaty of Economic Union (the Maastricht Treaty), the EEC then became the European Union. The Maastricht Treaty has since been amended to a certain degree by the Treaty of Amsterdam. Among other things, the Treaty of Amsterdam, which entered into force in 1999, meant a greater emphasis on citizenship and the rights of individuals.[5]

---

[4] There were originally two Treaties of Rome, but since the EEC Treaty turned out to be much more important than the Euratom Treaty commentators normally talk about just *the* Treaty of Rome.

[5] A useful introduction to the history and the organization of the European Court of Justice may be found on the Court's official webpage: http://curia.europa.eu/index.htm as well as on http://europa.eu/institutions/inst/justice/index_en.htm. As far as information about the European Court of Human Rights is concerned, it can be found on the Court's official webpage: http://www.echr.coe.int/echr/. Information on cases is available for the European Court of Justice at http://curia.europa.eu/en/

Within the European Union, the Court of Justice of the European Communities, usually called the European Court of Justice (ECJ), is the highest judicial body. It settles disputes between Member States, or between Member States and the European institutions, and sees to it that EU legislation is interpreted and applied in the same way in all EU countries. 'Its main responsibility is the interpretation of the treaties that establish the European Community and the EU. The Court is part of the EU, which consists of three "pillars" in the terminology of the 1992 Maastricht Treaty. The first of these pillars is the European Community itself . . . The other two pillars of the European Union are intergovernmental rather supranational.'[6] If the Treaty of Lisbon, signed in December 2007 and to which we shall come back in Chapter 5, is ever ratified, this pillar system will be abolished.

The ECJ was set up in 1952 and is based in Luxembourg City – not in Brussels like most of the other EU institutions. It is composed of one judge per Member State, and it is led by a president. It may sit as a full Court, in a Grand Chamber (thirteen Judges), or in chambers of three or five Judges. It sits in a Grand Chamber when a Member State or a Community institution that is a party to the proceedings so requests, or in particularly complex or important cases. Other cases are heard by a chamber of three or five Judges. The ECJ acts as a collegiate body: decisions are made by the court rather than by individual Judges, and no minority opinions are given. 'Because the Court deliberates in secret, national governments have no way of knowing with any certainty how "their" justices have acted. And despite periodic dissatisfaction with the Court, national governments have proved reluctant to curtail its authority.'[7]

Through its case law, the ECJ has identified an obligation on administrations and national courts first of all to apply EU law in full within their sphere of competence and secondly to protect the rights conferred on citizens by that law and to abolish any conflicting national provisions. Under the Rome Treaties, the ECJ is to

> 'ensure that in the interpretation and application of this Treaty the law is observed'. (Article 220, ex 164). Generally that application will in the first instance be by the courts of member states. The Court of Justice exercises different types of jurisdiction – for example, in cases brought against a state by another institution of the

transitpage.htm (case law), and for the European Court of Human Rights at: http://www.echr.coe.int/ECHR/EN/Header/Case-Law/HUDOC/HUDOC+database/ (last visited on 7 January 2009).

6 Shirley Williams, 'Human Rights in Europe', in Samantha Power and Graham Allison (eds.), *Realizing Human Rights: Moving from Inspiration to Impact* (New York: St. Martin's Press, 2000), 78–79.

7 Anand Menon, *Europe: The State of the Union* (London: Atlantic Books, 2008), 81.

European Community (such as the Commission) (Article 226, ex 169), or brought by one member state against another (article 227, ex 170). States 'are required to take the necessary measures to comply with the judgment' of the Court (Article 228, ex 171). Depending on its precise jurisdictional base, the Court may enter judgment against a party, annul an administrative act, award money damages, or afford other relief.

Article 234 (ex 177) grants the Court jurisdiction to give 'preliminary rulings' on matters including the Treaty's interpretation, and the validity and interpretation of acts of Community institutions.[8]

It was in the mid-1960s that the ECJ established the supremacy of European law vis-à-vis the legal systems of the Member States. It was a Dutch case, *van Gend & Loos v. Nederlandse Administratie der Belastingen* (1963), that got the ECJ started on the route toward 'what can only be termed a legal revolution'. The following year, the ECJ completed this revolution with its decision in the *Costa v. ENEL* case – an Italian case which challenged the supremacy of European law over Italian law. At stake was an Italian nationalization law, and the question was whether this law was in breach not only of the Italian Constitution, but also of the EEC Treaty. In its ruling, the ECJ invented a new doctrinal principle – namely that European law had '*internal primacy*, thereby conferring to national courts the task to enforce EC rules over conflicting national legislation'. This was a principle taken from international law where a treaty is traditionally considered to trump national law. Only, now, the ECJ 'turned treaty obligations directed towards member states into rights for member state citizens'. And the rest, as they say, 'is history. National courts would over time embrace these fundamental principles, thus allowing the ECJ to develop a comprehensive and strong case law and binding their respective governments to respect it. A European rule of law had been established.'[9]

In the area of human rights, too, the ECJ has made a difference. A bill of rights had been proposed in the early 1950s, but nothing ever came of this proposal; in none of the subsequent treaties was a bill of rights or even a list of enumerated rights included. The 1957 Rome Treaty was mostly concerned with protecting states' rights from encroachments by Community organizations; human rights were by and large seen as sufficiently protected by each individ-

[8] Henry J. Steiner and Philip Alston (eds.), *International Human Rights in Context: Law, Politics, Morals* (Oxford: Oxford University Press, 2000, 2nd edition), 860.

[9] These quotations are from Morten Rasmussen, 'From Costa v. ENEL to the Treaties of Rome – A Brief History of a Legal Revolution', in Miguel Poiares Maduro and Loïs Azoulai (eds.), *The Future of European Law: Revisiting the Classics in the 50th Anniversary of the Rome Treaty* (Oxford: Hart Publishing, 2009 – forthcoming).

ual nation state. In spite of the absence of a proper bill of rights, the ECJ 'began in 1969 to evolve a specific doctrine of human rights . . . Over the years during which the human rights doctrine has evolved, the Court has identified several different normative underpinnings for it. They include the Treaty of Rome, the constitutional traditions of the member states, and international treaties accepted by member states.'[10]

The ECJ doctrine of human rights has mainly been applied over the years to the actions of the EU itself, not to actions of the Member States. This came to be reflected in the amendments to the Treaty on European Union which came into force in 1999 in accordance with the Amsterdam Treaty. A new Article 6 was added, which reaffirmed that the EU 'is founded on the principles of liberty, democracy, respect for human rights and fundamental freedoms, and the rule of law, principles which are common to the Member States'. Article 6 furthermore states that '[t]he Union shall respect fundamental rights, as guaranteed by the European Convention for the Protection of Human Rights and Fundamental Freedoms signed in Rome on 4 November 1950 and as they result from the constitutional traditions common to the Member States, as general principle of Community law'.[11]

The European Convention on Human Rights (a Council of Europe treaty) has been accorded a privileged position within the EU legal order. Yet, the EU itself is not a member of the Council of Europe, even though the EU's accession to the Strasbourg convention has been a top priority for various EU politicians and policy makers for a number of years. The Treaty of Lisbon (as formerly the draft European constitution) states that the EU has legal personality, and Protocol No. 14 of the European Convention, which opened for signature in May 2004, explicitly announces that the EU may accede to the Convention. The way for such an accession has thus been prepared. At the moment, the Russian Federation remains the only Council of Europe member state which has not ratified Protocol No. 14. This delaying of its entry into force is not only a problem in terms of the question of the EU's accession to the European Convention; it is also, as we shall see, a major problem in that Protocol No. 14 amends the control system of the Convention. 'Although arrangements exist to facilitate consultation and coordination between the EU and the Council of Europe', as Steiner and Alston sum it up, 'they remain separate entities operating in very different settings despite the fact that the activities of each organization are very relevant to those of the other.'[12]

The ECJ only allows individual petitions in cases where the acts of Member States or of European institutions directly violate EU treaty law. 'Generally,

---

10 Steiner and Alston, supra n. 8, 790.

11 Cf. ibid., 790–791.

12 Ibid., 791.

therefore, an individual seeking redress from acts or omissions of a European government must look to the European Court of Human Rights in Strasbourg rather than to the European Court of Justice in Luxembourg for a remedy.'[13] In general, the ECtHR case law encompasses a far larger variety of human rights issues and is more value-based than the relevant case law of the ECJ which appears more technical, based as it is on the principles of non-discrimination and of the freedom of movement in the EU. It is accordingly to the ECtHR that we shall now turn.

The European Court of Human Rights (ECtHR)

The Council of Europe was founded in 1949. Based in Strasbourg, it is distinct from the European Union, but no country has ever joined the European Union without first having been a member of the Council of Europe. It currently counts forty-seven members (including among others Turkey, Russia and the nations of the Caucasus), and it has granted observer status to five more countries (the Holy See, the United States, Canada, Japan and Mexico). All in all, we are talking about some 800 million people, who speak at least twenty different languages. The aim of the Council of Europe 'is to achieve a greater unity between its members for the purpose of safeguarding and realizing the ideals and principles which are their common heritage and facilitating their economic and social progress. This aim shall be pursued through the organs of the Council by discussion of questions of common concern and by agreements and common action in economic, social, cultural, scientific, legal and administrative matters and in the maintenance and further realization of human rights and fundamental freedoms.'[14]

The Council of Europe's most significant achievement is the European Convention for the Protection of Human Rights and Fundamental Freedoms. It was adopted in 1950 and came into force in 1953, and it outlines the rights and freedoms which Member States must guarantee to everyone within their jurisdiction. Protocols – the above-mentioned Protocol No.14 being hitherto the latest of these – have since been added. To monitor compliance by Signatory Parties, the European Convention established the European Court of Human Rights (ECtHR). As a result of the entry into force of Protocol No. 11 in 1998, the Court was instituted as a permanent or full-time court. Under the old system, judges only worked part-time and the main examination of complaints was undertaken by the European Commission on Human Rights.

---

13 Williams, supra n. 6, 79.

14 Article 1 of the Statute of the Council of Europe (5 May 1949, ETS no. 001) – available at http://conventions.coe.int/Treaty/EN/Treaties/Html/001.htm (last visited on 7 January 2009).

The Commission ceased existence in 1999 'as a result of what has often been termed a merger or fusion of the old Court and Commission'.[15]

All member states of the Council of Europe have to sign and ratify the Convention. There are currently forty-seven judges, equal to the number of Signatory Parties. Each state is required to nominate three candidates, and interestingly enough, there are no nationality requirements for judges. Thus, 'the first Court saw a Swiss judge elected on the nomination of Liechtenstein and an Italian for San Marino'.[16] This is because judges are assumed to be impartial arbiters, rather than representatives of any particular country. The nominated candidates are elected by the Parliamentary Assembly of the Council of Europe.

The European Convention mentions two different procedures for holding member states accountable by the ECtHR for violations of rights: the individual petition procedure (Art. 34) and the interstate procedure (Art. 33). According to Article 33, one or more states may hold another state party accountable for breaches of the Convention. This hardly ever happens, however; by far the majority of cases brought before the ECtHR are Article 34 individual petitions. The ECtHR, it should be mentioned, is one of only two international courts in the world (the other being the Inter-American Court of Human Rights) to allow individual petitions against violations of human rights by the governments of its member states. Proceedings under the individual petitions procedure of Article 34 begin, Steiner and Alston explain,

> with a complaint by an individual, group or NGO against a state party. To be declared admissible a petition must not be anonymous, manifestly ill-founded, or constitute an abuse of the rights of petition. Domestic remedies must have been exhausted, it must be presented within six months of the final decision in the domestic forum and it must not concern a matter which is substantially the same as one which has already been examined under the [ECtHR] or submitted to another procedure of international investigation or settlement.[17]

Decisions are made by majority vote, and each judge may give his or her separate opinion, whether concurring or dissenting – a different procedure from the one employed by the ECJ.

The ECtHR works, as Goldhaber puts it, 'by shaming European nations. Technically, the court has two main powers.' It can order a state to pay compensation to an individual. More importantly, however, 'it can declare a state to be in violation of the European Convention on Human Rights – and require the state to give an "effective remedy." An effective remedy often

---

15 Steiner and Alston, supra n. 8, 798.
16 Ibid., 800.
17 Ibid.

means a change in law.'[18] It falls to the Committee of Ministers, the executive arm of the Council of Europe, to make sure that states comply. It is made up of a representative from each member state's foreign ministry and, according to Article 46 of the European Convention, '[t]he final judgment of the Court shall be transmitted to the Committee of Ministers, which shall supervise its execution'. A state in violation must produce reports on its progress to these representatives. In principle, by a two-thirds vote, the Committee of Ministers can even kick out non-complying members of the Council of Europe – a very serious threat indeed, as membership of the Council of Europe is a prerequisite to membership of the EU itself. This has never happened, though. 'In effect, the Council of Europe is the EU's antechamber.'[19]

In addition, it is the role of the Parliamentary Assembly, which consists of delegations from the legislature of each member state, to see to it that laws are brought into conformity with ECtHR decisions. The significance of the involvement of the Parliamentary Assembly in the task of supervising the execution of judgments 'lies above all in the ability of members of national parliaments to bring subsequent pressure to bear on the national legislature and executive to adopt the necessary measures, and also in their power to make formal recommendations to the national authorities in charge of policy making'.[20]

Today, after the United Kingdom's Human Rights Act in 1998 and the incorporation of the European Convention on Human Rights into Irish law in 2003, European human rights law 'is operative in the domestic courts of every member state. That makes domestic courts a driver of enforcement and uniformity in their own right.'[21] The ECtHR has, however, fallen prey to its own success. Its case-load is so formidable today that judges and scholars talk about a case-load crisis. At the end of 2006, approximately 90,000 individual petitions were pending before the Strasbourg court[22] – a result, first, of the acceptance by more and more member states of the right to individual petition and secondly adherence to it of the Eastern European countries since 1990.

The drafting of Protocol No. 14 is an attempt at reform. It proposes a general overhaul of the system – one suggestion being to simplify procedures

---

[18] Goldhaber, supra n. 1, 5.

[19] Ibid., 6.

[20] Elisabeth Lambert Abdelgawad, *The Execution of Judgments of the European Court of Human Rights* (Human rights files, No. 19, Council of Europe Publishing, 2nd edition, January 2008), 61.

[21] Goldhaber, supra n. 1, 6.

[22] This is the Council of Europe's own assessment – see *State of Human Rights and Democracy in Europe* (Strasbourg: Council of Europe Publishing, 2007), 40.

for dealing both with cases which have no chance of success (at least 90 per cent of all cases) and well-founded repetitive cases. Protocol No. 14 is, however, as we saw, still waiting for the Russian Federation to come on board. If or when this will happen is anyone's guess. Russia is holding up the system in other ways as well. In the Parliamentary Assembly's annual report on human rights and democracy in Europe, produced for the first time in 2007, it is noted that Russia also has not yet ratified Protocol No. 6 to the European Convention on the abolition of the death penalty, and that there have been problems in the Russian system with failing to give top priority to the implementation of judgments of the ECtHR as well as with pressuring NGOs to stop working for human rights (in the name of enhancing national security).

The fact that the Russian Federation still needs to ratify Protocol No. 6 is pretty bad, in that 'one of the greatest achievements of the Council of Europe, and of its Parliamentary Assembly in particular, is the de facto abolition of the death penalty in peacetime in all member states'.[23] As for not implementing the judgments of the Strasbourg court speedily enough, Russia is not the only culprit. In its first annual report, the Parliamentary Assembly notes that 'unacceptable delays' have occurred in a number of European Council member states. Belgium is one example, Italy another and Greece a third. Belgium still needs 'to complete the legislative reforms required to ensure full execution of the judgment of the [ECtHR] in the case of *Conka v. Belgium*' (2002), while 'Greece and Italy [are urged] to accelerate the adoption of general measures necessary to ensure full execution of the judgments of the Court and effectively prevent similar violations of the Convention'.[24]

All in all, the Council of Europe may well be proud of the fact that its 'achievements in the field of human rights and in the establishment and consolidation of democracy are unparalleled'. However, this should not blind us to the need, as it says in the Foreword to the Parliamentary Assembly's first annual report, 'to step up our efforts throughout Europe to combat a number of growing threats including racism, xenophobia and discrimination against minorities, poverty and social exclusion, trafficking in human beings and domestic violence'.[25] This is a depressingly long list of things to do. Not surprisingly, the biggest problems seem to occur in relation to combating terrorism – a topic we shall come back to shortly. 'Respect for Human Rights begins at Home', as another EU publication reminds us.[26]

---

23 Ibid., 15.

24 Ibid., 31, 33.

25 Ibid., 5.

26 European Commission, External Relations, *The European Union: Furthering*

OFFICIAL – AND UNOFFICIAL – HUMAN RIGHTS DIALOGUES

Respect for human rights should indeed begin at home – especially since the EU has made human rights and democracy a central aspect of all its external relations: in its political dialogues with third countries as well as through its development cooperation and assistance and its action in multilateral fora such as the United Nations. In addition, the EU is currently engaged in human rights dialogues with China and Iran. Detailed consultations are taking place with African, Caribbean and Pacific states, and the EU and Russia have started to hold consultations on human rights on a regular, bi-annual basis.[27] The underlying notion here is 'mainstreaming human rights and democratization' – a concept that the EU defines in this way: '[m]ainstreaming is the process of integrating human rights and democratization issues into all aspects of EU policy decision-making and implementation, including external assistance'.[28]

When it comes to the United States, the EU holds that there are 'broadly converging views' involved. 'Regular consultations on human rights issues are also held on the basis of broadly converging view[s] with countries such as the United States of America, Canada, Japan or New Zealand. These take the form of six-monthly meetings of experts, in the run up to key human rights meetings at the United Nations.'[29] Other than that, no official EU–US dialogues on human rights are taking place. From time to time, unofficial attempts are made, however. One recent example is 'the Transatlantic Dialogue Project', started in the autumn of 2004 by Morten Kjærum and David Weissbrodt, directors of the EU Agency for Fundamental Rights and the University of Minnesota Human Rights Centre, respectively. Morten Kjærum was heading the Danish Institute for Human Rights at the time. Along the way, Kevin Boyle, University of Essex Human Rights Centre, and Paul Martin from the Columbia Center for the Study of Human Rights in New York, also joined in.

The immediate motivation was the US Government's 'War on Terror' in the aftermath of 9/11. It seemed that neither at the intergovernmental level between the EU and the US nor at the level of bilateral contact between the US and individual European countries was there much dialogue on human rights going on. 'Could civil society fill the gap? Might efforts by the non-governmental sector to explore the possibility of dialogue across the Atlantic over human rights encourage the Governments to re-engage?', the initiators of 'the

---

Human Rights and Democracy Across the Globe (Luxembourg: Office for Official Publications of the European Communities, 2007), 5.

27 See ibid., 9.

28 Ibid., 13.

29 Ibid., 9.

Transatlantic Dialogue Project' asked themselves and each other. Well, the answers to these questions were never really found. After two preparatory meetings – one in New York in September 2004 and one in Copenhagen in January 2005 – the Project went 'on hold'.[30]

The beginning was auspicious enough. The meeting in New York was opened by none other than famed American scholar Louis Henkin and former UN High Commissioner for Human Rights, Mary Robinson. Hopes were expressed for annual conferences and dynamic (and not just academic) dialogues. 'However even at this early stage the challenge was obvious . . . The group that had come together, US and European, were in agreement on the issues. There was an absence of Republican voices or at least skeptics in sympathy with the current US Government stance on human rights and the "War on Terror." '[31] It was a little like preaching to the already converted, in other words. The project was put on hold – officially for lack of sufficient funding.

Quoting William Pfaff to the effect that the Bush administration has defended its unilateralist and pre-emptive attacks on other countries by referring to the 'exceptional' status of the US among nations, Kevin Boyle ends his account of the 'Transatlantic Dialogue Project' by stating, 'It was precisely these claims and assumptions that the Transatlantic Dialogue on Human Rights was intended to challenge. The need to do so is as urgent as ever.'[32] His statement is then followed by the question, 'is anyone ready for the challenge?'. Well, it is to be hoped that others will try their luck too. A transatlantic dialogue on human rights will have a chance only if both Americans and Europeans start out at the same level, with an interest in and a willingness to listen to each other.

If only for historical reasons, transatlantic dialogues on human rights ought to be in better shape than they currently are. As Goldhaber points out, 'the field of European human rights was pioneered by a handful of lawyers who studied American law during the civil rights era.' He mentions as examples the way in which some of the lawyers behind those early human rights cases that came before the ECtHR – Lord Anthony Lester and the aforementioned Kevin Boyle, for example, both of whom had studied at the Yale Law School – enlisted the help of and teamed up with well-known American lawyers and law professors. The ECtHR 'was roused by English and Irish barristers who were self-consciously influenced by the American civil rights movement' and

[30] Kevin Boyle, 'Transatlantic Human Rights Dialogue', in Rikke Frank Jørgensen and Klaus Slavensky (eds.), *Implementing Human Rights: Essays in Honour of Morten Kjærum* (Copenhagen: The Danish Institute for Human Rights, 2007), 271.

[31] Ibid., 275.

[32] Ibid., 276.

who would cite in their petitions landmark American Supreme Court opinions. The later campaign of Irish feminists for abortion information was, Goldhaber continues,

> expressly patterned on American precedents. So was the quest for religious freedom by Jehovah's Witnesses in Greece. And so is the incipient Roma crusade against police brutality and school segregation in Central Europe. In all three of these instances, there are strong organizational links between the European advocates and their American models.[33]

But whereas formerly the American influence was strong in Europe, the picture has now changed. By comparison to the US Supreme Court, it is now the ECtHR which is setting the pace, and 'Americans should care about European rights law because, on the whole, it presents a progressive parallel universe'. Examples abound: Europeans were twenty years ahead in legalizing gay sex, and in Europe there is a fundamental right to a healthy environment, just as a state may not limit public information on abortion. Europe has furthermore eliminated the death penalty, but most important of all, in Europe, the ban on torture is absolute. 'Strasbourg has long struggled to strike a balance between antiterror and civil rights. Its rulings on detention and torture, especially psychological torture, deserve study as the United States gropes for the war on terror's limits.'[34]

This is where inspiring figures like Zeki Aksoy and P.J. McClean, who were mentioned in the introduction to this chapter, come in. The former, a Turkish kurd who was tortured by Turkish secret police and applied to the ECtHR in May 1993, was the Aksoy in *Aksoy v. Turkey*. *Aksoy* was 'the first European Court of Human Right judgment to confirm a torture incident anywhere in Europe'.[35] Unfortunately, Zeki Aksoy did not live long enough to see his case become a legal landmark; he was killed by the Turkish secret police in April 1994. And as for P.J. McClean, he was one of the original fourteen 'hooded men' in Belfast, whom the British police suspected of terrorism in 1971 and on whom they used some of Stalin's KGB torture techniques: hooding, noise bombardment, food deprivation, sleep deprivation, and forced wall-standing in a painful position. In 1974 and 1975, McClean and the other hooded men were awarded compensation for false imprisonment, assault and torture, but this did not satisfy the Republic of Ireland, which went on to

---

33 Goldhaber, supra n. 1, 181, 182.

34 Ibid., 11, 182.

35 Ibid., 124. The story is somewhat more complicated than this, as Goldhaber relates in Chapter 12 of *A People's History of the European Court of Human Rights*, ('The tortures of Aksoy.')

pursue a rare interstate complaint at the ECtHR. While it took the Court another twenty years to recognize the existence of outright torture in Western Europe, it did recognize in *Ireland v. United Kingdom* that 'even subtle methods of making detainees confess can violate human rights'.[36] – On the whole, Goldhaber concludes on the basis of these two and other cases, that the ECtHR, routinely confronting 'nations over their most culturally sensitive, hot-button issues', has shown over the years 'an impressive record of political courage and achievement'.[37]

THE WORK OF THE TWO EUROPEAN COURTS IN CONTEXT

Goldhaber's favorable assessment of the work and the role of the ECtHR is borne out, by and large, by the first annual report (2007), by the Committee of Ministers of the Council of Europe, *Supervision of the execution of judgments of the European Court of Human Rights*, as well as by a Council of Europe Publication on *The Execution of Judgments of the European Court of Human Rights* of January 2008 by Elisabeth Lambert Abdelgawad. Once a judgment has been delivered by the ECtHR, as we saw, the state involved must answer to the Committee for its execution. Noting initially how supervision of execution is 'an essential element of the credibility of the system and the efficiency of the actions of the Court', the Committee of Ministers' annual report for 2007 goes on to state some 'undeniable achievement[s]':

> As attested by the final resolutions closing its supervision of execution, the Committee of Ministers has so far always been able to conclude that respondent states have fully executed the judgments rendered against them. Admittedly, execution has taken a considerable time in some cases, and has also required investment on the part of the Committee of Ministers and the member states. In rare cases execution has even been at a total standstill for certain periods, but the end result has always been full execution. Thus applicants have in all cases received the just satisfaction awarded by the ECtHR (plus adequate compensation for any delay, if need be) and have received, if applicable, any further individual measure required under Article 46 to erase, as far as possible, the consequences of the violation found (*restitution in integrum*). More than a thousand different general problems revealed by the Court's judgments have also been remedied, or are in the course of being remedied, through legal, administrative and/or other reforms.

This level of respect for an international treaty – even considering that it relates to human rights – is remarkable and deserves to be highlighted. It demonstrates the

---

36 Ibid., 114.
37 Ibid., 2.

> commitment of European states to human rights and also the quality of the work performed by the treaty institutions . . .[38]

That the Committee of Ministers may on the whole be proud of the efficiency of the system is confirmed by Elisabeth Lambert Abdelgawad. 'Now more than ever', she writes in her introduction to *The Execution of Judgments of the European Court of Human Rights*, 'enforcement of judgments is regarded as one of the keys to improving the European human rights system'. And after having in her short publication gone over, first, the content of the obligation to execute judgments of the ECtHR and, second, the supervisory system and its methods, she concludes that, 'although there are some flaws, the outcome of the execution of judgments has been broadly positive, so that the rare exceptions are even more unacceptable'.[39]

Non-compliance with judgments seems to be less of a problem than delays in the various member states. Even where there are set time-limits, delays happen – in fact, the time it takes for member states to execute judgments of the ECtHR has roughly trebled since the late 1990s. Such delays are, moreover, reflections of the exponential increase in the number of applications lodged before the Court – an increase which in turn has led to an enormous growth in the Committee of Ministers' workload: '[w]hile an average of 800 cases were on the agenda of each of its six Human Rights meetings in 2000, today that figure is over 3000. The number of cases pending shows the same trend; the total is now more than 6000. The number of cases for which final resolutions are submitted has risen accordingly.'[40]

As for the nature of the cases brought before the Committee of Ministers for execution, it seems very varied. Appendix 1 to the Committee of Ministers' first annual report provides an overview of the issues examined in 2007. Here there are cases listed which relate to the right to life and protection against torture and ill-treatment, to the prohibition of slavery and forced labour, to the protection of rights in detention, to issues related to aliens and to access to and efficient functioning of justice. Other cases listed relate to the protection of private and family life, to freedom of religion, freedom of expression and information, freedom of assembly and association, property rights, electoral rights, freedom of movement and discrimination. And then, there are the cases dealing with second and third generation rights: environmental protection and the right to education. These cases do indeed bear witness 'to a great variety

---

38 Council of Europe, Committee of Ministers, *Supervision of the execution of judgments of the European Court of Human Rights*, 1st annual report, 2007 (Strasbourg: Council of Europe, March 2008), 7, 10.

39 Abdelgawad, supra n. 20, 5, 71 (Strasbourg: Council of Europe Publishing).

40 Ibid., 65.

of situations', as it is noted in the report. And while the report furthermore notes that it is difficult to say anything definite about particular developments within 2007, it is interesting that 'certain groups of cases have started to become more frequent for certain states over recent years, not least cases involving children or those concerning environmental issues'.[41]

Not surprisingly, the list of cases in the Committee of Ministers' annual report for 2007 corresponds well with the list of key issues, trends and challenges provided in the other first annual report from the Council of Europe – that of the Parliamentary Assembly, previously referred to. In his explanatory memorandum on the 'State of Human Rights in Europe', rapporteur Christos Pourgourides has chosen to focus his report around the following six topics: upholding human rights in Europe, the rule of law, 'black holes', protecting human rights while fighting terrorism, human rights and the protection of vulnerable persons, and respect for diversity. As far as the first two topics are concerned, Pourgourides stresses, among other things, the challenges that certain human rights defenders are facing (ranging from direct use of violence to administrative obstacles and restrictive laws) and the undue political influence on the criminal justice systems and corruption that remain a concern in a number of Council of Europe member states.[42]

In Europe, moreover, Pourgourides reminds us, there are still geographical areas or 'black holes' where the Council of Europe human rights mechanisms cannot fully be implemented, and where secret detention, disappearances and extrajudicial killings are taking place. And he is not just talking about the usual suspects here. Poland and Romania run secret detention centres, for example; Germany, Turkey, Spain and Cyprus are 'staging points', just as Ireland, the United Kingdom, Portugal, Greece and Italy are 'stopovers' for 'flights involving the unlawful transfer of detainees'.[43]

Then, there are human rights and the protection of vulnerable persons, and respect for diversity. In part, the former concerns the treatment of persons deprived of their liberty. One of the most striking and shocking findings is, Pourgourides writes, that 'a number of prisoners and other persons deprived of their liberty are still being subjected to torture or other forms of inhuman and degrading treatment in Europe'. Roma, travellers and immigrants seem to be at particular risk, but the situation of individuals arriving illegally in Europe – for example seasonal agricultural workers – is also alarming. And when it comes to the respect for diversity, 'sixty years after the Second World War, Jews, Roma, and gay and lesbian people are still discriminated against in a number of Council of Europe member states. In other words, racism and intol-

41 Committee of Ministers' annual report, 2007, supra n. 38, 11.

42 *State of human rights and democracy in Europe*, supra n. 22, 38–61.

43 Ibid., 64.

erance based on racial, ethnic or religious origin, sex or sexual orientation has not yet been eradicated in Europe.'[44]

The overall issue of ethnic and racial discrimination is quite problematic in many member states. One of the new faces of discrimination, according to Pourgourides, is 'cultural racism'. This is especially interesting in light of the discussions concerning 'culture' that we encountered in Chapter 2.

Today, the idea of 'culture' appears increasingly to replace the idea of 'race', and take on the role it used to play in the field of racism and discrimination. According to this new form of racism, cultures make up predefined entities which are homogenous, rigid and, above all, incompatible with one another. Groups of persons are therefore defined by their culture, with some cultures being 'superior' to others.[45]

As it is used here, 'culture' has none of the positive connotations that we normally choose to assign to it. Instead, in this context, it becomes a means to exclude 'others' and 'otherness', the ultimate manifestation of which is the fight against terrorism and the justification of repressive measures against human rights defenders. And it is for the fight against terrorism that Pourgourides saves his fiercest criticism and warnings that something is decidedly wrong. The fight against terrorism is 'one of the recent major challenges for our society' and it 'has harmed the cause of human rights in different ways'. For example, 'the Court's case law reveals that the deaths in a large percentage of the cases in which the Court found violations of Article 2 of the [European Convention on Human Rights] (Right to life) had been caused during anti-terrorist operations', and reports also document 'the troublesome worldwide trend to question the absolute ban on torture and ill-treatment in the name of security'.[46]

Politics versus Law

All in all, therefore, 'constant vigilance is called for', as Abdelgawad writes in her conclusion to *The Execution of Judgments of the European Court of Human Rights*; 'particularly where fundamental rights are violated by states, nothing can ever really be taken for granted'.[47] As successful as the two European courts may be said to be, the question therefore is whether other ways of fighting are also called for. As some scholars see it, recourse to the judiciary may not always be sufficient. 'The courts are often seen as the primary defenders of fundamental rights in a constitutional polity', writes

44 Ibid., 74, 84.
45 Ibid., 84–85.
46 Ibid., 68–69.
47 Abdelgawad, supra n. 20, 71.

Kieran St C. Bradley, for example. This seems especially to be the case in relation to the European Community, where almost no attention is given to the activities of the political institutions when it comes to fighting for human rights:

> It is surely the case, however, that the legislative and executive branches of government should be considered the primary defenders of human rights. The definition of the rights to be protected, and especially the balance to be struck between conflicting values in a given situation, and of the methods of protection, falls in the first place to the legislature, possibly in accordance with guidelines established by a written constitution, while their implementation on the ground, where the citizen is first in contact with the State, is the task of the administration . . . Judicial forms of protection should therefore be seen as a solution of second-last resort, in cases of disputes concerning the existence or scope of a particular rights or rights; in short, prevention is better than cure.[48]

Bradley's views are seconded by Philip Alston and Joseph Weiler, who challenge the implicit premise that 'equipping individuals to pursue existing Community legal remedies . . . is, for the most part, not merely sufficient but is even an effective mechanism to guarantee that rights will not be violated within the Community legal sphere'. While judicial protection is important, it is by no means sufficient:

> Effective access to justice requires a variety of policies that would empower individuals to vindicate the judicially enforceable rights given to them. Ignorance, lack of resources, ineffective representation, inadequate legal standing and deficient remedies all have the capacity to render judicially enforceable rights illusory. In our view, therefore, too much faith is placed by the Community in the power of legal prohibitions and judicial enforcement.[49]

These views are voiced specifically in relation to the European Community and the EU, but they are also relevant in other contexts. In general, argues Bradley, 'scrutiny of human rights issues may be more palatable where undertaken by public representatives who are answerable to an electorate, rather than by "unelected bureaucrats" '.[50] The underlying discussion here is one of politics versus law – a discussion which, as we shall see in the following chapters, is of great importance when it comes to US views on international law, for example. But if we stay within the European context for now, it really was

---

48 Kieran St C. Bradley, 'Reflections on the Human Rights Role of the European Parliament', in Philip Alston (ed.), *The EU and Human Rights* (Oxford: Oxford University Press, 1999), 847.

49 Philip Alston and J.H.H. Weiler, 'An "Ever Closer Union" in Need of a Human Rights Policy: The European Union and Human Rights', in ibid., 12–13.

50 Ibid., 848.

not that long ago that the use of courts and lawyers to promote social policy (judicial activism) was looked upon with suspicion. Karl Marx famously castigated human rights as a vehicle for individual aggrandizement and enrichment of the privileged classes, just as the European socialist movement has traditionally been sceptical of the prioritization of the legal over the political.

There are still sceptics out there, as we just saw. To these we may add Irish law professor Conor Gearty. Speaking of the modern human rights movement he asks in *Can Human Rights Survive?*, for example, '[w]hich great social movement has ever before put lawyers in its front-line?'. Until fairly recently, the reactionary force of human rights law was a commonplace of left-wing thinking. It was really only with the end of the Cold War in 1989 that this hostility was replaced by a much more enthusiastic view of human rights. This should make us recognize, says Gearty,

> that we are relying on a largely speaking conservative force – the law, the judges, the legal profession – to carry our radical project through to completion . . . What kind of a war-strategy is it to entrust our greatest emancipatory tasks to judges, a sub-category of precisely the kind of well-off, already empowered person who ought to be terrified by the prospect of true human rights?[51]

His own 'journey to and from human rights', Gearty tells us, began when he got a job at a British law school in the early 1980s. He now had to assign to his students a number of cases most of which were 'dreadful, coercive decisions'. When he furthermore witnessed some very bad behaviour on the part of certain judges, he ended up thinking that 'judges were bad everywhere, not just in Britain. They had been even worse in the past – there had never been a golden age of judicial good conduct; this was just a liberal myth'.[52]

Today, Gearty has succeeded in reconstructing his belief in human rights – but only to a certain extent. He no longer lets himself be carried away by empty human rights rhetoric of the kind that promises the world, but changes nothing in practice. It is only if or when human rights are viewed as practical, political means toward bettering the conditions of the not so well-off among us that they retain their emancipatory power. The crucial thing is to see human rights as *a part of* politics – and not as *above* politics:

> The problem is that . . . in recovering its certainty in what is right and what is wrong, and in overseeing other laws for compatibility with this brand of the truth, human rights law seems invariably to find itself reverting to a particular philosophical tradition that has certainly had its uses in past generations but which is not particularly

---

[51] Conor Gearty, *Can Human Rights Survive?* (The Hamlyn Lectures 2005, Cambridge: Cambridge University Press, 2006), 12.

[52] Ibid., 2, 3.

> helpful or persuasive today. This is the line of thinking that essentially sees the idea of human rights not as an emancipatory political concept at all but rather as a pre- or supra-political ideal, as reflective of a truth beyond politics to which politics ought to be subject. On this view, our core or essential human rights are made up of a number of rights that people have which precede politics or which are above politics. They are not rights which are achieved (and sustained) through politics.[53]

To Gearty's point about human rights as political entities that ought to enter political discussion instead of trumping it, Finnish law professor Martti Koskenniemi would nod in agreement. What rights boil down to in the end are political interests, and when such interests are dressed in rights language, their political nature is obscured. Understanding and acting upon rights as absolute and universal has, Koskenniemi argues, certain negative, cultural effects on politics. First of all, it reduces politics to the declaration of insights or truths that have already been found elsewhere, and this, in turn, makes of politicians technically competent experts, rather than debaters who enter into dialogue on issues of importance to themselves and to their constituents. What this means, in the end, is that politics become

> the politics of procedure, a struggle for the power to define, for jurisdiction: the question is not so much whether a weighing of interests has to take place, but rather which authority in the final analysis is empowered to do the weighing.
>
> This aspect highlights the priority of process to substance in rights discourse. And for those immersed in that discourse the natural cultural preference is that 'only the Strasbourg organs are competent to conduct the weighing of interests involved in the Convention'.[54]

Secondly, the rhetoric of rights does not go beyond expressing the values or interests of the individual citizen. In fact, of course, no citizen lives in a vacuum, but it is only rarely the case that the values or interests of that larger community around him or her get expressed. Nor does the rhetoric of rights allow for a situation of doubt – of the individual finding him- or herself torn between competing values and interests. Expressing oneself in terms of rights makes for strong, non-ambivalent and also non-negotiable statements. 'Thinking of politics in terms of rights is unable to reach the process in which the interests of individuals (and their "individuality") are formed, omitting the question whether having such interests is good in the first place, and failing to discriminate between interests that conflict but which we feel equally strongly about.'[55]

---

53 Ibid., 72.

54 Martti Koskenniemi, 'The Effect of Rights on Political Culture', in Alston (ed.), supra n. 48, 114.

55 Ibid.

Finally, there is a real danger that the current rhetoric of rights will eventually lead to what Koskenniemi calls a 'political culture of bad faith'. With the deconstruction of natural law, unthinking faith in rights can no longer be taken for granted. People just simply know today that 'administration and adjudication have to do with discretion, and that, however much such discretion is dressed in the technical language of rights and "balancing", the outcomes reflect broad cultural and political preferences that have nothing inalienable about them'. People tend to cope with this knowledge in various ways. Some simply declare that rights are nothing but politics or, even, give up on rights talk altogether; others tend to make believe. They still use a version of rights talk even though they no longer really believe in the a-political or foundational nature of rights. Either way, the idea that human rights are important and necessary to the European project is jeopardized, and this ultimately seems to be the most serious problem for Koskenniemi:

> In this way, you may be compelled – in order to advance the cultural politics of a 'Europe' – to choose a purely strategic attitude towards rights. Even as you know that rights defer to policy, you cannot disclose this, as you would then seem to undermine what others (mistakenly) believe one of your most beneficial gifts to humanity (a non-political and universal rights rhetoric). It is hard to think of such an attitude as a beneficial basis from which to engage other cultures or to inaugurate a transcultural sphere of policies.[56]

The solution to this catch twenty-two situation is to let go of a rights discourse characterized by the use of rights as trumps, and instead further a political discourse in which discussions of 'deviating conceptions of the good – whether or not expressed in rights language' are encouraged.[57] The link here between European identity and human rights is very interesting. What is ultimately at stake for Koskenniemi is the question of how to move toward a common European identity once the belief in absolute and universal human rights has been lost.

CONCLUDING REMARKS

> To Germany's fearful neighbours, the *quid pro quo* for its rebirth was continuing American involvement in Europe, achieved through the Marshall Plan and, later, the North Atlantic Treaty of 1949. Both the United States and Germany's neighbours wanted a political framework as well, one that would encourage Germany to develop democratic institutions and the rule of law within a more closely integrated Europe.

---

[56] Ibid., 116.
[57] Ibid.

> The Federal Republic of Germany evolved rapidly into a rights-based democracy, much influenced by the American model... Drafted in part by Carl Joachim Friedrich, a German academic who had emigrated to the United States and become a distinguished professor at Harvard University, the [new basic constitution, the *Grundgesetz*] spelled out in detail the fundamental rights of German citizens...
>
> Germany's Constitutional Court has become as fierce a guardian of these rights as the US Supreme Court has been of the Bill of Rights and has critically influenced the evolution of human rights law in Europe...
>
> A democratic Federal Republic of Germany was a crucial element in the establishment of a stable democratic Western Europe, but it was not the only one. A framework was needed capable of embracing all the countries of Western Europe within a structure of respect for human rights. That framework was the Council of Europe and, at its center, the European Court of Human Rights.[58]

Describing the origins of European human rights law institutions in an article on 'Human rights in Europe', British politician and academic Shirley Williams explains the growth of human rights in Europe as, at least in part, due to a strong American influence. It was through an American insistence, right after the end of World War Two, that rights talk was introduced into Europe.[59] And later on, as we have seen in this chapter, some of the European lawyers behind the most important cases coming before the ECtHR – cases that would go on to become legal landmarks – were to receive the inspiration to use the law and the courts to fight for a better and more just world as foreign students at American law schools. One such European student was Mary Robinson, who went to the US in 1966 to get her LL.M. degree (master of laws degree) at the Harvard Law School (HLS). In a 1980 interview in the *Sunday Independent*, she recalled how social issues kept surfacing in debates with fellow students, and how the time at HLS had been one of the most influential experiences in her life:

> The Vietnam War forced a lot of young people to re-think. There was a great deal of discussion on socialism, on equality, civil rights, and poverty. Many of the very bright students were turning down large law firm salaries, to get involved in projects and counsel for legal education, which was a totally transformed approach. When I came home, I related all this to Ireland and have continued to do so.

What the later lawyer, member of the upper house of the Irish parliament, Irish president and United Nations High Commissioner for Human Rights

---

58 Williams, supra n. 6, 81–82.

59 Maybe it would have been more correct to say that rights talk was 're-introduced' into Europe at this point. According to German legal historian Michael Stolleis, Europe has its own long and proud history of rights talk. Stolleis outlines this history in *The Eye of the Law: Two Essays on Legal History* (Abingdon, UK: Birkbeck Law Press, 2009).

took home to Ireland with her was a greater awareness of the role of law in culture and society – law as the 'hidden infrastructure which conditions our society and pervades almost every aspect of our lives', as she was to put it much later. What she furthermore learned in the US was the power of judicial review. The example of the US Supreme Court under Earl Warren (1953–1969) was an inspiring one – one that made her aware of the need for Irish judges to play a more active role in policy making.[60]

An American influence this pervasive would, one might have thought, have led to a greater or better transatlantic understanding in the area of human rights and international law. This has not been the case, however. Dialogues on human rights have been established, but they primarily focus on issues to do with the fight against terror, and one of the few unofficial attempts that have been made to start a broader dialogue was not exactly a great success. Neither does there seem to be much cooperation going on across the Atlantic within the field of human rights. The main ingredients – the belief in the rule of law, democracy and human rights; the understanding of law's major cultural role and importance for identity formation – are certainly there on both sides. Yet, we have failed to put to good use this common ground. This may perhaps have something to do with Michael Goldhaber's argument – that by now the apprentice, the ECtHR, has become the more advanced, if not downright progressive, and has left the master, the US Supreme Court, behind. On neither side of the Atlantic has this led to a greater will to see the obvious parallels that exist between the role that law has historically played in American culture and society and the role that human rights law is increasingly beginning to play in Europe.

But there is more to it, I think. And it is to some of the possible explanations that we shall now turn.

---

60 The two Mary Robinson quotations as well as the history of her stay at the Harvard Law School, can be found in Michael Böss, 'American Links to Legal Reform in Ireland, 1937–1997: A Study in the International Impact of American Constitutional Law', in Helle Porsdam (ed.), *Folkways and Law Ways: Law in American Studies* (Odense: Odense University Press, 2001), 229–230.

5. Divergent transatlantic views on human rights: economic, social and cultural rights

The majority of the fifteen ECtHR cases with which Michael D. Goldhaber presents us in *A People's History of the European Court of Human Rights* concern political and civil rights. This may have something to do with the fact that these cases have been 'selected for their legal significance and personal drama' and that special attention has been given 'to contrasts between Europe and the United States' in order to make an American readership interested.[1] The choice of cases may perhaps also, one may speculate, reflect the general scepticism that many Americans show vis-à-vis second-generation rights, the economic, social and cultural rights.

In this and the following chapter we will look at two of the main differences between European human rights talk and American rights talk: the *kinds* of (human) rights emphasized, and the attitude toward international law and international human rights regimes. Whereas Americans tend to think that the core of human rights consists of first generation rights only (the civil and political rights), many Europeans tend also to believe in second generation rights (the economic, social and cultural rights), if for no other reason than that the welfare state and its future matter a great deal to them. This distinction is not watertight, of course; there are Americans who would never dream of questioning whether economic, social and cultural rights are something other than rights, just as there are Europeans who would still consider political and civil rights more 'real' than any other kinds of rights. We are dealing with generalizations here, but these will serve, I hope, to make an important point in relation to transatlantic dialogues on human rights.

In Chapter 6, we shall then look at the other human rights area or issue that radically divides the waters: the role of international law and institutions. Whereas on the European side, there is a strong feeling that supranational law

---

1 Michael D. Goldhaber, *A People's History of the European Court of Human Rights* (New Brunswick, NJ, and London: Rutgers University Press, 2007), 10.

and institutions are the way of the future, there is much less enthusiasm on the American side. Sovereignty is a big issue, as is federalism. But also more culturally related matters such as American exceptionalism and belief in the superiority of the American constitutional tradition play an important role.

In our analysis, we will take into consideration the various arguments made since 1948 by American scholars and policy makers regarding the pros and cons of American involvement in international human rights initiatives. These arguments provide an excellent example of the American side of things. They are interesting in this connection, furthermore, because they reflect back on the whole history of transatlantic debates and because they provide an excellent background for discussing the pros and cons of Europe presently taking over judicial activism and constitutional democracy, American style.

We have touched on these issues already in passing, in Chapters 1 and 2, but in this and the following chapter we will make the definition of the core of human rights as well as the discussion of the role of international law our focus of attention.

THE CORE OF HUMAN RIGHTS

Human rights, it is commonly agreed, 'are a core set of rights that human beings possess by simple virtue of their humanity'.[2] We find these rights set out in a number of international human rights instruments, most notably the so-called International Bill of Rights consisting of the Universal Declaration of Human Rights (UDHR), the International Covenant on Economic, Social, and Cultural Rights (ICESCR or Economic Covenant), and the International Covenant on Civil and Political Rights (ICCPR or Political Covenant). Of these, only the two Covenants are legally binding, although many international lawyers would argue that the UDHR has also by now become binding on all states through customary international law. The US ratified the Political Covenant only in 1992, as mentioned in Chapter 2, and to this day has not yet ratified the Economic Covenant.

Today, in human rights discourse, human rights are often divided into various layers. In his influential 1977 book, *Citizenship and Social Development*, T.H. Marshall mentioned three different layers of citizens' rights: civil rights, political rights and social rights. The civil rights were embedded in the constitutional state with its rule of law, the political rights in the system of democracy

---

[2] Mark Gibney, *International Human Rights Law: Returning to Universal Principles* (Lanham, MD: Rowman & Littlefield Publishers, Inc., 2008), 3.

and the social rights in the arrangements of the welfare state.[3] Another way of dividing up human rights that is often used (and that has been used throughout previous chapters) follows the distinction attributed to Czech lawyer Karel Vasak between different generations of human rights.[4] The civil and political rights make up the first generation of human rights, while the economic, social and cultural rights make up the second generation. The former deal essentially with liberty and with participation in political life. They are the ones mentioned in those early human rights documents, the American Declaration of Independence (1776) and the French Declaration of the Rights of Man and of the Citizen (1789), and they are sometimes also called 'negative rights' because they serve to protect the individual and his/her family from excesses of the state.

By comparison, the historical origins of the second generation rights, the economic, social and cultural rights – which are often also called 'positive rights' because they ask the state to play a role in the life of the individual citizen and his/her family, to guarantee a certain minimum standard – are somewhat blurred. One source seems to have been the major religions that have always preached concern for one's neighbour. Then there is the influence of political and philosophical writers such as Thomas Paine, Karl Marx, Immanuel Kant and John Rawls. In addition, scholars mention various political and social movements of the 19th and 20th centuries: the Fabian socialists in Great Britain, Chancellor Bismarck in Germany and his introduction in the 1880s of social insurance and the American New Dealers. Finally, the Mexican Constitution of 1917, the various Soviet Constitutions and the Weimar Republic Constitution of 1919 are often referred to as constitutional inspirations.[5] Today, some scholars and activists talk about a third generation of human rights emerging: the 'solidarity' (or group) rights. These include the right to a clean environment, the right to development and the rights of minority cultures and of indigenous peoples.

In the Universal Declaration of Human Rights, first and second generation rights are mentioned side by side. The UDHR not itself being a legally binding document, the original idea within the United Nations was to create a follow-up document that would transform the political and moral statements

---

3 T.H. Marshall, *Citizenship and Social Development* (London and Chicago, IL: University of Chicago Press, 1977).

4 Felipe Gómez Isa and Koen de Feyter (eds.), *International Protection of Human Rights: Achievements and Challenges* (Bilbao: University of Deusto, 2007), 35, 37, 130.

5 Henry J. Steiner and Philip Alston (eds.), *International Human Rights in Context: Law, Politics, Morals* (Oxford: Oxford University Press, 2000, 2nd edition), 242.

of the UDHR into 'real' law. In part as a result of the cold war, the east and the west could not agree on such a project, however. While the east, headed by the USSR, argued that the core of human rights consisted of economic and social rights, the west, headed by the US, argued just the opposite: the real and important human rights were the civil and political ones. In the end, two documents were drafted in 1966 (but ratified only in 1976) – the Political and Economic Covenants. Both are legally binding documents; yet, the discussion about what makes up the core of human rights is still very much with us.

Officially, the Political and Economic Covenants and their two sets of rights are, in the wording adopted by the second World Conference on Human Rights in Vienna in 1993, 'universal, indivisible and interdependent and interrelated. The international community must treat human rights globally in a fair and equal manner, on the same footing, and with the same emphasis.'[6] But this official consensus does not always hold up. It masks, as Steiner and Alston put it,

> a deep and enduring disagreement over the proper status of economic, social and cultural rights. At one extreme lies the view that these rights are superior to civil and political rights in terms of an appropriate value hierarchy and in chronological terms. Of what use is the right to free speech to those who are starving and illiterate? At the other extreme we find the view that economic and social rights do not constitute rights (as properly understood) at all. Treating them as rights undermines the enjoyment of individual freedom, distorts the functioning of free markets by justifying large-scale state intervention in the economy, and provides an excuse to downgrade the importance of civil and political rights.[7]

While the view that economic and social rights do not constitute rights (as properly understood) at all is the one often voiced by Americans to explain their antipathy towards second-generation human rights, the view that these rights are superior to civil and political rights represents the position of certain developing countries which would like to see a greater emphasis being placed on the right to development and other second- and third-generation rights. The European view most often presented by human rights scholars and activists is that the truth is somewhere in between these two extremes – that first and second-generation human rights are equally important, that they are indeed 'universal, indivisible and interdependent and interrelated'. In legal theory, moreover, efforts have been made over the past few years 'to wipe out the distinction between the two sets of rights by replacing the traditional positive/negative dichotomy with a tripartite terminology, to *respect*, *protect* and *fulfil*, showing that compliance with human rights – social and civil – can

---

6 Vienna Declaration, 5, quoted in ibid., 237.
7 Ibid., 237.

require various measures from (passive) non-interference to (active) ensuring satisfaction of individual needs depending on the given circumstances.'[8]

ECONOMIC, SOCIAL AND CULTURAL RIGHTS IN THE EUROPEAN CONTEXT

The Development of a Social Europe?

Economic and social rights were mentioned in the post-World War Two constitutions of France, Germany and Italy – but not in the European Convention of Human Rights. The decision not to include these rights was made because key drafters of the document felt that it was necessary first, in the words of Pierre-Henri Teitgen, 'to guarantee political democracy in the European Union and then to co-ordinate our economies, before undertaking the generalisation of social democracy'.[9] The economic and social rights had to wait until the European Social Charter in 1961 to be officially recognized. Often referred to as the social counterpart of the European Convention on Human Rights, the Social Charter has since been revised and amended by various protocols, but whereas every member of the Council of Europe has ratified the European Convention, as we saw, only about a third have also ratified the Social Charter instruments. For the possible development of a Social Europe, we therefore have to look elsewhere.

Within the context of the European Union, social rights have, as Miguel Poiares Maduro puts is, 'been developed as a function of market integration, not as an element of European citizenship'. From the very start of Community law in 1958, a major aim has been to promote the freedom of movement for workers – a freedom which has

> been developed as a function of economic efficiency: the intent is an optimal allocation of labour under the mechanisms generated by market integration. There is no free movement of persons conceived as a right to choose between different models of life and regulatory regimes (including social protection)... Persons can move only as market agents: workers, self-employed persons, and companies.[10]

---

[8] Ida Elisabeth Koch, 'Economic, Social and Cultural Rights as Components in Civil and Political Rights: A Hermeneutic Perspective', 10 *The International Journal of Human Rights* (2006), 406.

[9] Pierre-Henri Teitgen, quoted in Steiner and Alston, supra n. 5, 794.

[10] Miguel Poiares Maduro, 'Striking the Elusive Balance Between Economic Freedom and Social Rights in the EU', in Philip Alston (ed.), *The EU and Human Rights* (Oxford: Oxford University Press, 1999), 462.

This drive toward market integration has, some critics maintain, furthered not only economic freedom at the cost of social rights and policies, but also EU law and policy at the cost of national welfare laws. Social welfare laws have typically been the privilege or duty of the various member states – solidarity being 'traditionally a national concept, especially for those forms of financial solidarity not linked to insurance or the payment of contributions'. In principle, member states do still have sovereign power to define their social policies, and it is settled case law that member states can set up their social protection systems any way they wish. 'However, the ECJ has always emphasized that the Member States must nevertheless comply with Community law when exercising those powers.'[11]

Today, as a result, the responsibility for the regulation and delivery of social protection and welfare arguably no longer belongs solely to the states, but increasingly also to the EU. There are, Gráinne de Búrca argues, 'two main aspects to the claim that the EU has an important impact in this field. The first relates to the impact that EU economic law and policy have on existing national laws and policies in the area of social welfare and the second relates to the gradual emergence of elements, albeit still in fragmented form, of a distinctive EU welfare dimension.'[12] As far as the impact of EU law on existing national welfare laws is concerned, it is especially the internal market and competition law which have brought about changes to national laws, as we saw.

The European project started as an economic project. The fundamental aim from the very beginning has been the creation of an inner market in which there would be a free movement of goods, persons, services and capital, and over the years the ECJ and the EU legislature have between them created a body of law intended to further such free movement. 'And gradually, but in particular in recent years, the effect of the treaty provisions on the free movement of workers and services, and of EC competition and state aids law on the provision of important national services, have exposed the vulnerability of national welfare institutions to the varying influence of a range of European norms.'[13] Such influence can operate more or less directly, but pressures are invariably built to adapt national welfare law accordingly. And it is not just the economic dimension of things that is affected; internal market and competition

---

[11] Herwig Verschueren, 'European (Internal) Migration Law as an Instrument for Defining the Boundaries of National Solidarity Systems', 9 *European Journal of Migration and Law* (2007), 308.

[12] Gráinne de Búrca, 'Towards European Welfare?', in Gráinne de Búrca (ed.), *EU Law and the Welfare State: In Search of Solidarity* (Oxford: Oxford University Press, 2005), 1.

[13] Ibid., 1–2.

law has a tendency also to carry over into other areas of life. De Búrca mentions as examples access to information on abortion, access to higher education, and access to cross-border medical assistance – all of which have been impacted on by ECJ case law in ways that exceed the merely commercial.[14]

Far-reaching as such impact of EU law on existing national laws may be, the second aspect emphasized by de Búrca – the gradual emergence of a distinctive EU welfare dimension 'through deliberate action . . . at the European level and not only in the impact of other EU policies on national welfare institutions' – may be even more important. Such deliberate action includes first of all 'the provisions of EU citizenship and more specifically . . . the ECJ case [law] which has evolved around them'. In addition it includes 'even if only faintly so far, given the limited justiciability of some of the most relevant provisions – . . . parts of the EU Charter on Fundamental Rights, particularly . . . the titles on "Solidarity", "Equality", and "Citizens' Rights" '. Then, there is 'the complicated body of EC legislation regulating the coordination of social security benefits' as well as 'the large and expanding body of EC equality law'. And finally, the deliberate EU action may be said to manifest itself in certain attempts to create within the EU a range of common national social policies in areas such as employment, anti-poverty, pensions and health.[15]

The way in which the EU system itself makes use of a discourse around the concept of the 'European social model' that would seem to suggest a conscious European welfare programme is interesting, moreover. When that concept was referred to in the past, people normally meant to suggest certain principles that the different European welfare states would have in common. Now, what the 'European social model' seems to suggest is instead the existence of one single system or model in Europe. 'Indeed the renewal and "modernization" of the European social model has', says de Búrca, 'been a theme of EU social policy over the last decade in particular. Even if the notion of the European social model is thus rather vague and diffuse, it suggests something which is simultaneously based on and drawn from various national welfare systems, but which is also promoted by the EU and independently shaped by developments at transnational and supranational level.'[16]

EU citizenship was introduced in the Treaty on European Union which was signed in Maastricht in 1992 and appears to be 'a new type of citizenship, a *sui generis* creation'. Citizenship is normally associated with membership of

---

14 Ibid., 2.
15 Ibid.
16 Ibid., 3.

a nation state and with the rights and duties such membership gives to the individual. Citizenship of the Union gives the individual rights and duties not only in the Member State to which he or she belongs, but also in the EU at large. It aims partly at providing an increased protection to the individual, and partly at furthering a closer union and sense of belonging among the peoples of Europe. 'It constitutes', write Ulf Bernitz and Hedvig Lokrantz Bernitz, 'a part of the endeavour to create a "People's Europe". The purpose is to bring the EU closer to the citizens in the Member States and to give the EU a new political and social dimension.'[17]

Citizenship of the Union confers certain specific rights on the individual. Among these are rights of a political nature as well as rights of an economic nature. Citizens of the Union may now vote and run for office at municipal elections as well as at elections to the European Parliament (Art. 19 of the Maastricht Treaty). They furthermore have the right to diplomatic and consular protection in third countries where their own country is not represented (Art. 20), just as they have the right to petition the European Parliament and the right to apply to the European Ombudsman (Art. 21). The right to vote and the right to diplomatic protection are new rights in the EU context. The right to petition the European Parliament and the right to apply to the European Ombudsman are important democratic contributions to the EU – focusing 'directly on the Community', they 'concern the relationship between the individual and the Community . . . When these rights are exercised, a direct legal relationship arises between the individual and the Community.'[18]

Significant as these political rights are, the economic rights outlined in Article 18 concerning the right to move and to reside freely within the territory of all Member States are arguably even more important. It is these rights which have been the foundation for the ECJ's development of the status of EU citizenship and the rights such citizenship entails. Versions of these rights did exist prior to the Maastricht Treaty – especially for persons pursuing an economic activity – but corresponding rights have gradually been developed also for economically non-active individuals, even third-country nationals, in the case law of the ECJ and in secondary legislation to the point where, with the consolidation of these rights by Union citizenship, as Dorte Sindbjerg Martinsen puts it, 'rights are gradually decoupled from a person's status as a worker'.[19]

---

[17] Ulf Bernitz and Hedvig Lokrantz Bernitz, 'Human Rights and European Identity: The Debate about European Citizenship', in de Búrca, supra n. 12, 505.

[18] Ibid., 517.

[19] Dorte Sindbjerg Martinsen, 'Social Security Regulation in the EU: The De-Territorialization of Welfare?', in de Búrca, supra n. 12, 90.

One piece of such relevant EU legislation is Community Regulation 1408/71, a social security co-ordination mechanism, which has recently been revised with the adoption of Regulation 883/2004, likely to come into force in 2009. 'The provisions of Regulation 1408/71 now co-ordinate the social security systems of 31 European states: 27 EU Member States, 3 EEA States and Switzerland, covering the nationals of these states as well as third-country nationals legally resident in a Member State.'[20] The primary aim of this co-ordination system has been to ensure the free movement of persons, but to do so in a way which would also respect national social security legislation. The definition of social security legislation having traditionally been the privilege of the Member States themselves, as we saw, the EU has abstained from finding ways of harmonizing the legislation of the various Member States. Instead, the underlying principles of coordination used have been equality of treatment for all persons and benefits covered by the Regulation and exportability within the geographical scope of the Regulation of acquired rights.[21]

With the adoption of Regulation 883/2004, the scope of the Regulation has been extended so as to apply to all European citizens[22] when it comes to social security legislation on sickness benefits, maternity and equivalent paternity benefits, invalidity benefits, old-age benefits, survivors' benefits, benefits in respect of accidents at work and occupational diseases, death grants, unemployment benefits, pre-retirement benefits, and family benefits.[23] This development, argues Martinsen, 'is thus a specific reflection of the general development from economic community to political union . . . The extension of intra-European social security rights to all Community nationals adds substantial rights to the skeleton of European citizenship, since cross-border

---

20 Verschueren, supra n. 11, 309.

21 These principles are, explains Verschueren, 'essential: the absence of Community wide social security schemes and the preservation of differences between the Member States' social protection policy and legislation can only be acceptable in a Community context of free movement of persons, if Member States ban all discrimination on grounds of nationality and even non-discriminatory obstacles to such movement.' Ibid., 312.

22 The conditions for legally residing third-country nationals have also been somewhat expanded with Regulation 859/2003 – 'Apparently, the amendment adopted in 2003 put an end to an intense debate between the Commission, Council, Parliament, and Court on the status of third-country nationals, and finally granted equal rights to a previously deprived group. However radical such an extension may seem, it should be noted that in practice it is not of much use. Third-country nationals legally residing in Member States have no right to free movement, but they can *only* invoke the rights under Regulation 1408/71 if they *do move* between member States'. Martinsen, supra n. 19, 96).

23 Ibid., 91.

social rights are, finally, granted irrespective of economic activity.'[24] We may now talk about a 'de-territorialization of welfare'. Due to the activities of both the ECJ and the political bodies of the EU, what counts today is residence (where a person lives), rather than nationality (where a person comes from) – 'the autonomy to define welfare policy means and objectives is compromised by Community law'.[25]

The most recent step toward such a de-territorialization of welfare is the EU Charter on Fundamental Rights of 2000 which sets out in a single text, for the first time in the European Union's history, the whole range of civil, political, economic, social and cultural rights of European citizens and all persons resident in the EU. These rights are divided into six sections: dignity, freedoms, equality, solidarity, citizens' rights and justice. They are based on the fundamental rights and freedoms outlined in the European Convention on Human Rights, the constitutional traditions of the EU Member States, the Council of Europe's Social Charter, the Community Charter of Fundamental Social Rights of Workers and other international conventions to which the European Union or its Member States are parties.

The EU Charter was included as Part II of the Treaty Establishing a Constitution for Europe, adopted in Dublin in 2004, the ratification process of which was stalemated with the French and Dutch 'no' in the spring of 2005. A 'Reform Treaty' was subsequently proposed. It has since come to be known as the Treaty of Lisbon because it was signed by the twenty-seven heads of state and government in Lisbon in December 2007. The Lisbon Treaty had to be ratified by all twenty-seven member states before 1 January 2009 if it was to enter into force. The June 2008 Irish referendum on the Treaty, which ended in a 'no', has left matters somewhat up in the air. The Charter of Fundamental Rights was to be retained, although not in full. A clause would simply refer to it and this would be legally binding (except in the United Kingdom and Poland which had negotiated certain exceptions). The Treaty of Lisbon furthermore contained a 'social clause' whereby social issues such as the promotion of a high level of employment and adequate social protection must be taken into account when defining and implementing all policies.[26]

Despite the fact that the Charter is not (yet) legally binding, both the ECJ and the European legislature have already referred to it.[27] To what extent the Charter would strengthen the process of full constitutionalization of citizenship rights

---

24 Ibid., 95, 97.

25 Ibid., 105.

26 Useful, basic information on the Lisbon Treaty, provided by the French think tank, Fondation Robert Schuman, is available at http://www.robert-schuman.org/tout-comprendre-sur-le-traite-de-lisbonne.php (last visited on 8 January 2009).

27 See Verschueren, supra n. 11, 341.

we cannot know, of course. But 'the sheer fact that something akin to a bill of rights – including social rights – has been codified in the Constitutional Treaty [now the Lisbon Treaty] must be regarded as a very significant (some have said "spectacular") innovation'.[28] Whether or not the emergence of an EU welfare policy is something Europeans should be happy about is a question on which people disagree, however. Whereas some see in the new Charter a reinforcement of the EU's commitment to fundamental rights and a possible help to clarify the legal basis of the rights already protected by the ECJ, others are of the opinion that solidarity cannot be stretched beyond the nation state to include all of Europe, that EU citizens already enjoy too much judicial protection of their rights – the ECJ having become altogether too judicially activist, to the point of defying the will of the legislature – and that a second written catalogue of rights may increase rather than lessen tension with the European Convention as well as with its 'other' interpreter, the European Court of Human Rights.[29]

'The question remains', writes Goldhaber, 'which is really supreme – the EU court or the [ECtHR]?'[30] So far, collision between these two seems to have been avoided. The ECJ has even on occasion taken Strasbourg case law into account and seems more inclined toward doing so today than was earlier the case.[31] The Charter may give rise to new conflicts, though, as it will make it more likely that the ECJ will have to 'trespass' onto the human rights turf of the Strasbourg court. Were the EU to accede to the European Convention, as is suggested in the Lisbon Treaty, this might effectively solve the problem in favour of the ECtHR.

ECONOMIC, SOCIAL AND CULTURAL RIGHTS IN THE AMERICAN CONTEXT

American Antipathies Towards Second Generation Rights

As we saw in Chapter 2 in connection with the European Social Model, the move of the EU toward the protection of welfare rights seems to have the

---

[28] Maurizio Ferrera, 'Towards an "Open" Social Citizenship? The New Boundaries of Welfare in the European Union', in de Búrca, supra n. 12, 37.

[29] Síofra O'Leary, 'Solidarity and Citizenship Rights in the Charter of Fundamental Rights of the European Union', ibid., 45, note 22.

[30] Goldhaber, supra n. 1, 177.

[31] Dean Spielman mentions four such occasions. See Dean Spielman, 'Human Rights Case Law in the Strasbourg and Luxembourg Courts: Conflicts, Inconsistencies, and Complementarities', in Alston, supra n. 10, 772–775.

support of several European intellectuals, who have argued that it is possible to stretch solidarity beyond current nation-state borders. This is somewhat ironic, perhaps, in that some of these very same intellectuals used to be fierce opponents of the EU. When it comes to European welfare, though, the general consensus seems to be that this is what Europe is (or should be) all about, and that such welfare may perhaps best be safeguarded today at the European level.

Not so in the United States. Whereas in Europe an economic efficiency and property discourse has eventually led to the protection of the social rights of workers and their families, as we saw, this does not seem to have happened in the American context.[32] 'Why does the American Constitution lack social and economic guarantees?', asks Cass Sunstein in a recent article – an article that is based on his book on FDR's proposed 'Second Bill of Rights' to which we briefly referred in Chapter 2.[33] He comes up with four possible answers to this question, and we shall use a couple of these possible answers in the following as a point of departure and framework for an exploration of American antipathies toward second generation rights. Sunstein's first possible answer concerns the age of the US Constitution, the oldest still in force in the world. 'When it was drawn up, the American approach was entirely standard, and hence the absence of social and economic rights is simply a matter of timing.'[34] Another of his possible answers (and the one he himself finds the most important) concerns the effect on the Supreme Court of the election to the presidency in 1968 of Richard Nixon, as we saw in Chapter 2. For a brief period from 1970 to 1973, he argues, the Court seemed to be heading in the direction of recognizing at least some economic and social rights. But then Nixon nominated Chief Justice Warren Burger and Associate Justices Blackmun, Powell and Rehnquist, and these four effectively 'cut the ground from under an emerging movement' in favour of economic and social rights in the US.[35]

When it comes to civil and political rights, the Constitution has come, over the years, to be interpreted in ways that depart significantly from its original meaning. But this has not happened in the case of those second-generation rights. Nor have there been any major attempts to amend the Constitution to

---

32 In the American context, the Supreme Court's use of the Commerce Clause has been extended to include various *civil* rights, however.

33 Cass R. Sunstein, *The Second Bill of Rights: FDR's Unfinished Revolution and Why We Need It More Than Ever* (New York: Basic Books, 2004).

34 Cass R. Sunstein, 'Why Does the American Constitution Lack Social and Economic Guarantees?', in Michael Ignatieff (ed.), *American Exceptionalism and Human Rights* (Princeton, NJ, and Oxford: Princeton University Press, 2005), 96.

35 Ibid., 108.

include them. Between them, presidents Franklin Delano Roosevelt and Harry Truman succeeded in sharply reducing the gap between the rich and the working class as well as in reducing wage differentials among workers, for example. 'America in the 1950s was a middle-class society, to a far greater extent than it had been in the 1920s – or than it is today', argues Nobel Laureate, professor of economics and columnist in the *New York Times*, Paul Krugman. We remember the Great Depression, but we have largely forgotten 'the Great Compression', the narrowing of income gaps that took place between the 1920s and the 1950s. Krugman owes this phrase to economic historians Glaudia Goldin and Robert Margo, who use it about the policies that were very consciously used by FDR, and after him also by Truman, to create middle-class America: huge increases in taxes on the rich, support for a vast expansion of union power, a period of wage controls used to greatly narrow pay differentials, to mention three.[36]

The thing is, though, that FDR neither proposed any constitutional amendment nor encouraged the judiciary to play a role in relation to his Second Bill of Rights and the Great Compression in general. He wanted to work with and through the Congress, to use political rather than judicial processes. 'Part of the reason for this strategy', writes Sunstein, 'was the sheer difficulty of producing constitutional amendments. Part of it was great suspicion of the conservative judiciary. For those interested in creating the Second Bill of Rights, constitutional amendment did not seem an attractive option in light of the inevitable fact that any such amendment would increase the authority of judges.'[37] FDR was right, of course, to distrust the judiciary, especially the Supreme Court, which by the end of the 1936 term had declared New Deal laws unconstitutional in seven of the nine major cases which came before it. He felt that the 1936 election had given him a mandate for further reform – but that such reform was now jeopardized by the Court, which had left 'a "no-man's land" where no Government – State or Federal' could now act.[38]

But there was more to it than this. Like so many American politicians before and after him, FDR was of the opinion that economic, social and cultural rights are a political, not a judicial project. In his 1941 'four freedoms'

---

[36] Paul Krugman, *The Conscience of a Liberal* (New York and London: W.W. Norton & Co., 2007), 38–39, 53.

[37] Sunstein, supra n. 34, 101. Interestingly, Sunstein later adds, 'in my view, Roosevelt was right to say that decent opportunity and minimal security should be provided politically rather than judicially' (at 109).

[38] FDR, quoted in George Brown Tindall and David E. Shi, *America: A Narrative History* (New York and London: W.W. Norton & Co., Fourth Edition, 1996), Vol. II, 1185. – On the infamous 'court-packing' manoeuvre that followed and the way in which it made FDR lose the battle but win the war, as he was to put it, please see ibid., 1185–1186.

speech, he had suggested that economic and social security in the modern world was a 'basic thing' that people expected from their political and economic systems. But three years later, when he introduced the idea of a 'second bill of rights', he did make use of a rights discourse.[39] The social contract that he had in mind was one between the government and the people, though, his conception of constitutions being what Sunstein calls 'pragmatic', rather than 'aspirational'. Unlike some people – and Sunstein, erroneously in my opinion, points especially to Europeans here – who consider constitutions symbolic declarations of their nation's or region's hopes and aspirations, Americans like FDR tend to take a more direct, pragmatic approach. 'What will this provision do, in fact? How will the courts interpret this provision, in fact?', they will ask.[40]

This is especially the case when it comes to economic, social and cultural rights. The interdependence of the two categories or generations of rights has been part of the doctrine of the United Nations from the very start, and this was reflected, as we saw, in the Universal Declaration of Human Rights of 1948. Both in regard to first- and second-generation rights, the UDHR uses the phrase, 'everyone has the right to . . .'. This wording was followed in the Political Covenant – but not in the Economic Covenant which instead employs the formula 'States Parties recognize the right of everyone to . . .'. In terms of these obligations, moreover, Article 2(1) of the Economic Covenant states that '[e]ach State Party . . . undertakes to take steps . . . *to the maximum of its available resources*, with a view to *achieving progressively* the full realization of the rights recognized in the present Covenant by all appropriate means . . .' (emphases added). And finally, the monitoring procedures of the two categories of rights also differ; by comparison to those of the Political Covenant, the procedures called for by the Economic Covenant are somewhat weak.[41]

These differences have given rise to much criticism – especially along the lines that the wording used in the Economic Covenant is so vague and programmatic that it becomes very difficult to determine when and to what degree those obligations of progressive realization can be or have been met. Besides, the rights outlined, critics argue, are not justiciable – that is, there is no effective legal basis for legal action. In 'What Future for Economic and

---

39 Daniel J. Whelan, 'The United States and economic and social rights: past, presents . . . and future?', Human Rights & Human Welfare, Working Paper No. 26 (2005), available at http://www.du.edu/korbel/hrhw/working/2005/26-whelan-2005.pdf , 4 – (last visited on 8 January 2009). I am quoting from this paper with Daniel Whelan's permission.

40 Sunstein, supra n. 34, 101.

41 See Rob Buitenweg, *Human Rights, Human Plights in a Global Village* (Atlanta, GA: Clarity Press, Inc., 2007), 63–66.

Social Rights?', David Beetham summarizes this line of criticism in the following way:

> It is argued, typically, that the list of so-called 'rights' in the [UDHR and the Economic Covenant] can at most be a statement of aspirations or goals rather than properly of *rights*. For an entitlement to be a human right it must satisfy a number of conditions: it must be fundamental and universal; it must in principle be definable in justiciable form; it should be clear who has the duty to uphold or implement the right; and the responsible agency should possess the capacity to fulfil its obligations. The rights specified in the Covenant . . . would seem to fail on every count. They confuse the fundamental with the merely desirable, or that which is specific to the advanced economies . . . Even those that are fundamental cannot in principle be definable in justiciable form. At what level can the deprivation of nutrition, sanitation or health care be sufficient to trigger legal redress? And whose duty is it to see that these 'rights' are met – national governments, international institutions, the UN itself?[42]

The most openly hostile reaction to the second-generation rights and to the Economic Covenant has come from the US. It did not take long, in fact, before the first positive American reaction in the UN – built, at least in part, around Roosevelt's popularity and legacy on economic and social guarantees (his New Deal programmes, proposal for a Second Bill of Rights and GI Bill of Rights) – eroded. As the UN's Commission on Human Rights was discussing in 1947 how to go about writing an international bill of rights, its elected chairperson, Eleanor Roosevelt, was instructed by her government not to commit the US too heavily. When the Declaration of Human Rights was adopted, she accordingly clarified that 'the United States Government does not consider that economic, social and cultural rights imply an obligation on governments to assure the enjoyment of these rights by direct government action'.[43] And in 1953, with two more years of her term still remaining, Eleanor Roosevelt was then dismissed from her position as chairperson of the Commission on Human Rights. It was also around this time that the Eisenhower administration declared that the US would not become a party to any UN human rights treaties. Here matters lay until President Carter decided to give it another try.

There were, argues David Whelan, basically three reasons for this early American opposition: '[t]he first was that the [Economic Covenant] would violate domestic jurisdiction or sovereignty by allowing international scrutiny of human rights problems in the US. Second, by virtue of the Supremacy Clause of the Constitution, the obligations of the covenant would require the expansion of the powers of the federal government to the detriment of states'

---

42 David Beetham, 'What Future for Economic and Social Rights?', 43 *Political Studies* (1995) 41, quoted in Steiner and Alston, supra n. 5, 255.

43 Quoted in Whelan, supra n. 39, 7.

rights. Finally, the covenant would enhance communist influence in the US, and usher in socialism.'[44]

In this first phase, arguments against the second generation human rights took on a domestic angle. But after President Carter had signed the Economic Covenant in 1978 and sent it to the Senate for its advice and consent to ratification – which, of course, he never received – arguments would also focus on the implications for US foreign policy. The important thing to stress in this context is the way in which hostility to loss of sovereignty was mixed up with, first of all, a fear that US ratification of the Economic Covenant would encourage the emerging civil rights movement in the US (based largely on federal initiatives – something which was not popular among supporters of states' rights) and, second, a fear that such a ratification would lead to 'back-door communism'.[45] In relation to the former, Andrew Moravcsik and others have argued, also, that among conservatives (especially southern conservatives) support of states' rights was a sort of code for concerns about race. International human rights would tend to reinforce the pattern known from the civil rights era according to which more and more rights would be given to blacks and other minorities.[46]

Much later, to this fear was added another fear – namely that international human rights instruments would guarantee unlimited government interference in family life. Thus, the most vocal opponents of the ratification of the Convention on the Rights of the Child (CRC), in the drafting process of which the US had participated and to which it became a signatory in 1995, were conservative religious organizations. These described the CRC as 'the most dangerous attack on parents' rights in the history of the United States', 'the ultimate program to annihilate parental authority' and a 'tool for perverts',[47] and they were so efficient in their attacks on the Convention that the US never ratified it. Unlike certain other treaties, the CRC is characterized by containing both first- and second-generation rights. The only other country in the world besides the US never to have ratified the CRC is Somalia.

This is a good example of the power that conservative groups, especially religious groups, have been able to wield since the 1960s and 1970s – a power that is out of proportion to the actual size of such groups, but that is furthered, among other things, by the fragmented nature of American political institutions which allow 'veto players' to block particular government actions. It is a cliché of comparative politics, explains Moravcsik,

---

44 Ibid., 8.

45 Ibid.

46 Andrew Moravcsik, 'The Paradox of US Human Rights Policy', in Ignatieff, supra n. 34, 178.

47 Quoted in Susan Kilbourne, 'Placing the Convention on the Rights of the Child in an American Context', in Steiner and Alston, supra n. 5, 519.

> that the American system of government stands out in comparative perspective for its extreme commitment to the Madisonian schema of 'separation of powers' and 'checks and balances.' All other things equal, the greater the number of 'veto players', as political scientists refer to those who can impede or block a particular government action, the more difficult it is for a national government to accept international obligations. The US political system is in most respects exceptionally decentralized, with the consequence that a large number of domestic political actors must approve major decisions. Three such characteristics of the US political system are of particular importance to an understanding of US human rights policy: supermajoritarian voting rules and the committee structure of the Senate, federalism, and the salient role of the judiciary in adjudicating questions of human rights.[48]

We shall come back to these characteristics of the US political system in the following chapter. Mixed with these concerns, moreover, were fears that economic, social and cultural rights would give rise to a more collectivist way of thinking which might in the end undermine the enjoyment of individual freedom and downplay the importance of civil and political rights. Most importantly, such a collectivist way of thinking might call for large-scale state intervention in the economy which might seriously impair the functioning of free markets, as mentioned above. On the issue of 'back-door communism', the American Bar Association (ABA) played quite a significant role, as we shall see. In general, the ABA was opposed to promoting human rights through treaty law – an opposition that would later help create among senators support for the Bricker Amendment – but its members were especially critical of the idea of economic and social rights. In 1948, the new ABA president, Frank Holman, began writing a series of articles which focused on the draft Economic Covenant and basically argued that 'this program, if adopted, will promote state socialism, if not communism, throughout the world'.[49] What was at stake was nothing less than the idea of America and especially that sacred document which more than any other document down through American history has been responsible for creating this idea, the Constitution.

The Cultural or American Exceptionalism Explanation

This takes us to what Sunstein calls the cultural or American exceptionalism explanation. He is referring here not so much to the sense of America being different from and implicitly better than other countries, and therefore entitled to special treatment on the world scene, to which we referred in Chapter 3, but rather to the more specific fact that socialism has never been very powerful in the US. Since Werner Sombart asked in his 1906 book, *Why No Socialism in*

---

48 See Moravcsik, in Ignatieff, supra n. 34, 186–187.
49 Frank Holman, quoted in Whelan, supra n. 39, 7.

America?, many scholars have commented on the fact that the US is the only advanced industrial country that has had neither a strong socialist movement nor a proper labour party. This has indeed made the US exceptional, and many have advanced explanations of the underlying causes for this: a high degree of upward mobility, the lack of a feudal past, and the electoral system with its two major parties and its checks and balances which has made it difficult for a third, socialist party to become successful, for example. To these we may add what Michael Ignatieff has called the 'legal isolationism' of the US: 'American mainstream values . . . are structured legally by a rights tradition that has always been different from those of other democratic states and increasingly diverges from international human rights norms'.[50]

We have referred to this American rights tradition and rights talk in previous chapters and to what American legal scholar Kenneth Karst once called 'law's promise': the potential of law and the courts to reshape the social meanings of race, gender and religion and 'to promote the enactment of millions of individual narratives of inclusion'.[51] While law's language is that of power, it can at times also be *empowering*, as several individual Americans but also minority groups discovered after having successfully taken their fight to be taken seriously to the country's courts.[52] Historically, American judges have not allowed themselves to be inspired by foreign human rights law. The attitude has been that, precisely because of its strong rights tradition, the US has nothing to learn from others about rights. If international law conflicts with the Constitution – then something is wrong, not with the Constitution, but with international law.

The so-called Feeney/Goodlatte Resolution is an interesting case in point. On 17 March 2004 Congressman Tom Feeney, a Republican representing Florida's 24th Congressional District, submitted House Resolution 568 (now 372) to his colleagues in the US Congress. Co-sponsored by US Representative Bob Goodlatte, a fellow Republican from Virginia, the Feeney/Goodlatte resolution or the 'Reaffirmation of American Independence Resolution' was a response to the tendency by certain Supreme Court justices to rely upon the decisions of foreign judicial tribunals when deciding American constitutional and statutory cases. 'Increasingly, Supreme Court

---

[50] Michael Ignatieff, 'Introduction: American Exceptionalism and Human Rights', in Ignatieff, supra n. 34, 10.

[51] Kenneth L. Karst, *Law's Promise, Law's Expression: Visions of Power in the Politics of Race, Gender, and Religion* (New Haven, CT: Yale University Press, 1993), 107.

[52] This is mostly true of the period after World War Two. Before the Warren Court (1953–1969), the Supreme Court did not work toward bettering the conditions of minority groups – unless we consider the wealthier tiers of American society a minority group.

justices have relied upon numerous foreign sources to overturn anti-sodomy laws, uphold affirmative action admissions processes, and prohibit the death penalty', Feeney and Goodlatte commented when they reintroduced the resolution on 3 May 2007. And they continued:

> These justices have written or joined opinions that cited foreign authorities such as the European Court of Human Rights, the European Union, including foreign courts in Jamaica, India, and Zimbabwe, to justify its decisions. In one case, Justice Breyer even cited to Zimbabwe, that bastion of human rights…
>
> Congressman Goodlatte and I have authored the "*Reaffirmation of American Independence Resolution*" advising the federal courts that their role is interpreting U.S. law, not import foreign laws – a clear violation of the separation of powers. This resolution affirms the sense of Congress that judicial decisions interpreting the U.S. Constitution should not be based on any foreign laws, court decisions, or pronouncements of foreign governments unless they are expressly approved by Congress. We encourage you to become co-sponsors to this important resolution.[53]

The Feeney/Goodlatte resolution is a good illustration of a festering dispute which has to do with when (if at all) it is appropriate for the Supreme Court to discuss foreign legal materials.[54] And while some judges – chiefly Justice

---

53 Support the Feeney/Goodlatte 'Reaffirmation of American Independence Resolution', May 3, 2007 – available at http://www.house.gov/hensarling/rsc/doc/CA_012907_feeneygoodlatteforeignlaw.doc (last visited on 29 March 2009). – Cameron Smith in Congressman Feeney's office informs me that as of 23 May 2008 H.Res. 372 has 49 cosponsors and has been referred to the House Judiciary Committee, and that no further action has been taken.

54 The response by E.E. Edwards and Prof. Speedy Rice to the proposed legislation in 2004 on behalf of the National Association of Criminal Defense Lawyers in the following joint statement is interesting:

> Since the founding of the United States, our government, in all three branches, has maintained American independence while at the same time properly reflecting on world views and opinions. Our founding fathers, while rejecting the tyranny of King George, incorporated the vision and philosophy of many foreign intellectuals, scholars and governments to create the most unique and free people in the world. That we still today examine and consider myriad worldviews is not only correct, but necessary to continue our fine internationalist tradition. In areas such as maritime law, foreign trade, telecommunication, transportation, contracts, tort law and social justice, the consideration of enlightened views is not only the American way, but fundamental to the survival of our country and our own way of life. Our Constitution protects us from being bound by foreign laws but its original intent was never to blind us to foreign law.
>
> Any attempt to close the courts to comity and full and transparent implementation of the rule of law, whatever the source, resembles obstinate isolationism in a globally-networked world. NACDL doubts that is what Congress intends, but we are sure it is what Congress will get if it passes H.RES.568 – available at

Scalia – are of the opinion that it is hardly ever appropriate, other members of the Court see comparative constitutionalism in a much more positive light. 'To a court already divided along every ideological position imaginable, add judicial foreign policy as the latest fault line!', one commentator noted with reference to the Feeney/Goodlatte resolution.[55]

US rights guarantees have, Ignatieff writes, 'been employed in the service of a political tradition that has been consistently more critical of government, more insistent on individual responsibility, and more concerned to defend individual freedom than the European socialist, social democratic, or Christian democratic traditions.'[56] Changes may slowly be happening, though. Noting how some American lawyers and judges seem increasingly willing to 'travel abroad to help train their counterparts in fledgling or transitory democracies' and to 'travel to participate in colloquies with their peers', Anne-Marie Slaughter has predicted that 'American judicial narcissism, understood as a desire to be the best on any playing field, is likely to lead American judges toward participation in global judicial dialogues'.[57]

CONCLUDING REMARKS

We may attribute a good part of US reluctance to commit itself to international human rights, especially the economic, social and cultural rights, to the success of a conservative minority in imposing its own conservative viewpoints on its fellow Americans – a success that has, in turn, a lot to do with the institutional decentralization of the American political system. Or so argues Andrew Moravcsik:

> From 1945 to 1970, the dominant substantive concern motivating such conservative opposition was undoubtedly race, and, like conservative opposition to expansion in the jurisdiction of the federal government, it aimed primarily to defend segregation and racial discrimination. Since then the relevant conservative agenda has broadened to include issues often connected with race, but also lifestyle issues of greatest importance to a religious minority: abortion, the traditional family, religion, capital punishment, and criminal procedure.[58]

---

http://www.nacdl.org/public.nsf/newsreleases/2004mn009?opendocument (last visited on 9 January 2009).

55 T. Wu, 'Foreign Exchange: Should the Supreme Court care what other countries think?', *Slate*, posted Friday, 9 April 2004 – available at http://www.slate.com/id/2098559/ (last visited on 9 January 2009).

56 Ignatieff, supra n. 34, 11.

57 Anne-Marie Slaughter, 'A Brave New Judicial World', in ibid., *supra* n. 34, 302–303.

58 Moravcsik, in ibid., supra n. 34, 196.

Affecting change thus will not be easy. In fact, continues Moravcsik,

> to reverse current trends would require an epochal constitutional rupture… such as those wrought in the United States by the Great Depression and the resulting Democratic 'New Deal' majority; in Germany, France, and Italy by the end of World War II; and in all European countries through a half century of European human rights jurisprudence.[59]

Moravcsik is not the only American scholar to point to the legacy of Franklin Delano Roosevelt and to link this legacy to what has happened in the European context since 1945. This is an obvious link to make, in the sense that FDR's 'four freedoms' and thoughts on a Second Bill of Rights had a major impact on, first, the Atlantic Charter and then, through the International Bill of Rights, on the European Declaration on Human Rights. It is interesting to see, for example, how in her Foreword to the EU publication, *Furthering Human Rights and Democracy across the Globe* of 2007, Commissioner Benita Ferrero-Waldner uses a decidedly Rooseveltian choice of words: '[c]entral to the EU's approach is the concept of human security – an idea of security which places people at the heart of our policies. It means looking at the comprehensive security of people, not the security of states, encompassing both freedom from fear and freedom from want.'[60]

'Could we go back to an understanding of economic and social "rights" that Franklin Delano Roosevelt had?', asks Daniel Whelan. Roosevelt, being most definitely not a socialist, believed in some kind of interaction between the state and the market in the realization of economic and social rights. The role of the state was to make sure that opportunities existed for the able-bodied to take good care of themselves, but also to care for those who had neither the talent nor the physical ability to do so on their own. Today, according to Whelan, if we wish to communicate with the most ardent critics of second generation rights, we need to use a discourse that they understand and of which they approve – a market language or property discourse:

> In order to more effectively counter the critics of economic and social rights, proponents of those rights will need to reconsider the language of rights, and speak to their opponents in their own language – the language of the market. They need to demonstrate – as Sunstein has – that the state is vital to the survival of the market, and the state has obligations to live up to so the market can survive, and protect our ability to meet our economic and social needs. The idea of a 'free market' is a myth;

---

59 Ibid., 197.

60 European Commission, External Relations, *The European Union: Furthering Human Rights and Democracy across the Globe* (Luxembourg: Office for Official Publications of the European Communities, 2007), 3.

> the market only exists because the state regulates it. Unregulated capitalism would eat itself alive – as recent 'corporate scandals' amply demonstrate.[61]

In this endeavour, the story of how a Social Europe of sorts is currently being created may be an inspiration. As we have seen in this chapter, the expansion of social rights for workers and their families has happened against the background of a drive toward market integration. There is even a parallel of sorts in American history – in the way in which important civil rights have been argued for on the basis of the Commerce Clause (Art. 1, Section 8 of the Constitution) which gives to Congress the exclusive authority to manage commerce between the states, with foreign nations, and Indian tribes. During the New Deal era – after Roosevelt had successfully 'persuaded' members of the Supreme Court no longer systematically to block vital New Deal legislation – the scope of the Commerce Clause was expanded. This happened again after the passing of the Civil Rights Act of 1964, which had as one of its aims the prevention of discriminating against black customers.

When it comes to civil rights, that is, the precedence seems to be there.

---

61 Whelan, supra n. 39, 13.

6. Divergent transatlantic views on human rights: the role of international law

When it comes to the international situation, Europeans are, again generally speaking, more willing to promote international law and human rights institutions than are Americans – even at the 'cost' of subsuming national law and national concerns under those of supranational law.

It was Winston Churchill who famously said in a speech in Zürich in 1946:

> We must re-create the European Family in a regional structure called, it may be, the United States of Europe. If at first all the States of Europe are not willing or able to join the Union, we must nevertheless proceed to assemble and combine those who will and those who can. The salvation of the common people of every race and of every land from war or servitude must be established on solid foundations and must be guarded by the readiness of all men and women to die rather than submit to tyranny. Therefore I say to you: let Europe arise![1]

The idea of the United States of Europe has a long history, as Stefan Collignon points out in his introduction to Guy Verhofstadt's *The United States of Europe: Manifesto for a New Europe* (2006). Jean-Jacques Rousseau envisaged a Europe, where 'there are no more French, German, Spanish, even Englishmen whatever one says, there are only Europeans. They all have the same tastes, the same passions the same habits.' To Montesquieu, 'matters are such in Europe that all states need each other. Europe's a state made up of several provinces', just as Kant thought the creation of a confederation of European states might be a step toward a 'world republic'. Then there was Victor Hugo, who dreamed about the day 'when you France, you Russia, you England, you Germany, when all you Nations of the continent, without losing distinctive qualities or your individual glories, will bind yourself tightly together into a single entity and you will come to constitute a European fraternity, as absolutely as Brittany, Burgundy and Alsace are now bound together

---

1 Winston Churchill, quoted in Guy Verhofstadt, *The United States of Europe: Manifesto for a New Europe* (London: Federal Trust for Education and Research, 2006), 3.

with France'. A 'European Federal Republic is established', Hugo furthermore thought, 'in right and is waiting to be established in fact'.[2]

After the disaster of World War One, moreover,

> the German Social Democratic Party put the creation of the United States of Europe into its 1926 party programme in Heidelberg and it reiterated this commitment again after 1945. In 1930, the United States of Europe became the title of a book by Edouard Herriot – Prime Minister in France's Third Republic – and constituted a serious attempt at practically envisioning a unified Europe. Within the framework of the erstwhile League of Nations, it promoted the idea of a coalition of all willing European states to foster the organisation of economic and security policies in Europe . . . Jean Monnet founded the Action Committee for the United States of Europe in 1955 after the French Assemblée Nationale had rejected the Treaty on the European Defence Community.[3]

As for a Council of Europe, it was also Churchill who presented a vision for such a forum in some of his wartime speeches. If a Council could be established and 'eventually embrace the whole of Europe, and all the main branches of the European family', this would create hope for 'the enthronement of human rights'. Later still, Churchill proposed the creation of a court which might bring abuses of human rights 'to the judgment of the civilised world'.[4] When another influential figure at the time, the previously mentioned French lawyer and politician Pierre-Henri Teitgen, opened the convention that created the Council of Europe, he argued that 'the sovereignty of justice' is the only sovereignty worth dying for. And during a debate the following month, writes Michael D. Goldhaber, 'Teitgen proclaimed it the role of the court to be the conscience of Europe'.[5]

THE ROLE OF INTERNATIONAL LAW IN THE EUROPEAN CONTEXT

Sovereignty and European Values

When it came to the adoption of a European Convention, there were at least three different factors at work:

---

2 Quoted in Stefan Collignon, 'Introduction' to ibid., 9.

3 Ibid.

4 Winston Churchill, quoted in Michael D. Goldhaber, *A People's History of the European Court of Human Rights* (New Brunswick, NJ, and London: Rutgers University Press, 2007), 3.

5 Ibid., 4.

> It was first a regional response to the atrocities committed in Europe during the Second World War and an affirmation of the belief that governments respecting human rights are less likely to wage war on their neighbours. Secondly, both the Council of Europe, which was set up in 1949 (and under whose auspices the Convention was adopted), and the European Union (previously the European Community or Communities, the first of which was established in 1952) were partly based on the assumption that the best way to ensure that Germany would be a force for peace, in partnership with France, the United Kingdom and other Western European states, was through regional integration and the institutionalization of common values . . . [T]he third major impetus towards a Convention [was] the desire to bring the non-Communist countries of Europe together within a common ideological framework and to consolidate their unity in the face of the Communist threat.[6]

The whole idea, in other words, was to avoid the sort of problems recent European history had been so full of by means of creating a supranational framework. Whereas the American Dream, as we saw Jeremy Rifkin argue in Chapter 2, was based on property rights, markets, and nation-state governance, the new European Dream was and is centred around human rights, networks, and multilevel governance.

The drafters were not blind to the fact that those visions for a supranational Europe would alienate some – that there would be concerns over sovereignty as well as over the (perceived) distance, geographical and also psychological, between the individual citizen and European politicians and bureaucrats. Those concerns have lasted to this day – two obvious examples being the French and Dutch voters turning down the first attempt at a European constitution in 2005 and the Irish 'no' to the Lisbon Treaty in 2008. Europe has had its own version of a federalism debate, that is. How do matters currently stand? In terms of the perceived distance to European centralized politics, according to a recent Standard Eurobarometer (Eurobarometer 69, Spring 2008), a majority of 52 per cent of all European citizens support their country's membership of the EU and 54 per cent think that, on balance, their country benefits from membership. Needless to say, such support is higher in some countries than in others, but the interesting thing is that in virtually all countries support outstrips opposition. The overall trust in the EU stands at 50 per cent – not exactly great. However, it is higher than that placed in national institutions.[7]

---

6 Henry J. Steiner and Philip Alston (eds.), *International Human Rights in Context: Law, Politics, Morals* (Oxford: Oxford University Press, 2000, 2nd edition), 786–787.

7 Eurobarometer is a series of surveys regularly performed on behalf of the European Commission since 1973. *Eurobarometer 69: The European Union and its Citizens, Fieldwork: March–May 2008* (published in November 2008) – available at http://ec.europa.eu/public_opinion/archives/eb/eb69/eb69_part3_en.pdf (last visited on 11 January 2009).

According to Eurobarometer 69, moreover, the majority of Europeans believe that it makes sense to talk about a set of common European values, but they also think that such values should be seen in the wider context of Western values. When asked about the most important values for them personally, Europeans mentioned peace (45 per cent) followed by human rights (42 per cent) and respect for human life (41 per cent). When it comes to the values most representative for these Europeans of the European Union, the three values heading the list are human rights (37 per cent), peace (35 per cent) and democracy (34 per cent). Overall, the belief that certain issues are better dealt with jointly at the EU level than by national governments alone seems to be on the rise. Asked to decide in relation to twenty different issues whether these ought to be decided at the national or the EU level, an absolute majority answered for eleven of these issues that they should be decided jointly at the EU level. As many as 79 per cent thought that this was the case for fighting terrorism, 71 per cent for protecting the environment and 70 per cent for scientific and technological research. By contrast, in policy areas such as pensions, health and social welfare – the areas that have concerned us in Chapter 5 – 73 per cent, 64 per cent and 67 per cent, respectively, believed that these are better managed at the national level.[8]

However, in a special Eurobarometer report on European cultural values, published only a year earlier (in September 2007), when presented with a list of nine values and asked to choose up to three which they would like to see furthered in society, respondents selected peace (61 per cent), respect for nature and the environment (50 per cent) and social equality and solidarity (37 per cent). And later, when they were asked to assess which of those same values could best be considered European (as opposed to being represented by other countries in the world), these respondents chose peace (57 per cent), freedom of opinion (54 per cent) and social equality and solidarity (53 per cent).[9] To a majority of Europeans, it would thus seem, social equality and solidarity are distinctly European values in the sense that Europeans care about them – even though they are not necessarily interested in decisions concerning these values being taken at the EU level by European politicians whom they otherwise trust more than their own national politicians.

[8] *Standard Eurobarometer/ Eurobarometer 69: The European Union Today and Tomorrow, Fieldwork: March–May 2008* (published in November 2008) – available at http://ec.europa.eu/public_opinion/archives/eb/eb69/eb69_part3_en.pdf (last visited on 11 January 2009).

[9] *Special Eurobarometer: European Cultural Values, Summary Report, Fieldwork: 14/02–18/03 2007* (published in September 2007) – available at http://ec.europa.eu/public_opinion/archives/ebs/ebs_278_sum_en.pdf (last visited on 11 January 2009).

For the average European, the problem thus does not so much seem to be connected to sovereignty as such. Certain issues are better taken care of at the European level while others belong at the more local level. It is precisely such a balancing act that the two European courts have been engaged in for many years: figuring out which areas of societal concern belong where, when it comes to the protection of human rights. The ECJ, as we saw in Chapter 5, has been able over the years to negotiate a space for Social Europe in between the Member States and the supranational EU system. And when it comes to the ECtHR, this has happened under the legal category of 'the margin of appreciation'.

The term 'margin of appreciation' has been used in a number of decisions by the Strasbourg court to refer to the 'room for manoeuvre' which national authorities may be allowed when fulfilling their obligations under the European Convention on Human Rights. It is not listed anywhere in the European Convention, but has been simply asserted or read 'between the lines' of the Convention by the ECtHR. Having originally been used 'to address provisional State derogations of rights outlined in the [European Convention, ECHR], which were justified by exigent circumstances within the offending States' – circumstances usually involving risks to state security – the doctrine has since evolved 'into one of the ECtHR's primary tools for accommodating diversity within Europe, national sovereignty, and the will of domestic majorities, while still effectively enforcing the rights elucidated within the ECHR . . . striking a long term balance among conflicting domestic social interests'.[10]

It is interesting, moreover, that the Court's use of the margin of appreciation depends on the extent to which there is consensus on whether the right(s) in question are covered by the Convention. The more consensus there seems to be, the less latitude the ECtHR is willing to grant the national authorities involved. 'This is in keeping with the notion that the court is trying to preserve core European values', argues Aaron A. Ostrovsky. 'As more and more States agree on what is included within those values, the court is less and less likely to allow derogation. Consensus then becomes a gauge by which the court may read whether a certain activity has become part of Europe's core rights.'[11]

To those less enamoured with the notion of 'the margin of appreciation', there is an element of feigned modesty involved on the part of the ECtHR – an attempt to make it look as if the individual European state has more power and influence than it actually has.

---

[10] Aaron A. Ostrovsky, 'What's So Funny About Peace, Love, and Understanding? How the Margin of Appreciation Doctrine Preserves Core Human Rights within Cultural Diversity and Legitimises International Human Rights Tribunals', *Hanse Law Review* (2005), 50–51. – (available at SSRN: http://ssrn.com/abstract=716242 – last visited on 12 January 2009).

[11] Ibid., 50–51.

Also, the way in which the Court has interpreted the Convention as a living document and has relied less on the original intent of the drafters than on an assessment of developing consensus is deeply problematic. It seems less than clear, such critics maintain, how the Court arrives at its definition of such consensus among European states. It is important, Laurence Helfer has argued, for example, that the ECtHR develop 'a more comprehensive and rigorous methodology for applying the European consensus inquiry'. The factors that seem to have counted as 'evidence of consensus' are legal consensus expressed through statutes and regional agreements, expert consensus and European public consensus. But such 'evidence of consensus' is not very solid – how many member states will have to change their laws 'before a right-enhancing norm will achieve consensus status?', Helfer asks, for example.[12] Experts notoriously disagree about almost anything, and as for that European public consensus, how do we go about measuring it – will the twice-yearly Eurobarometer reports, first published by the European Commission in 1973, do as evidence for the Court, one wonders.

Furthermore, the application of such perceived consensus would, if used in its extreme, 'exclude the possibility of finding any national legislation in violation of the [European Convention]'. Adapting its interpretation of the Convention to societal changes only if enough member states (whatever that means) have adopted the new ideas under review – views on the rights of homosexuals, say – is 'in principle not consistent with the Court's mission to protect the individual against the collectivity and to do so by elaborating common standards . . . [I]f a collectivity oppresses an individual because it does not want to recognize societal changes, the Court should take care not to yield too readily to arguments based on a country's cultural and historical particularities.'[13] As a result, the margin of appreciation jeopardizes the idea of universality. The typical situation in which the ECtHR will apply the doctrine involves a minority confronting a majority – 'the exact situation where an international tribunal should be responsible for protecting deeper universal rights and not deferring to state (majority) preferences'.[14]

Finally, the issue of consensus ties in with the principle of subsidiarity which 'requires that decisions should always be taken at the level closest to the citizen at which they can be taken effectively, thus creating a presumption in favour of action at the level of the Member States except where exclusive Community competence has already been granted'.[15] As some see it, this

12 Laurence Helfer, quoted in Steiner and Alston, supra n. 6, 857.

13 P. Van Dijk, quoted in ibid., 858.

14 Ibid., 57.

15 Philip Alston (ed.), *The EU and Human Rights* (Oxford: Oxford University Press, 1999), 27.

ensures that democratically elected, representative political bodies have the main responsibility. According to Paul Mahoney, for example, government by judges is 'quite alien to our conception of "law" in democracy'. International authorities such as the ECtHR are 'subsidiary' to human rights protection at the local level, and the doctrine of margin of appreciation addresses the question of 'what in the instant context is the area of retained democratic discretion' – 'where societal values are still the subject of debate and controversy at national level, they should not easily be converted by the Court into protected Convention values allowing of only one approach'.[16] We should not get to the point where the political bodies in Europe come to rely on the ECtHR to do everything – eventually to settle every political and/or legal question. This is not how democracies are supposed to work.

To this, others would counter that the judicial restraint called for by the principle of subsidiarity is not 'a one-way street'. The guidelines attached to the Protocol on the application of the principle of subsidiarity and proportionality, annexed to the Amsterdam Treaty, indicates that Community action is justified when the objectives in question cannot adequately be achieved by member states' action or when those objectives includes a transnational dimension. Besides, argue Philip Alston and Joseph Weiler:

> where the measures in question are taken by the Community within the field of Community law it makes no sense to argue that individual Member States are best placed to ensure not only that those measures do not violate human rights but that they do whatever they can to promote respect for them.[17]

As with so many other issues connected with (human) rights, in both the American and the European context, the discussion concerning the doctrine of the margin of appreciation also touches on law versus politics – judicial activism versus judicial restraint, constitutional democracy versus parliamentary democracy. Toward the end of this chapter, we shall return to this discussion.

Such criticism notwithstanding, the margin of appreciation doctrine has been applied over the past few years also by tribunals outside Europe, both international and domestic. The same is true for other features of ECtHR jurisprudence, and today among the world's systems of human rights the European system is viewed as one of the most fully developed and successful.

---

16 Paul Mahoney, quoted in Steiner and Alston, supra n. 6, 854.

17 Philip Alston and J.H.H. Weiler, 'An "Ever Closer Union" in Need of a Human Rights Policy: The European Union and Human Rights', in Alston, supra n. 15, 27.

Law: Europe's best Foreign Policy Tool?

To some, law has become Europe's best foreign policy tool. Picking up the gauntlet thrown to Europe by Robert Kagan in *Of Paradise and Power: America and Europe in the New World Order* (2003), Mark Leonhard has argued, for example, that 'the European project is based on a desire to move beyond a world of power politics, where "might makes right", to a community based on the rules of law. Europeans have used this desire to turn a lot of the basic rules of sovereignty on their head.' Rather than staying within an old-fashioned nation-state paradigm, Europeans have turned the relationship between the different European nation-states into domestic policy – a policy which is based on thousands of common standards and laws, together known as the *acquis communautaire*. And 'because each member state wants its fellow members to obey the law, they are forced to obey it themselves'.[18]

Europeans have a strong interest in defending international law and legal institutions, in part because the EU was itself founded on the basis of an international treaty. They have seen this system work at home, so to speak, and now also believe in using law on the international scene as a means toward creating a peaceful and democratic order:

> At the same time, the EU builds provisions about human rights, the sanctity of contracts, and European competition policy into all of its dealings with other countries. In order to comprehensively change the countries it comes into contact with, European diplomacy starts not with military strategy, but domestic politics. Europeans believe that the best way to win the war on terror, control the proliferation of weapons of mass destruction, or wipe out organized crime and drugs is to spread the international rule of law. By helping to transform weak or autocratic states into well-governed allies, Europeans hope to be able to defend themselves from the greatest threats to their security.[19]

This European preference for long-term involvement with the aim of providing political, economic and legal bases of stability as opposed to removing what are perceived to be imminent security threats by military means only is one we have seen other European intellectuals express as well in earlier chapters. As a strategy, the European talk of 'conflict and threat prevention' can also be seen as an answer to President George W. Bush's doctrine of 'preventive war'.[20] In 'The European Security Strategy: A Secure Europe in a Better World' of December 2003, we are told how

---

[18] Mark Leonhard, *Why Europe will Run the 21st Century* (London and New York: Fourth Estate, 2005), 41, 42.

[19] Ibid., 47.

[20] Ibid., 63. Leonard is referring, here, to the wording used in the European

> We are committed to upholding and developing International Law . . . It is a condition of a rule-based international order that law evolves in response to developments such as proliferation, terrorism and global warming. We have an interest in further developing existing institutions such as the World Trade Organisation and in supporting new ones such as the International Criminal Court . . . The quality of international society depends on the quality of the governments that are its foundation. The best promotion of our security is a world of well-governed democratic states. Spreading good governance, supporting social and political reform, dealing with corruption and abuse of power, establishing the rule of law and protecting human rights are the best means of strengthening the international order.[21]

Another, more recent example is a resolution on the fight against terrorism adopted by the European Parliament in December 2007. Having outlined the firm commitment of the EU to the 'fight against terrorism in all its dimensions', the report goes on to stress that there must be no areas in this fight against terrorism 'in which fundamental rights are not respected'. Dismay is shown that abuse of powers seems to have occurred under the pretext of counter-terrorism – extreme interrogation techniques have been applied on terror suspects, for example – and a need is expressed to pay 'considerably more attention in the EU counter-terrorism strategy to the causes of terrorism and the EU's role therein'. As far as 'prevention' is concerned, the report states that the European Parliament

> Believes, further, that an important element in preventing terrorism is an EU and Member State development aid policy that also functions as a security policy; considers that promoting civil society and helping to achieve social peace and prosperity are a suitable means of showing people their opportunities and restricting the spread of fundamentalist ideologies; believes, therefore, that the development of education, health and social security systems in countries often identified as the origin of terrorist activities should be made a much greater priority than before in development aid policy . . .[22]

In the European no less than the American context, it would thus seem, views on the role of international law have quite an impact on views concerning the importance of second generation human rights – and vice versa. René Cassin's wish to 'desacralize' claims of state sovereignty has borne fruit in

---

Security Strategy which was signed in December 2003 (The European Security Strategy: A Secure Europe in a Better World), Brussels, 12 December 2003, 8 – available at http://consilium.europa.eu/uedocs/cmsUpload/78367.pdf (last visited on 11 January 2009).

21 The European Security Strategy, ibid., 9–10.

22 European Parliament resolution of 12 December 2007 on the fight against terrorism – available at http://www.europarl.europa.eu/sides/getDoc.do?pubRef=-//EP//TEXT+TA+P6-TA-2007-0612+0+DOC+XML+V0//EN&language=EN – last visited on 12 January 2009.

Europe, in no small part due to the promotion of Social Europe. Such limitations on sovereignty are an inconceivable prospect to most Americans, especially when they are brought about by the pursuit of second-generation rights.

THE ROLE OF INTERNATIONAL LAW IN THE AMERICAN CONTEXT

The Problem of Treaty Ratification

'No court can have jurisdiction over a sovereign nation', Thomas Jefferson wrote in 1791, and this still pretty much sums up the attitude of many of his countrymen. The United States is now, in effect, as Timothy Garton Ash puts it,

> the last truly sovereign European nation-state. This respect for sovereignty does not, however, apply equally to foreign states, especially those from which the United Sates sees threats to its own security . . . Uniquely, America will continue to define its national purpose in idealistic terms originally drafted by a group of often Francophile Englishmen more than two centuries ago. Of course the content of this American creed has developed with time, but its central commandments remain remarkably constant.[23]

The reasons for the American distrust of international law are many and varied. In the following, we shall look first at certain structural obstacles to US adherence to international law that are independent of the transitory opinion of members of the US government, the courts as well as of the American public, and then we shall turn to some of those definitions of national purpose in idealistic terms which Ash points to.

With the exception of Article VI, which declares treaties of the United States (in addition to the Constitution itself and the laws of the US) to be 'the supreme law of the land' and Article III, Section 2, which proclaims cases arising under treaties to be within the judicial power of the US, the Constitution is fairly vague in its references to international law and to the status of such law under US law. In its use under the Constitution, moreover, the word 'treaty' has a more restricted meaning than it does in international law. 'That is', explains international lawyer John F. Murphy, 'under Article II (2) (1), the term "treaty" is applied only to international agreements, however denominated, that become binding on the United States through ratification by the

---

[23] Timothy Garton Ash, *Free World: America, Europe, and the Surprising Future of the West* (New York: Vintage Books, 2005), 119.

president with the advice and consent of the Senate through a two-thirds vote of that body'.[24]

The constitutional requirement of a two-thirds majority vote in the Senate is unique and makes of the Senate one of those potential 'veto groups', mentioned by Andrew Moravcsik, that are able to block particular government actions due to the fragmented nature of American political institutions (see Chapter 5). Here, the support of the chairman of the Foreign Relations Committee is crucial, and if he or she happens to hold conservative views (which has been the case for most chairmen since 1945), then it is virtually impossible to override his/her decision to block consideration of a treaty on the floor. From Woodrow Wilson's proposal for a League of Nations in 1919 to the present, 20th century American history has seen numerous examples of Senate minorities, disproportionately representative of conservative southern and rural mid-western or western states and suspicious of liberal multilateralism, blocking attempts to ratify international agreements – even in cases where a simple majority support in the Senate was in fact in place. The role assigned to the Senate by the Constitution, writes Moravcsik,

> helps explain why robust US action to support international human rights norms – whether unilateral or multilateral – tends typically to originate in either the executive branch or the House of Representatives, and often uses budgetary, regulatory, or diplomatic instruments, rather than the process of ratification and domestic legal change.[25]

One example of such conservative Senate action is the – nearly successful (one of the proposed amendments fell just one vote short of actually obtaining the required two-thirds vote) – attempt made by members of the American Bar Association (ABA), mentioned in Chapter 5, to pressure key senators into taking action so as to prevent the US from becoming a party to the two UN Covenants in the early 1950s. These members found an ally in Senator John Bricker, a Republican from Ohio, whom they helped draft various amendments commonly referred to collectively as the Bricker Amendment in 1953. At this period, 61 per cent of the Senators were lawyers and presumably members of the ABA – a fact which must have been helpful to the organization.[26] This was the height of the McCarthy period – a period during which

---

[24] John F. Murphy, *The United States and the Rule of Law in International Affairs* (Cambridge: Cambridge University Press, 2004/2005), 76–77.

[25] Andrew Moravcsik, 'The paradox of U.S. human rights policy', in Michael Ignatieff (ed.), *American Exceptionalism and Human Rights* (Princeton and Oxford: Princeton University Press, 2005), 187–188.

[26] Daniel J. Whelan, 'The United States and Economic and Social Rights: Past, Present . . . and Future?', Human Rights & Human Welfare, Working Paper No. 26 –

'the historic fear of foreign entanglements with respect to self-determination erupted again' – and what Bricker (and the ABA) did not like was the wording of Article VI of the Constitution, according to which treaty law is placed at the same level as constitutional law and statute law. Their aim was to see to it that treaties would no longer be self-executing and would no longer override the reserved powers of the states.

The proposed amendment had three sections:

> Sec. 1. A provision of a treaty which conflicts with this Constitution shall not be of any force or effect.
> Sec. 2. A treaty shall become effective as internal law in the United States only through legislation which would be valid in the absence of treaty.
> Sec. 3. Congress shall have power to regulate all executive and other agreements with any foreign power or international organization. All such agreements shall be subject to the limitations imposed on treaties by this article.[27]

During the debate in the Senate, Bricker told his colleagues: 'I do not want any of the international groups, and especially the group headed by Mrs. Eleanor Roosevelt, which has drafted the covenant of Human Rights, to betray the fundamental, inalienable, and God-given rights of American citizens enjoyed under the Constitution. That is really what I am driving at.'[28] The incoming Eisenhower administration saw the proposed amendment as an attempt to curb the president's power to conduct foreign policy and vigorously opposed its adoption. The result was that support withered away – the proposed amendment never made it out of the Senate. However, as Murphy writes, 'Senator Bricker lost the battle but won the war.'[29] A lasting legacy of the Bricker Amendment has been the package of reservations, understandings and declarations (RUDs) which invariably accompanies any US ratification of international agreements.

In 1977, President Carter signed four human rights treaties – two of them being the two UN Covenants, for example. He sent them on to the Senate for its consent, proposing that members of the Senate adopt a number of RUDs in the process. A legal adviser in the State Department at the time, Robert Owen, summarized the objections raised during the Senate hearings in this way:

---

available at http://www.du.edu/korbel/hrhw/working/2005/26-whelan-2005.pdf, 8 (last visited on 8 January 2009). I am quoting from and referring to this paper with Daniel Whelan's permission.

27 Bricker Amendment, 1953, quoted in Stanley N. Katz, 'US Constitutionalism and International Human Rights: Incompatible?' – used to be available at http://web.ceu.hu/legal/universalism%20and%20local%20knowledge%20in%20HR%202003/Katz_paper. htm, 3–4 (last visited on 21 May 2008).

28 Ibid., 4.

29 Murphy, supra n. 24, 82.

> [Objections to the human rights treaties] tend to fall into three categories. First, it is said that the human rights treaties could serve to change our laws as they are, allowing individuals in courts of law to invoke the treaty terms where inconsistent with domestic law or even with the Constitution. The second type of objection is that the treaties could be used to alter the jurisdictional balance between our federal and state institutions . . . The third type of objection is that the relationship between a government and its citizens is not a proper subject for the treaty-making powers at all, but ought to be left entirely to domestic legislative processes . . .[30]

The treaties were never voted on and nothing further happened until President Bush made another – and this time successful – attempt to get the Political Covenant ratified in 1991. The Bush administration sent only the Political Covenant to the Senate for ratification, not the other three treaties (among them the Economic Covenant). Among the formal reservations submitted to the Senate Foreign Relations Committee was one that concerned free speech and another that dealt with capital punishment – two of the areas that have always caused problems because the US differs from many other countries in its insistence on more or less absolute freedom of speech as well as on the use of the death penalty.

In terms of free speech, the Bush administration recommended this reservation: 'Article 20 does not authorize or require legislation or other action by the United States that would restrict the right of free speech and association protected by the Constitution and laws of the United States'. And to Article 6, which prohibits the death penalty for crimes committed by minors as well as by pregnant women, the Bush administration would 'reserve the right, subject to Constitutional constraints, to impose capital punishment on any person (other than a pregnant woman) duly convicted under existing or future laws permitting the imposition of capital punishment, including such punishment for crime committed by persons below eighteen years of age'.[31]

Among the declarations mentioned by the Bush administration was one that spoke to the self-execution of the Convention. 'For reasons of prudence', it stated, 'we recommend including a declaration that the substantive provisions of the Covenant are not self-executing.' Senator Bricker would have been pleased! A number of states parties to the Political Convention were not pleased, however, at what they saw as a total dilution of the Convention due to such RUDs. The American reservation to Article 20 was found by many states to be especially incompatible with the object and purpose of the Convention, and several of the American NGOs participating in the Senate hearings strongly criticized that some of the most important provisions of the

---

30 Robert Owen, quoted in Steiner and Alston, supra n. 6, 1035.

31 Proposals by the Bush Administration of Reservations to the International Covenant on Civil and Political Rights, quoted in ibid., 1039–1040.

Covenant would not be self-executing. The result, wrote Human Rights Watch and the American Civil Liberties Union in a joint report, was that 'ratification became an empty act for Americans: the endorsement of the most important treaty for the protection of civil rights yielded not a single additional enforceable right to citizens and residents of the United States'.[32]

President Bush obtained the consent of the Senate to ratify the Political Covenant in 1992. The US has since improved its record somewhat by also ratifying the Convention on the Prevention and Punishment of the Crime of Genocide; the Convention against Torture and other Cruel, Inhuman or Degrading Treatment or Punishment; and the International Convention on the Elimination of all Forms of Racial Discrimination. But there has never been much talk about ratifying such important treaties as the Convention on the Elimination of All Forms of Discrimination against Women (CEDAW) or the American Convention on Human Rights.[33]

Customary Law and the Distrust of Centralized Power

The distinction between self-executing and non-self-executing treaties and the use of RUDs is among the most important structural obstacles to US adherence to international law, but a couple of others could also be mentioned.[34] Together, they 'have all contributed to "treaties" enjoying a lowly and problematical status under US law and practice'.[35]

When it comes to the second primary source of international law, customary law, things do not look much better, moreover. The oldest source of international law, customary international law 'results from a general and consistent practice of states followed by them from a sense of legal obligation', as stated in Section 102 of the Restatement (Third), Foreign Relations Law of the United States.[36] In terms of where to look for evidence of such law, international lawyers normally mention the actual practice of states, a state's laws and judicial decisions, the writings of international lawyers as well as the judgments of national and international tribunals. In addition, treaties – especially multilateral treaties – can be evidence of customary international law.

---

[32] Ibid., 1041–1042.

[33] Ibid., 1033.

[34] Murphy also mentions the extensive constitutional authority of the president in foreign affairs to suspend, terminate or deviate from treaty obligations as well as the uncertain status of presidential executive agreements under US law (supra n. 24, 87–90).

[35] Ibid., 90.

[36] Steiner and Alston, supra n. 6, 70.

And this is where things get especially tricky as far as the US is concerned. When the UN was in its infancy, there were around sixty member states among which Western states – and especially the US – were the dominant ones. Many of the states that would become members later on were Western colonies, and the Soviet Union did not play much of a role in the UN context. The number of states upon whose customs and usages customary international law was to be built was therefore comparatively small – and these states consisted, for the most part, of 'civilized nations', to use a phrase from the 1900 US Supreme Court decision in *The Paquete Habana* to which we shall return shortly. 'Today, by contrast, there are 191 member states of the United Nations and close to 200 states in the world community, and these states have raised a serious challenge to the dominance of the international legal process to the West.'[37] This not only makes it increasingly difficult to figure out what constitutes relevant state practice; it also means that what the US would consider 'rogue states' have a say in this process. And it also means that the US might find itself in a situation where parts of the International Bill of Rights – the Economic Covenant, say – would be forced on the country as customary international law despite the fact that the US is strongly opposed to them. Customary international law, that is, would tend to spin the US into a web of human rights law, not of its own making and perceived not to be in its best interest – a situation in which all the most carefully thought-out RUDs would not amount to much!

Take the Human Rights Council, a subsidiary organ of the UN General Assembly based in Geneva, which replaced the Commission on Human Rights in June 2006, for example. Several states with doubtful human rights records, to put it mildly, have been accepted as members. And in 2008 – the year that marked the 60th anniversary of the Universal Declaration of Human Rights – the Council failed to speak out against events in Tibet. It withdrew one of its experts from the Congo as if the crisis in that country were now solved, and it praised the good will of the government of the Sudan concerning Darfur even though manifestly, problems in that province are by no means over. How can anyone take seriously the work of the Council or pretend that it is a voice for good in this world, many Americans now ask.

In addition, there is the question of what status customary international law has under US law – a question which becomes increasingly relevant as its scope of coverage expands. In an often quoted passage from its 1900 decision in *The Paquete Habana*, the US Supreme Court stated:

---

37 Murphy, supra n. 24, 14.

> International law is part of our law, and must be ascertained and administered by the courts of justice of appropriate jurisdiction, as often as questions of right depending upon it are duly presented for their determination. For this purpose, where there is no treaty, and no controlling executive or legislative act or judicial decision, resort must be had to the customs and usages of civilized nations; and, as evidence of these, to the works of jurists and commentators, who by years of labor, research and experience, have made themselves peculiarly well acquainted with the subjects of which they treat. Such works are resorted to by judicial tribunals, not for the speculations of their authors concerning what the law ought to be, but for trustworthy evidence of what the law really is.[38]

The Paquete Habana is a classic case that is a 'must-read' for American students of international law, first of all 'to demonstrate the process of ascertaining a norm of customary international law' and secondly 'to raise the issue of the status of customary international law under US law'.[39] The language used in the opinion is clearly ambiguous, however – how and when did international law become 'part of [American] law', and what did the Court mean by a 'controlling executive or legislative act or judicial decision', are but two of the questions American lawyers have since wrestled with. They have received virtually no help from the courts. There is only one reference to customary international law in the Constitution: Article 1, section 8, clause 10, which says that Congress has the power 'to define and punish . . . [o]ffenses against the Law of Nations'. Using norms of customary international law in the interpretation of the Constitution has always been controversial, and the Supreme Court has 'never explicitly upheld the use of international law as a guide to interpreting the US Constitution'.[40]

Finally, in our attempt to explain why the US has been critical of international law, we also have to factor in what Murphy calls US triumphalism, exceptionalism and provincialism:

> The collapse of the Soviet Union . . . left the US as the 'sole remaining superpower' and has encouraged an attitude of triumphalism that has irritated the governments of other countries . . . Accompanying this triumphalism and closely related to it is an attitude of 'exceptionalism', that is, that the US bears special burdens and is entitled to special privileges because of its status as the sole surviving superpower. The collapse of the Soviet Union also brought about a [revival] of US provincialism and isolationism as well as of a preference to act unilaterally rather than multilaterally.[41]

---

38 Quoted in Murphy, supra n. 24, 95–96.
39 Ibid., 96.
40 Ibid., 93.
41 Ibid., 7.

More fundamentally, perhaps, what we are looking at here, Murphy furthermore suggests, is a distrust of power, and especially of centralized power that runs deep in American history. Americans have tended to distrust such centralized power even more when it has been claimed and exercised abroad – especially when the US itself has had no say in the matter. Thus, it has been against the establishment of the International Criminal Court, for example, which may put American citizens on trial according to a new legal order over which the US has no control. However, when it comes to international institutions and organs such as the UN Security Council, the Yugoslav and Rwanda Tribunals, and the International Monetary Fund and the World Bank, over which it has been able to secure some measure of control, the US has taken a much more positive attitude.[42]

It is against this background that Europeans have often accused the US of being both inconsistent and hypocritical. Yet, to the historical distrust of centralized power we should add another deep-seated concern – namely, that many international human rights systems suffer from a democratic deficit. There is no legislative body on the international scene. Neither international human rights lawyers nor NGOs are democratically elected – so where does their legitimacy come from and whom do they answer to? In an interesting article on 'US Constitutionalism and International Human Rights: Incompatible?', well-known legal historian Stanley N. Katz refers to a 'historic Federalist sense of the tight fit between popular sovereignty and constitutional validity' – a tight fit which

> makes it hard for us to accept the constitutional legitimacy of even the most admirable exogenous constitutional institutions and norms. We simply do not accept that the United Nations or any other international body embodies the will of the American people sufficiently for it to establish rules enforceable in American courts. We are all Brickerites, to this extent, especially wary of the possibility that exogenous norms will be bootstrapped into the domestic order, by treaty, executive agreement, or otherwise. This is an integral part of our historic constitutional personality that is increasingly in tension with the globalism of higher values. For us Americans, international human rights as they might be simply assimilated into our Constitution threaten the creation of a disturbing democratic deficit. For us, the adoption of such important values (at least insofar as they are new values) requires a formal constitutional act invoking popular sovereignty.[43]

It is in fact, Jeremy Rabkin continues this line of thinking, only a sovereign state which can make and enforce law in a reliable way and thereby protect the rights of its citizens. Moving from civil rights to human rights is at odds with

---

[42] Ibid., 354–355.
[43] Katz, supra n. 27, 8.

the basic principles of American thought and the broader traditions of liberal political thought on which the American Founders drew. The driving force in the world for this move toward human rights and global governance is Europe, and Rabkin's disdain for what is happening on the other side of the Atlantic Ocean is hard to miss in this quotation from one of his many books, *Law Without Nations?*, of 2005:

> The idea that the world could be reformed by human rights crusaders – properly anointed by international human rights authorities – was too inspiring, too comforting, to question in public. European governments no longer anchored in traditional religion were very ready to embrace new pieties. Rights talk escaped from the confines of settled constitutional orders, first into the neverland of international conferences, then on to the real world of deadly conflict. But it would all turn out well if only people believed in the magic words 'human rights.' Hocus pocus![44]

The kind of human rights law that the Europeans are so fond of generates a cloud of (mostly empty) rhetoric that does little to secure human rights in practice and that tends to undermine American principles such as the separation of powers doctrine and federalism.

CONCLUDING REMARKS: POLITICS VERSUS LAW, PARLIAMENTARY VERSUS CONSTITUTIONAL DEMOCRACY

There is something slightly ironic about these domestic American discourses on federalism and the separation of powers doctrine finding their way into or being echoed in discussions concerning the international domain, just as many European democracies are changing from a democracy *without* to a democracy *with* constitutionalism. The tendencies in Europe toward more human rights talk, which Rabkin and others find so terrible, are accompanied by political and judicial changes which are, at least to a certain extent, due to an American influence. We have already touched upon this influence in previous chapters, especially Chapter 4, but it bears repeating with Anne-Marie Slaughter that

> America's greatest judicial exports all revolve around the protection of minority rights. The institution of judicial review itself is designed to prevent the will of the majority from ever overriding the rights guaranteed in a democratically approved

[44] Jeremy Rabkin, *Law Without Nations? Why Constitutional Government Requires Sovereign States* (Princeton, NJ, and Oxford: Princeton University Press, 2005), 164.

> constitution. The United States directly ensured that the high courts of Germany and Japan would exercise judicial review; the chief architects of the European Court of Justice's assertion of the equivalent of judicial review were European judges educated in the United States . . .[45]

American politics has always been highly Constitution-centred. Another way of putting it is to say that American democracy is a constitutional democracy. Modern constitutionalism is generally considered to have its practical beginnings in the making of the American and the French constitutions during the late 18th century. The ideology of constitutionalism can be traced back to the theories of John Locke (1632–1704), Charles Montesquieu (1689–1755) and Jean Jacques Rousseau (1712–1778), its three key elements being the rule of law, the separation of powers and human rights (in the liberal tradition).

From the beginning, constitutionalism has developed into two quite different main directions. 'The Americans chose a way which stabilised constitutionalism based on judicial review and checks and balances, whereas the citizens of Western European countries chose a way which brought them towards modern democracy and close to unlimited parliamentarism.'[46] In its political version, the American Dream – that is, the personalized or individualized version of American exceptionalism – is very much about having rights: the rights and freedoms outlined in the Constitution. It is this originally European idea that Europeans are getting back today in the shape of constitutionalism. As they too are becoming multiethnic and rights-oriented, they are beginning to listen to the view that the solution to the gravest flaws of majoritarian democracy may be found in constitutionalism in the form of a judicial review. 'In order to reconcile democracy and human rights', argues Michael Ignatieff, 'Western policy will have to put more emphasis not on democracy alone but on constitutionalism, the entrenchment of a balance of powers, judicial review of executive decisions, and enforceable minority rights guarantees. Democracy without constitutionalism is simply ethnic majority tyranny.'[47]

According to Henry Steiner and Philip Alston, the spread of constitutionalism can be approached from two different perspectives: '[f]irst, the adoption of liberal-style constitutions (or at least constitutions with a significant liberal component) can be seen as a *horizontal* trend among states, a consequence of

---

45 Anne-Marie Slaughter, 'A brave new judicial world', in Ignatieff, supra n. 25, 301.

46 Ágúst Thór Árnason, 'Constitutionalism: Popular Legitimacy of the State?', in Martin Scheinin (ed.), *Welfare State and Constitutionalism – Nordic Perspectives* (Copenhagen: Nordic Council of Ministers, 2001), 46 – this and the previous paragraph build on Árnason's article.

47 Michael Ignatieff, 'Human Rights as Politics', in Amy Gutman (ed.), *Human Rights as Politics and Idolatry* (Princeton, NJ: Princeton University Press, 2001), 30.

the influence and pressures exerted by powerful countries in the liberal constitutional tradition like the United States'. The second perspective is *vertical* rather than horizontal in character, in that it 'stresses the links between the spread of such types of constitutions and the achievements of the human rights movement in constructing an international system of norms, institutions and processes'. Here, we are talking about influences from international law and institutions that are 'above' the state rather than influences between states – the European Union being a prime example.[48]

Most European scholars tend to emphasize the *vertical* approach to the spread of constitutionalism. 'Earlier on', comments Jens Elo Rytter in relation to the Scandinavian context, for example, 'the very existence of judicial review of legislation was controversial. Today, the major issue is its extent . . . The Nordic constitutional tradition is now in a process of development towards a more permissive approach to basic rights and judicial review, influenced by the general development in Europe.'[49] Consequently, those who are against this change in the constitutional balance of powers between the courts and the legislatures have focused their criticism on developments in Europe. Several of Rytter's colleagues have openly questioned present tendencies toward giving the ECtHR in Strasbourg more and more power – political power, that is. The Court's decisions are too political; it changes political issues into legal ones. Its judges are political 'super judges', wielding significant power through decisions which are not re-examined or checked by elected politicians, or so the argument goes.

As we have seen in the previous chapters, these European scholars are certainly justified in looking toward Europe and its two courts. However, this sometimes makes them underestimate the American influence which is also at play – perhaps in an act of wishful thinking, wanting international law and international institutions to count for more than the pull of American culture and American dreams. In constitutionalizing their political systems, the individual member states are becoming not only Europeanized, but also Americanized – to a certain extent, they are also falling victims to American attempts at legal hegemony.

I am taking my cue here from Detlev N. Vagts who, in an influential article in the *American Journal of International Law* of 2001, has talked about 'hegemonic international law'. Tracing this concept to three German international law scholars in the early part of the twentieth century – Heinrich Triepel, Carl Scmitt and Wilhelm Grewe – Vagts points out that a shift to 'hegemonic international law' means first of all 'setting aside the norm of nonintervention into

---

48 Steiner and Alston, supra n. 6, 988.

49 Jens Elo Rytter, 'Judicial Review of Legislation – a Sustainable Strategy on the Enforcement of Basic Rights', in Scheinin, supra n. 46, 140, 138.

the internal affairs of states'; second, avoiding 'agreements creating international regimes or organizations that might enable lesser powers to form coalitions that might frustrate the hegemon'; third, putting 'internal law above international law' as a matter of constitutional doctrine; and fourth, abstaining from customary international law in order to prevent the emerging rule in question from becoming part of custom.[50] Detlev Vagts is careful to say that he does not 'take a position as to whether the United States is or should be a hegemon but merely addresses the lawyer's question of what the legal implications would be if it is'.[51] He clearly suggests, however, that we are presently watching the US moving toward hegemony by adapting international law to its own purposes.

Vagts' point is well-taken, I think. Americans are not against international law if such international law means, in effect, American law globalized. It is only when such globalization backfires, when Europeans proceed to move from civil to human rights – that is, takes the initial American influence and develops it further towards something that intends to submerge individual nation-state interests under those of international human rights law – that they become worried. For a while, after the fall of the iron curtains all over Eastern Europe, it did look as if history had ended, to paraphrase Francis Fukuyma, and that American ways had been more or less universally accepted.[52] This included the American legal way or American constitutionalism. 'Following the end of the Cold War', writes Andreas Paulus, 'some Americans are – or have been – in no less a jubilant mood than their European counterparts . . . Most of the American enthusiasm for globalization – and even more so the disillusionment which followed – is nurtured, [however,] not by an effort to institutionalise and legalize international relations, but by another impulse: the advent of the global liberal age.'[53]

With the advent of the global liberal age, these Americans thought, universal history was culminating in liberal democracy – with the United States and its constitutional democracy as its chief embodiment. What they had perhaps not quite anticipated was the way in which, toward the end of the 1990s and especially after 11 September 2001 and the following war by the American-led 'coalition of the willing' against Iraq and terrorism in general, the European

---

50 Detlev N. Vagts, 'Hegemonic International Law', 95 *American Journal of International Law* (2001), 845–847.

51 Ibid., 843.

52 See Francis Fukuyama, *The End of History and the Last Man* (London and New York: Penguin Books, 1992).

53 Andreas Paulus, 'The Influence of the United States on the Concept of the "International Community" ', in Michael Byers and Georg Nolte (eds.), *United States Hegemony and the Foundations of International Law* (Cambridge: Cambridge University Press, 2003), 69–70.

model, embodied by or in the EU, has developed into an alternative to the American model/Dream. Only time will tell which of the two – if indeed either of them – will in the end become the more popular and/or the more enduring.

'As in the past, the American view differs from ideas prevailing in Europe', Jeremy Rabkin notes in his introduction to the book on *Law Without Nations?*. 'But difference can be the beginning of reflection.'[54] Rabkin would be the first to recognize the kinds of discussions currently going on among European legal scholars and policy professionals about the legitimacy of judicial review in a democracy, the limits of judicial activism and the national judicial reinforcement of international norms. The European debates concerning the doctrines of federalism and separation of powers are every bit as poignant as their American counterparts, even if they are different in certain crucial respects. But if those differences can be recognized on both sides of the Atlantic, then this may indeed be the beginning of reflection. The basis for both rights dialects – the American and the European – was originally 'drafted by a group of often Francophile Englishmen more than two centuries ago' (Ash's phrase, as we saw above). It was in the new United States, though, that that basis came to be realized in practice, and it was the US which had, after World War Two, to prevail on the Europeans to take their own original ideas seriously – a fine example of the way in which influences have always gone back and forth over the Atlantic. And even though these Europeans have now taken those ideas one step further – have turned civil rights into human rights – the original rights discourse should make an obvious starting point for the beginning of reflection.

---

[54] Rabkin, supra n. 44.

7. Transatlantic dialogues on copyright: cultural rights and access to knowledge

One of the questions which American historian Lynn Hunt tries to answer in her highly readable *Inventing Human Rights: A History* of 2007 is how rights became 'self-evident'. Rights emerged during the 18th century. When the Declaration of Independence declared 'these truths to be self-evident, that all men are created equal, that they are endowed by their Creator with certain unalienable Rights, that among these are Life, Liberty and the pursuit of Happiness', and when the French issued their own Declaration of the Rights of Man in connection with their revolution, a whole new moral standard was created for political conduct.

We normally focus on the thinkers of the Enlightenment to explain how the 'truths' set out in these documents became 'self-evident'. This is only one part of the story, though, argues Hunt. There is another part as well – a part which has to do with a change of feeling and sentiment among ordinary people:

> Human rights are difficult to pin down because their definition, indeed their very existence, depends on emotions as much as on reason . . . Human rights are not just a doctrine formulated in documents; they rest on a disposition toward other people, a set of convictions about what people are like and how they know right and wrong in the secular world. Philosophical ideas, legal traditions, and revolutionary politics had to have this kind of inner emotional reference point for human rights to be truly 'self-evident.'[1]

Hunt traces the rise of rights in part to the changing idea of human relationships displayed by novelists, playwrights and artists. Novels such as Samuel Richardson's *Pamela* (1740) and *Clarissa* (1747–1748) and Jean-Jacques Rousseau's *Julie* (1761) sensitized people to the needs of their fellow human beings, including those not of their own gender or class: '[n]ovels made the point that all people are fundamentally similar because of their inner feelings, and many novels showcased in particular the desire for autonomy. In this way, reading novels created a sense of equality and empathy through

[1] Lynn Hunt, *Inventing Human Rights: A History* (New York and London: W.W. Norton & Co., 2007), 26–27.

passionate involvement in the narrative.'[2] The spread of empathy beyond local communities would in the end make people reject torture as a means of finding out whether or not those charged with a crime were guilty, for example, just as it would make them push for the expansion of self-determination for various disenfranchised groups.

If we are to believe Hunt, in other words, the belief in law's empowerment is grounded in empathy and understanding of how others think and feel. We have seen, in previous chapters, other scholars (Beck, Giddens, Held and Habermas) talk about solidarity, even cosmopolitan solidarity. What is interesting about Hunt's work is the way in which she points to the role of art and literature – or, in other words, culture – in promoting such solidarity. In this and the following two chapters, we shall stay within the realm of culture. We shall start by looking, in this chapter, at cultural rights as these relate to the formation of identity – local, European and global. The belief in law's empowerment, as we saw in Chapter 2, is clearly expressed in the discussions concerning that 'neglected' or 'underdeveloped' category of human rights, that 'poor relative' of economic and social rights, cultural rights.

We shall then focus on one of the major battlefields for fighting out cultural battles these days: the movement for access to knowledge. Ostensibly about who owns the right to knowledge – and thus about issues having to do with copyright protection – the fight for access to knowledge has everything to do with cultural pride. The underlying issue is cultural copyright: gaining respect and recognition beyond one's own insular community for one's cultural traditions – or, to put it in another way, seeking acceptance to be who one is.

We shall then follow up the discussion of access to knowledge by looking at other copyright-related issues. There has been a tendency in recent times for human rights discourse to trespass into areas in which it was previously unknown. Copyright (and intellectual property as a whole) is a prime example of such an area – a reflection, in our current knowledge societies or economies, of the importance of cultural issues, especially as these relate to identity and cultural pride. 'Human rights and intellectual property', writes Paul Torremans in the Foreword to his edited volume *Intellectual Property and Human Rights* of 2008, 'is clearly a field in full expansion and development'.[3] In the copyright area, no less than in other areas in which 'culture' has become an 'issue', there are certain interesting transatlantic angles that reflect back on several of the transatlantic themes we have looked at in previous chapters.

---

2 Ibid., 39.

3 Paul L.C. Torremans (ed.), *Intellectual Property and Human Rights*, Enhanced Edition of *Copyright and Human Rights* (Alphen aan den Reijn: Kluwer Law International, 2008), p. xxiv.

CULTURAL RIGHTS AND THE FIGHT FOR ACCESS TO KNOWLEDGE

Culture as Capacity and Empowerment

'So are arts and heritage only auxiliary functions, icing on the cake, nice to have but not essential to the nutritional needs of society?', asks Dick Stanley in a study prepared for the Council of Europe (2006). No, he answers, 'not at all. What arts and heritage contribute is cultural diversity, the rich variety of social understanding that modern societies and their citizens need to adapt their repertoires to their constantly changing conditions.'[4] Diversity, as we have seen in previous chapters, has long been a priority for the Council of Europe, the EU and European intellectuals. Europe has always been characterized by many different cultures, but now, also, there is the issue of all the many immigrants seeking a better life for themselves and their families in Europe. Managing change – on the part both of those who immigrate and of those who stay put – has therefore become more important than ever, and 'if you have a repertoire and tradition of sufficient richness and diversity, you can manage change . . . A society with a diverse repertoire can much more easily cope with change and sustain itself.'[5]

Cultural adaptation to new needs and fundamental changes can, Stanley argues, come about in three different ways. 'First, obviously, cultural flows from outside bring new information, new interpretations and new world views.' The problem is, though, that it is precisely to deal with and to process such new cultural flows that adaptation mechanisms are needed. Something else has to be added, that is. Ordinary members of society do have a certain 'creativity' at their disposal from simply 'daily using the symbolic resources of their repertoire to come to terms with everyday variability in their lives'. This second source of adaptation will not do the trick either, not being 'nimble enough' for something bigger than the small changes needed in every day life. Luckily, 'there is a third way: the repertoire, which we need to understand cultural flows from outside, is enriched through the workings of the arts and heritage'.[6]

As far as those staying put are concerned (those who must be taught to cope with and welcome newcomers and change in their lives), 'culture is not enter-

---

4 Dick Stanley, *Recondita Armonia – A Reflection on the Function of Culture in Building Citizenship Capacity*, a study prepared for the Council of Europe in the framework of the European Year of Citizenship, Policy Note No. 10 (Strasbourg: Council of Europe Publishing, 2006), 34.

5 Ibid., 36.

6 Ibid., 37–38.

tainment: it is capacity' – capacity that gives 'sufficient conceptual stability and self confidence to appropriate change without becoming confused and feeling threatened'.[7] And for those who are newcomers, culture may help create nothing less than citizenship capacity. Participating in cultural life can lead to a feeling of belonging to a group, thereby helping to create or validate one's identity. Cultural misunderstandings can be fatal, not just to the individuals involved, but to society as a whole. Society therefore has a stake in cultural politics and this, at least in principle, makes 'policy intervention to promote cultural vitality... justifiable'.[8]

Arts, heritage and culture in general are forms of continuing education: '[a] citizen's ongoing participation in culture, whether as artist or curator, or as "passive" recipient (audience), continuously challenges established notions and expands his or her citizenship vocabulary and repertoire. Culture is about both education and citizenship'.[9] All in all, concludes Stanley, the long-term trend of arts, heritage and culture in general 'is towards more sustainable social values'. The sustainable social values he has in mind are the ones associated with the UN Universal Declaration of Human Rights – 'contrary values, such as exclusionary patriotism, racial purity, worship of leaders, military superiority, millenarianism, hav[ing] generally proven to be dead ends'.[10]

If *A Reflection of Culture in Building Citizenship Capacity* implicitly sounds like a continuation of the Council of Europe's *In from the margins* of 1997, which we analysed in Chapter 2, the final synthesis report, by Kevin Robins, of the Council of Europe project on Cultural Policy and Cultural Diversity carried out between 2000 and 2004, *The Challenge of Transcultural Diversities,* explicitly states that 'what are put forward in this report are propositions that aim to build on . . . *In from the margins* . . .'.[11] As the title implies, Robins's final report stresses the development of transcultural perspectives. When it comes to the cultural landscape of Europe, two key developments may be identified. The first of these developments concerns a change in the way in which minorities are approached and talked about. Whereas formerly the question of minorities was considered to pose a problem for the European cultural order, there seems recently, Robins writes, to have been 'something of a discursive shift, in which the language of "minorities" has begun to be

---

7 Ibid., 9, 8.

8 Ibid., 46.

9 Ibid., 43.

10 Ibid., 30–31.

11 Kevin Robins, *The Challenge of Transcultural Diversities: Transversal Study on the Theme of Cultural Policy and Cultural Diversity*, Final report (Strasbourg: Council of Europe Publishing, 2006), 41.

displaced by a new conceptual frame concerned with "diversity" '.[12] The discursive shift from 'minority' to 'cultural diversity' is a positive one, Robins continues. It signals a realization, on the one hand, that diversity is here to stay – has become 'a constitutive aspect of all cultural orders and spaces' – and that diversity has become, on the other, de-ethnicised so as also to include other kinds of difference (gender and age, say). This means that difference is no longer only perceived as problematical, 'but actually as a positive asset and resource for any cultural order. It has validated difference'.[13]

In addition, there has been a development toward framing issues having to do with cultural diversity as transcultural, rather than national issues.

> Recent developments in patterns of migration, as well as in life strategies of migrant populations, have made it clear that minority issues – which are increasingly coming to be cast as diversity issues – can no longer be easily contained within the national frame of reference. What are increasingly apparent are the ways in which diversity policies are being pulled into both an international and a transnational frame of reference.[14]

Throughout the 1990s – and we saw this in the earlier *In from the margins* report – there was much talk of making sure that minorities were given access to cultural life. This gave rise to a growing awareness of the cultural dimension of citizenship, and claims for cultural rights were put forward by minority groups, both national and ethnic. 'What began to be recognized was the value of cultural empowerment in the citizen body as a whole, involving the capacity on the part of all citizens to participate fully and creatively in national cultural life – accepted as a diverse and complex cultural life.'[15] The problem today is, however, argues Robins, that for many people in Europe access to the cultural life of one nation may not be enough, many of their cultural reference points actually being outside their current country of residence. People in Europe live transcultural lives; both physically and mentally, they constantly move between cultural spaces. What these people want is no longer simply 'culture-as-belonging' or 'culture-as-groupishness', but instead 'culture-as-creativity' – 'a new kind of social membership, in which the individual can be accepted as an active agent with respect to cultural choices'.[16]

For such a new kind of social membership to come about, a more flexible approach to citizenship as well as to the principle of individual cultural rights in the context of transnational change is needed, according to Robins. Such

---

12 Ibid., 12.
13 Ibid.
14 Ibid.
15 Ibid., 31.
16 Ibid., 37.

cultural rights must be sustained and further developed, and one way to go is to invoke universal principles of human rights. Robins ends his final report on *The Challenge of Transcultural Diversities* by proposing a number of recommendations, many of which are phrased in terms of cultural rights:

> . . . the recognition of the centrality and importance of culture to the meaning of European citizenship; the right for all people living in Europe to exercise choice and agency in defining their own cultural identities; . . . the right of individuals, irrespective of legal status, to participate in the cultural life of their choice and to exercise free choice with respect to their cultural practices, whether this be in terms of expression and creativity, or in terms of consumption; . . . ensuring the right to culture of all residents, regardless of status, and safeguarding democratic access to cultural goods; . . .[17]

It is interesting to note that Robins lists 'consumption' among these cultural rights, and this is something we shall come back to presently. In this context, it is worth mentioning that the right to culture is linked, for Robins as it is for some of the other writers on European culture(s) whose work we have discussed in previous chapters, to access to and active participation in cultural life. Ultimately, for these writers, cultural diversity can be promoted in Europe only when everyone is ensured access to 'information with respect to all processes of production and consumption; training; communications media; cultural history; local, national and international civil society' and 'creative production and exchange'.[18]

Access to Knowledge (A2K)

One of the areas of cultural life which has lent itself to discussions of cultural rights and access to culture these past few years is the movement for access to knowledge (A2K). A variety of A2K initiatives have seen the light of day. The ones that we shall take a look at in the following are the Berlin Declaration on Open Access to Knowledge in the Sciences and Humanities of 2003, the Yale A2K Initiative of 2006, and the Cultural Rights: Fribourg Declaration of 2007.

In October 2003, the well-known and highly respected German Max Planck Society let the world know, by means of a press release entitled 'Science and Culture Accessible to All Internet Users',[19] that together with other representatives from leading German and international cultural and research institutions its president, Peter Gruss, had just signed a new declaration, the Berlin

---

17 Ibid., 43.

18 Ibid., 44.

19 The press release is available at http://oa.mpg.de/openaccess-berlin/pressstatement.html.

Declaration on Open Access to Knowledge in the Sciences and Humanities.[20] This had happened during what was to be the first in a series of conferences on open access to knowledge – conferences that have as their point of departure the need to think through and debate some of the fundamental changes that the spread of research-related knowledge and cultural heritage via the Internet have led to. The Internet provides certain possibilities for realizing dreams of free access to knowledge, and this is something that the creators of such knowledge – scholars and their institutions – must necessarily take into consideration.

As it says in the statement accompanying the press release, the Berlin Declaration is in part inspired by the Budapest Open Access Initiative of 2002. This is one of the Hungarian-born American financial speculator and philanthropist George Soros' Open Society Institute initiatives, and it talks about knowledge as a public good which ought to be available for everybody via the Internet:

> An old tradition and a new technology have converged to make possible an unprecedented public good. The old tradition is the willingness of scientists and scholars to publish the fruits of their research in scholarly journals without payment, for the sake of inquiry and knowledge. The new technology is the internet. The public good they make possible is the world-wide electronic distribution of the peer-reviewed journal literature and completely free and unrestricted access to it by all scientists, scholars, teachers, students, and other curious minds. Removing access barriers to this literature will accelerate research, enrich education, share the learning of the rich with the poor and the poor with the rich, make this literature as useful as it can be, and lay the foundation for uniting humanity in a common intellectual conversation and quest for knowledge.[21]

Another inspiration for the Berlin Declaration is the ECHO (European Cultural Heritage Online) initiative, a pilot project supported by the EU Commission. Whereas the Budapest Initiative is mostly geared towards the publication of scientific knowledge, the ECHO initiative deals with cultural knowledge or knowledge that comes out of the humanities. As the name implies, the Berlin Declaration on Open Access to Knowledge in the Sciences and Humanities shows an interest in both kinds of knowledge. The conference that gave birth to the Declaration was only the first in a whole series of conferences, as briefly mentioned. Every year, there has been a new Berlin Open

---

20 Berlin Declaration on Open Access to Knowledge in the Sciences and Humanities, signed on 22 October, 2003, available at: http://oa.mpg.de/openaccess-berlin/berlindeclaration.html (last visited on 12 January 2009 – as of January 2009, 257 organizations from all over the world have signed the Berlin Declaration).

21 Budapest Open Access Initiative – available at http://www.soros.org/openaccess/read.shtml (last visited on 12 January 2009).

Access conference. The 'Berlin 2 Open Access' conference, which was held in Geneva in 2004, was a follow-up meeting on the implementation of the recommendations in the Berlin Declaration. One central result of the conference was the drafting of a roadmap with concrete implementation steps to open access – a revised version of which was submitted for final approval at the 'Berlin 3 Open Access' conference in Southampton, England, in 2005.

According to this roadmap or guide to the implementation of the Berlin Declaration, 'the signatories of the Berlin Declaration are committed to achieving full open access to scholarly communication in order to realize the benefits of world-wide access to knowledge'. To this end, organizations 'committing to open access should establish an open web-site repository into which their researchers may deposit copies of journal articles and research reports', and 'a legal framework should be established for the organizational repository governing the relationship with authors, publishers and users of the repository content'. One possible candidate for such a legal framework might, the Roadmap suggests, be 'a scholarship-friendly licence such as Creative Commons'.[22]

Founded by law professor Lawrence Lessig, Creative Commons is a non-profit-making organization which allows authors or creators certain standardized choices when it comes to putting together the kind of licence they want. They can choose, for example, to limit the commercial use of their own work or to allow or prevent others from making changes to it later on. These choices then produce a licence which makes

> the freedoms associated with content on the net understandable, unchallengeable and usable. And by so marking content, we can encourage a wide range of creativity consistent with the underlying copyright law. Or put differently, we can encourage a kind of creativity that encourages others to build on the creative work of others, consistent with the underlying regime of intellectual property.[23]

At the Berlin 4 and Berlin 5 Open Access conferences, which took place in Golm, Germany, in 2006 and Padua, Italy, in 2007, respectively, the main issues on the agenda were how to move 'From Promise to Practice' (the theme of Berlin 4) and 'From Practice to Impact' (the theme of Berlin 5). And when the Berlin 6 Open Access conference convened in November 2008 in

---

[22] 'The Road to Open Access: A Guide to the Implementation of the Berlin Declaration', Berlin 3 Open Access – available at http://oa.mpg.de/openaccess-berlin/roadmap.html (last visited on 12 January 2009). On Creative Commons, please see http://creativecommons.org.

[23] Lawrence Lessig, '(Re)creativity: how Creativity Lives', in Helle Porsdam (ed.), *Copyright and Other Fairy Tales: Hans Christian Andersen and the Commodification of Creativity* (Cheltenham, UK and Northampton, MA, USA: Edward Elgar), 21.

Düsseldorf, Germany, the focus was on 'Changing Scholarly Communication in the Knowledge Society'. Five years after the Berlin Declaration, 'the range of Open Access activities is constantly widening due to constant technical development and the perceivable drift within the different scholarly communities towards new forms of communication and collaboration', and this makes it necessary to discuss both technical and political aspects of Open Access.[24]

For the president of the Max Planck Society as for the other people behind the Berlin Declaration, there are two different concerns involved. First, there is an activist, grass-roots-like interest in promoting free access to scientific knowledge. The Internet having 'fundamentally changed the practical and economic realities of distributing scientific knowledge and cultural heritage . . . [o]ur mission of disseminating knowledge is only half complete if the information is not made widely and readily available to society . . . In order to realize the vision of a global and accessible representation of knowledge, the future Web has to be sustainable, interactive, and transparent. Content and software tools must be openly accessible and compatible.'[25] Second, there is a more intellectual concern involved which has to do with the interests and the working conditions of the scholars producing the knowledge that is made freely accessible. At issue here is both the reputation of scholars whose careers (especially in the sciences) may depend on citation indexes and what could be called a right to be quoted, as well as the often considerable possibilities for financial gain involved in patents and copyright. And what is furthermore at stake is the discourse of copyright itself – how to solve the perennial problem of technological development invariably being way ahead of legal regulation of such development.

This 'double interest', as it were, in the issue of access to knowledge is also noticeable in another A2K initiative, the 'Yale A2K' initiative, which developed out of the 'Yale Information Society' project at the Yale Law School:

> The Yale Access to Knowledge (A2K) Initiative aims to build an intellectual framework that will protect access to knowledge both as the basis for sustainable human development and to safeguard human rights… Multinational corporations, elite policymakers, and other proponents of expansive intellectual property regimes argue that increasing intellectual property rights and corporate control over knowledge best serve society's interests. Yet ample evidence suggests that the reverse is true: increasingly, widespread access to knowledge and preservation of a healthy knowledge commons are the real basis of sustainable human development. Despite

---

24 A description of 'Berlin 6 – Changing Scholarly Communication in the Knowledge Society' – is available at http://oa.mpg.de/openaccess-dus/index.html (last visited on 12 January 2009).

25 Supra, n. 19, 'Preface' and 'Goals'.

> a growing body of evidence suggesting that maximizing intellectual property monopolies, disabling communication infrastructures, and restricting the development of essential technology with digital rights management schemes are harmful and misguided, these outmoded approaches continue to dictate global legal norms and shape national legal infrastructures. Not surprisingly, incumbent property owners desire to maintain their preeminence and resist sharing the intellectual property which they view as the source of their power.
>
> The goal of the A2K Initiative is to counterbalance the distorting force of these tendencies by supporting the adoption and development of effective access to knowledge policies.[26]

Building an intellectual framework which will be capable of solving some of the legal issues involved and at the same time creating free access at the grassroots level to the knowledge generated at institutions of learning such as Yale – that is the goal. Human rights are directly referred to here, if only abstractly, in connection with a healthy knowledge commons and sustainable human development. For access to knowledge to be directly defined as a cultural right we have to look toward the 2007 Cultural Rights: Fribourg Declaration. The Fribourg Declaration is the fruit of many years' work with cultural diversity and the place of cultural rights within the international human rights arena, and it builds on an earlier declaration of 1998, drawn up by the so-called 'Fribourg group' for UNESCO.[27]

At the presentation of the Declaration, the head of the Fribourg group Professor Patrice Meyer-Bisch drew attention to the fact that it is only during the last few years that there has been any interest in cultural rights. They have been mentioned together with economic and social rights, but it has been these other rights that have received by far the most attention. The Fribourg Declaration marks, Professor Meyer-Bisch continued, an attempt, not so much at defining new rights but rather at making already existing

---

[26] The Yale Information Society Project used to be available at http://isp.law.yale.edu/projects_knowledge/ (last visited on 28 June 2008).

[27] Another initiative worth mentioning in this connection is the Google Global Network Initiative: Protecting and Advancing Freedom of Expression and Privacy in Information and Communications Technologies, which was launched in October 2008 (in the 60th Anniversary year of the Universal Declaration of Human Rights). This Initiative 'is founded upon new Principles on Freedom of Expression and Privacy – supported by specific implementation commitments and a framework for accountability and learning – that provide a systematic approach for companies, NGOs, investors, academics and others to work together in resisting efforts by governments that seek to enlist companies in acts of censorship and surveillance that violate international standards'. For more information on the Initiative, please see http://www.globalnetworkinitiative.org/newsandevents/Diverse_Coalition_Launches_New_Effort_To_Respond_to_Government_Censorship_and_Threats_to_Privacy.php.

rights more visible.[28] There has been disagreement over the years as to what constitutes such cultural rights, but a sort of consensus seems to be currently forming that among these are the right to education, the right to linguistic freedom, the right freely to participate in cultural life as well as the right to benefit from scientific progress.[29] And this is where access to knowledge comes in.

The Fribourg Declaration is divided into twelve parts, each of which describes a particular theme or area. In Article 5, 'Access to and participation in cultural life', one of the freedoms mentioned is 'the freedom to develop and share knowledge and cultural expressions, to conduct research and to participate in different forms of creation as well as to benefit from these'. And in Article 6, entitled 'Education and training', we find a reference to the right to 'knowledge related to one's own culture and other cultures', just as Article 7 ('Communication and information') talks about the right to 'seek, receive or impart information'.[30]

As far as the people of the Fribourg group are concerned, there is no doubt: access to knowledge is a human right, a cultural human right. This view is shared by the Association for Progressive Communication (APC). In the work of the APC, the link between access to knowledge and cultural human rights is even more clearly expressed. In 2001–2002, the association organized various workshops around the world on 'Internet rights', and these resulted in a document, the APC Internet Rights Charter. The background for this Charter is the view that human rights, as laid down in the International Bill of Rights, cannot be realized unless information can be freely shared and communicated on the Internet. The Charter has six different themes. Theme number three, 'access to knowledge', specifically mentions the right to access to knowledge and to freedom of information and refers to Article 27 of the UN Universal Declaration: '[e]veryone has the right freely to participate in the cultural life of the community, to enjoy the arts and to share in scientific advancement and

---

[28] '*Considering also* that cultural rights, as expressed in the present Declaration, are currently recognized in a dispersed manner in a large number of human rights instruments and that it is important to group these rights together in order to ensure their visibility and coherence and to encourage their full realization . . .'; Preamble to 'Cultural Rights: Fribourg Declaration'. The Declaration is available at http://www.equalrightstrust.org/ertdocumentbank/Fribourg-declaration.pdf (last visited on 13 January 2009). The human rights instruments specifically referred to are the Universal Declaration, the two Covenants and the UNESCO Convention on the Protection and Promotion of the Diversity of Cultural Expressions.

[29] The very difficulty of defining cultural rights has also given rise to a second problem: their non-justiciability. There is no effective legal basis for legal action; like economic and social rights, cultural rights are therefore perceived as a challenge for advocacy.

[30] Fribourg Declaration, supra n. 28.

its benefits'. Towards the end, theme number three talks about 'the right to access to publicly-funded information', moreover, '[a]ll information, including scientific and social research, that is produced with the support of public funds should be freely available to all'.[31] This may be said to be of special relevance and importance to the European countries that have well-developed welfare states in which many scholars are employed in public universities and research institutions.

In the Preamble to the Fribourg Declaration, the conviction is stated that 'violations of cultural rights give rise to identity related conflicts which are some of the main causes of violence, wars and terrorism'. 'Culture' is a part of every human being's growth and development, and unless each individual is given the chance to experience cultural growth the result can be catastrophic. Lack of respect for each individual human being and his or her cultural self-determination unfortunately seems to be a part of the terrorism and war discourses of our time, and it is therefore absolutely necessary to draw attention to how this can lead to humiliation, hatred and reductionist, even fundamentalist, ways of thinking and reacting. According to the people behind the Fribourg Declaration, that is, cultural human rights are about much more than intellectual word games. Violation of these rights can lead to precisely the kind of 'clash of civilizations' that the American historian Samuel Huntington (in)famously wrote about a few years ago.[32]

Human dignity and respect for cultural autonomy being ultimately at stake, it is no wonder that cultural rights have from the very start been associated with the belief in and demand for cultural diversity. It was the UNESCO Convention on the Protection and Promotion of the Diversity of Cultural Expressions of 2005 which gave concrete form to the idea that the protection of cultural diversity and self-determination ought to become an international legal obligation. It is interesting, therefore (and in line with the opinions expressed by Janusz Symonides in Chapter 2), that the Fribourg Declaration explicitly observes how 'cultural rights have been asserted primarily in the context of the rights of minorities and indigenous peoples', but that it is now 'essential to guarantee these rights in a universal manner, notably for the most destitute'. Cultural relativism must be avoided and a clarification of cultural rights as they are already present in various human rights instruments constitutes the most efficient means of preventing them 'from becoming a pretext for pitting communities or peoples against one another'. The cultural rights outlined in the Declaration, it is furthermore stated, are for 'everyone, alone or

---

31 'APC Internet Charter', available at http://rights.apc.org/charter.shtml#3 – last visited on 13 January 2009.

32 This reference is to Samuel Huntington, *The Clash of Civilizations* (New York: Free Press, 2002).

in community with others' – cultural rights are individual, but may potentially also have a collective connotation, according to the Fribourg group.[33]

COPYRIGHT AND TRANSATLANTIC DIALOGUES

Before 2005 and the UNESCO convention, the demand for protection of cultural diversity was made with reference to relevant passages in the Universal Declaration and the two International Covenants. Among these was Article 19 of the Political Covenant which states that:

1. Everyone shall have the right to hold opinions without interference.
2. Everyone shall have the right to freedom of expression; this right shall include freedom to seek, receive and impart information and ideas of all kinds, regardless of frontiers, either orally, in writing or in print, in the form of art, or through any other media of his choice.

Article 15.1 of the Economic Covenant was also sometimes mentioned in this connection. It states that:

1. The States Parties to the present Covenant recognize the right of everyone:
   (a) To take part in cultural life;
   (b) To enjoy the benefits of scientific progress and its applications;
   (c) To benefit from the protection of the moral and material interests resulting from any scientific, literary or artistic production of which he is the author.

The interesting thing is, however, that this very Article also is often claimed as 'proof' that copyright is a human right for the individual author or creator. The same is true for its predecessor, the already mentioned Article 27 of the Universal Declaration which not only states that '1) everyone has the right freely to participate in the cultural life of the community, to enjoy the arts and to share in scientific advancement and its benefits', but also that '2) everyone has the right to the protection of the moral and material interests resulting from any scientific, literary or artistic production of which he is the author'. It would thus seem that one and the same Article refers both to the copyright of the individual author/creator and to the right to access of the general public to the work produced by this very author/creator.

As it was originally thought and set up, the copyright system of protection consisted of what we could call an equilateral triangle the three legs of which were made up of the rights of the author/creator, of the publisher/exploiter of the author/creator's work, and of the general public. The author/creator would

33 Fribourg Declaration, supra n. 28.

receive money for the work created by selling it to the publisher/exploiter who would then supply the means, technical and financial, to make the work in question available for purchase by the public – and everybody would benefit. The public would receive the latest knowledge available, the publisher/exploiter would make some money from producing and selling the work in question, and the author/creator would receive enough incentive to keep on creating good work. Unfortunately, as many see it, the triangle of actors involved in copyright is no longer equilateral. Christophe Geiger and other copyright scholars talk about a 'change of paradigm' – 'copyright, originally designed to protect the author and to provide incentives for him to create for the benefit of society, is nowadays more and more used as a mechanism to protect investment, without taking into account the impact on future creativity'.[34]

The movement for access to knowledge is a response to what is perceived to be an onslaught on the public domain by means of a gradual privatization of information through copyright. 'Born in the Age of the Enlightenment', Geiger explains,

> copyright was intended as a means of guaranteeing the author a sphere of liberty, allowing him to create freely while protecting him from any interference from the powers that be and from all risk of censorship. To this end, a wise balance was conceived between property and freedom, the former, in the individualist approach of the age, being presented as the means of ensuring the latter, with the overall aim of ensuring the common good – a dose of property to enable the author to live from his works, a dose of freedom to allow authors to build on what exists in order to create something new.[35]

There are actually two authors and their interests involved: the actual author who has created some piece of work from which (s)he wants to profit, and the future or potential author who will one day create a piece of work. The interests of the latter are not served by putting all kinds of obstacles in the way of the creative process. In order to avoid this, Geiger continues,

> the monopoly that has been created contains a certain number of limits aimed at permitting future creativity: the right only covers the form and not the content; the works are only protected for a certain period of time, at the expiry of which they

---

34 Christophe Geiger, 'Flexibilising Copyright – Remedies to the Privatisation of Information to Copyright Law', 39 *International Review of Intellectual Property and Competition Law* (IIC) (2008), 178.

35 Christophe Geiger, 'Copyright and the Freedom to Create – A Fragile Balance', 38 *International Review of Intellectual Property and Competition Law* (IIC) (2007), 707.

> become part of the public domain; and certain 'creative' uses are expressly permitted by the legislature under what are normally referred to (in a number of European countries at least) as 'exceptions' to copyright.[36]

Now, what seems to be happening is that this original paradigm is being abandoned. Exclusive copyrights are being constantly expanded while the copyright exceptions are becoming more and more restricted in scope. First, there is the length of copyright protection which is being steadily expanded. Take the situation in the United States, for example. Article 1, Section 8, Clause 8 of the US Constitution states that the Congress shall have the power 'to promote the Progress of Science and useful Arts, by securing for limited Times to Authors and Inventors the exclusive Right to their respective Writings and Discoveries'. Even though neither the word 'copyright' nor the word 'patent' is directly mentioned, this clause has been understood from the very beginning to cover both. What has been much debated, however, is what the words 'for limited times' mean. Originally, for copyright, limited times meant fourteen years – this is how long an author could get his work copyrighted for. Today, 'limited times' in relation to copyright means more than seventy years (in the US as also in Europe) – seventy years from the death of the author, which often makes the protection much longer in practice – and there are even those who argue that this is not long enough!

Second, works of a more technical kind for which people would not seek copyright protection in the past are increasingly being copyrighted. This too means an expansion of copyright protection. In the European systems (but less so in the American, as we shall see) copyright used to be associated with concepts of genius and creativity, yet today copyright law grants protection to works which have little, if anything at all, to do with any accepted notions of creativity. As a requirement, a sense of creativity is on the decline; indeed,

> copyright protection disassociates itself more and more from the fine arts and is becoming a suitable mode of protection for a number of creations which often neither have much to do with the creator's personality nor last for a very long time. Concerning such creations, however, other systems of protection that are more demanding – because of necessary registration – and less protecting (such as design law) have become less attractive in cases where copyright law may be applied.[37]

Traditionally, in the European systems, copyright was about 'creations' and not 'products'; today, a 'product' does not necessarily imply any creative or innovative effort; indeed, writes Geiger, 'the term "product" often presupposes investment. Thus, by granting copyright protection to a product, copyright law

---

36 Ibid., 708.
37 Geiger, supra n. 34, 183.

becomes implicitly a mechanism of investment protection.'[38] Originality in the sense of origin, i.e. that the work originates with the creator and is not copied, is still a condition, but creativity (or originality in the non-legal sense or uniqueness) seems to be less of a precondition now than it was before.

From a European point of view, this is potentially problematical. Culturally speaking, however, this move toward something that is better known in the Anglo-American systems, which see copyright as a property right that can be freely traded (the alienability of the copyright interest), as we shall see, may at least to a certain extent further cultural rights concerning the possibility of active participation in cultural life. The paradox here is that the more copyright dissociates itself from the fine arts and starts protecting creations which have nothing or very little to do with the creator's personality, the more it becomes, again culturally speaking, the sort of 'cultural leveler' that Jane M. Gaines has talked about – a leveller that furthers those 'citizens' rights as consumer participation and consumer rights' mentioned by Anne M. Cronin. We shall come back to both Gaines's and Cronin's arguments shortly.

Third, there are the copyright exceptions or limitations which are becoming more restricted. The so-called fair use or fair dealing laws are a good example. 'Fair use' is an American term which allows limited use of copyright material without requiring permission from the rights holders, such as use for scholarship or review. It is based on a First Amendment right to free speech. 'Fair dealing' is the term used for a similar principle in certain other common-law countries.[39] Over recent years, judges have tended toward less and less open interpretations of these copyright limitations, and this is of serious concern, writes Fiona Macmillan: '[w]hat is happening here is that copyright is failing to secure what has been described as the cultural or intellectual commons. This is because one way of safeguarding the intellectual commons is by strong fair dealing or fair use laws. It is arguable that a diverse and vigorous cultural development cannot occur without safeguarding the intellectual commons.'[40]

The result has been a commodification of copyright and a build-up of private power over cultural output. Macmillan lists two additional reasons for this commodification currently happening, especially in Anglo-American

---

[38] Ibid.

[39] Though similar, there are certain important legal differences between fair dealing and fair use. Generally speaking, fair use is broader, and a number of scholars have argued that it is more beneficial to users.

[40] Fiona Macmillan, 'What might Hans Christian Andersen say about Copyright Today?', in Helle Porsdam (ed.), *Copyright and Other Fairy Tales: Hans Christian Andersen and the Commodification of Creativity* (Cheltenham, UK and Northampton, MA, USA: Edward Elgar, 2006), 85.

copyright law: the alienability of the copyright interest and the vertical expansion of commercial distribution rights which increases the copyright holder's control over imports and rental rights. This commodification, as we shall see later, is especially noticeable in the area of film and the media and entertainment sector. As for the former, this concerns the law's concept of the meaning of property as a divestible or alienable right. The author normally does not hold this right for very long – the name of the game is to find a publisher who can exploit the work and make it profitable in the market. Most authors do not have the financial means to publish their work themselves; they need a publisher who is willing to run the risk of putting up the capital needed – on condition that the author signs over the copyright, or a part of it, to the publisher.[41]

What more than anything made the commodification of copyright visible, according to Macmillan, was the World Trade Organization's Agreement on Trade Related Aspects of Intellectual Property Rights (the TRIPs Agreement), negotiated in the 1986–1994 Uruguay Round, which introduced intellectual property rules into the multilateral trading system for the first time. TRIPs is arguably 'the central normative force in global copyright law' today, and it has led to changes in intellectual property discourses which consolidate the instrumental or trade-related approach.[42] It was the US that was the prime mover behind the negotiation and conclusion of TRIPs, and in support of the US government was a large and powerful coalition of US-based multinational corporate interests. 'The truth is', Macmillan writes, 'that, at least in the Anglo-Saxon model of copyright law, we had already gone a long way down the instrumental and trade-related road before the US did us the favour of bringing it all out into the open'.[43]

The move toward commodification and trade-related instrumentalism thus seems to be rooted in the Anglo-American view of copyright as a piece of property which can be bought and sold at will. As some scholars see it, the continental European *droit d'auteur* or authors' rights paradigm might help move copyright in a more non-instrumental direction. We shall look at, first, some European and, then, some American attempts to curb commodification by means of promoting the use of a human rights approach in the next section, but before we do so I want to draw attention, as promised, to what Anne M. Cronin has called 'a key innovation' in recent European politics – namely, 'the centrality of discourses of consumerism and consumer rights'. What seems to be happening is that European citizenship is increasingly connected by

---

41 Ibid., 86.
42 Ibid.
43 Ibid.

European institutions to the right to consume, and that cultural freedom is 'reframed as free access to citizenship rights as consumer rights'.[44]

Cronin argues that we may now in fact talk about a new European 'consumer citizen' whose most important human right seems to be the right to consume. This right is constructed by means of a cultural rights discourse – the relevant rights including the right to self-expression, the right to an identity and the right to have this identity recognized by others as well as by the state. In the Council of Europe final synthesis report, by Kevin Robins, of the Council of Europe project on Cultural Policy and Cultural Diversity, carried out between 2000 and 2004, *The Challenge of Transcultural Diversities,* as we saw above, the right to consumption figures on the list of important cultural rights to promote in the future. In this as well as in the earlier Council of Europe report on which it builds, *In from the margins*, the importance of active participation in and access to cultural life is stressed.

It is against this background that we must see what Anne Cronin calls 'the emergence of new consumer discourses that draw on liberal notions of self-expressive identity politics'.[45] By articulating citizens' participation in community life and citizens' rights as consumer participation and consumer rights, these reports aim at flattening differences – cultural differences (high-brow and state-subsidized versus lowbrow and more market-oriented), but also those of a social and/or ethnic kind. As consumers we are all equal before God, as it were, and as consumer-citizens we share the same rights of access to culture and cultural legitimacy.

Throughout *In from the margins*, consumer participation as cultural activity is portrayed as something active – 'a creative act in itself' – and as something that has 'a "political" dimension' and is 'an instrument of active citizenship'.[46] In the end, as Cronin points out, 'the report calls not for a redistribution of wealth through welfare provisions or other means, but rather a redistribution of cultural legitimacy through consumerism'.[47] The same argument could be made for the later report, I think, and the reason why I bring up Cronin and her argument about the European 'consumer citizen' in this context

---

44 Anne M. Cronin, 'Consumer Rights/Cultural Rights: A New Politics of European Belonging', 5(3) *European Journal of Cultural Studies* (2002), 308, 310. This and the next four paragraphs on Cronin and her work are taken from my article, 'On European Narratives of Human Rights and their Possible Implications for Copyright', in Fiona Macmillan (ed.), *New Directions in Copyright Law, Volume 6* (Cheltenham, UK and Northampton, MA, USA: Edward Elgar, 2007), 335–359.

45 Cronin, supra n. 44, 316.

46 The European Task Force on Culture and Development, *In from the margins: A contribution to the debate on Culture and Development in Europe* (Strasbourg: Council of Europe, 1997), 267, 50.

47 Cronin, supra n. 44, 320–321.

is that, in terms of furthering this redistribution of cultural legitimacy through consumerism, copyright Anglo-American-style provides a better instrument than does an author's rights paradigm. As Jane M. Gaines points out in *Contested Culture*:

> if the individual author produces property in the work in the Lockean sense, then every act of production is an act of origination, every work is an original work, regardless of whether it is aesthetically unoriginal, banal, or, in some cases, imitative. Every individual person is also a potential 'author' whose 'writing' will be as 'original' as those of a renowned or acclaimed literary figure.

Anglo-American copyrights's minimal point of origin requirement (greater willingness to grant copyright protection to products which may not be all that creative) thus performs a critique of authorial creativity – or, if we want to put it in cultural terms – of highbrow notions of the unique. 'Copyright law', Gaines concludes, 'is a great cultural leveler'.[48] In terms of active access to knowledge and culture, generally speaking, the Anglo-American copyright paradigm works better, in that it does not have all the connotations of originality and exceptionality (associated with the work of the true genius) that the continental author's rights paradigm has.[49] In cultural terms, it is far more lowbrow than its European cousin. 'In the eyes of the law', as Andreas Rahmatian puts it, 'it is irrelevant whether this "author" is a self-styled author-genius who should make way for the reader, and whether in literary criticism and art a concept of the "Romantic author" is rightly or wrongly maintained'.[50]

And precisely because cultural levelling or democratization is at stake, it can be very difficult to argue for the importance of supporting a cultural production which is not oriented toward exclusively commercial ends – for the need, say, to subsidize those cultural products that are not popular enough to hold their own in the market place. 'Indeed', as Pierre Bourdieu argues:

---

48 Jane M. Gaines, *Contested Culture: The Image, the Voice, and the Law* (London: The British Film Institute, 1992), 63–64.

49 It should be noted that Justice O'Connnor specifically mentioned originality as being 'the *sine qua non* of copyright' in *Feist Publications, Inc. v. Rural Telephone Service* (499 U.S. 340, 111 S. Ct. 1282, 113 L. Ed. 2d 358, 1991). 'To be sure', she then continued, 'the requisite level of creativity is extremely low; even a slight amount will suffice. The vast majority of works make the grade quite easily, as they possess some creative spark, "no matter how crude, humble or obvious" it might be' – quoted in Robert A. Gorman and Jane C. Ginsburg (eds.), *Copyright for the Nineties: Cases and Materials* (Charlottesville, VA: The Michie Company, 1993, 4th edition), 112–113.

50 Andreas Rahmatian, 'Universalist Norms for a Globalised Diversity: On the Protection of Traditional Cultural Expressions', in Macmillan (ed.), supra n. 44, 219.

> one of the difficulties of the battle that must be fought on this front is that it may assume antidemocratic appearances insofar as the mass productions of the culture industry do in a sense have the backing of the general public, and particularly of young people the world over, both because they are more accessible (the consumption of these products requires less cultural capital) and because they are the object of a kind of inverted snobbery. Indeed, it is the first time in history that the cheapest products of a popular culture (of a society which is economically and politically dominant) are imposing themselves as chic.[51]

We are back, it would seem, to some of those issues we looked at in Chapter 2 in connection with our discussion of European culture and in Chapter 3 in connection with transatlantic dialogues, past and present – issues which may roughly be summarized as highbrow culture (often European and often being in need of subsidy) versus popular culture (often American and often being commercially successful). When it comes to that old debate concerning the Americanization of European culture, for example, Professor Winfried Fluck suggested, as we saw, that the most important thing to consider today is whether European countries, in this case Germany, are taking over American models of financing culture:

> The major issue at stake in the relationship of, and comparison between, American and German culture today is the question of how, or on what principles, culture should be organized and financed. In the US, the organizing principle is mainly commercial . . . In Germany, on the other hand, there still exists a public consensus that such cultural forms should be supported by direct or indirect forms of taxation . . .[52]

In discussions concerning the future of copyright and intellectual property law in general, these issues form an (often unacknowledged) subtext.

WHERE DO WE GO FROM HERE?

'The information age is not about technology', Mike Holderness wrote for an international gathering of freelance journalists in 1995, 'it is about information – about content'. And when it comes to the differences between Anglo-American copyright and continental European authors' rights, he continues:

---

[51] Pierre Bourdieu, *Firing Back: Against the Tyranny of the Market* (New York and London: The New Press, 2003 Vol. 2, 70–71.

[52] Winfried Fluck, 'The Americanization of German Culture? The Strange, Paradoxical Ways of Modernity', in Agnes C. Mueller (ed.), *German Pop Culture: How 'American' Is It?* (Ann Arbor, MI: University of Michigan Press, 2004), 30–31.

> in brief, US and UK laws define 'copyright' as a 'property right'. Mainland European law, in general, defines authors' rights as human rights. The key difference, as we see it, is that a property right is by definition something which can be 'freely traded'. In this context, 'free trade' means that the transfer of rights is governed only by economic power.
>
> US and UK law then define moral rights – essentially a poor translation of the French '*droit moral*' subdivision of '*droit d'auteur*'. These are a source of confusion to many UK creators, and of total bafflement to most in the US. This is hardly surprising. 'Moral rights' represent a grudging and heavily-qualified recognition of an entirely different legal philosophy to 'copyright'.
>
> Authors' rights are, in the jargon, 'inalienable'. As the lawyer Alistair Kelman puts it, 'you can no more sell your author's rights in what you create than you can (legally) sell your soul'. You can, however, rent it for fair reward. This is what employment and work under contract are about – as contrasted with slavery, or being a feudal serf or peon![53]

Several copyright scholars have warned against exaggerating the differences between European *droit d'auteur* and Anglo-American copyright.[54] In light of the fact that copyright scholars promoting the use of a human rights approach explicitly refer to the need to check what they see as certain bad influences from the Anglo-American property paradigm of copyright, however, I will use the traditional division in the following pages.

Several possible solutions to the problems posed by the commodification of copyright have been advanced. These range between the suggestion, made by

---

53 Mike Holderness, 'Copyright and Authors' Rights' – available at http://media.gn.apc.org/c-rights.html#proper (last visited on 13 January 2009). 'Moral rights' are generally associated with civil law jurisdictions. Even though they also concern the rights of creators of copyright works, they are different from the economic rights associated with copyrights. They include the right of attribution, the right to have a work published anonymously or pseudonymously as well as the right to the integrity of the work. The preserving of the integrity of the work prevents the work from being altered, distorted or mutilated. The idea is that even if an artist has assigned his or her rights to a work to a third party, he or she may still maintain the moral rights to the work.

54 See e.g. Jane C. Ginsburg, 'A Tale of Two Copyrights: Literary Property in Revolutionary France and America', in Brad Sherman and Alain Strowel (eds.), *Of Authors and Origins: Essays on Copyright* (Oxford: Clarendon Press, 1994), 131–158. In *Værkslæren i ophavsretten* (The Concept of 'Work' in Copyright Law) (Copenhagen: Jurist- og Økonomforbundets Forlag, 2001), Danish copyright scholar Morten Rosenmeier warns that when it comes to the originality requirement in Continental European and Anglo-American copyright law, it is difficult to talk about anything else other than tendencies. In practice, today the two systems are growing more and more alike, and this means that scholars should be careful not to come up with too many abstract arguments.

Dutch scholars Marieke van Schijndel and Joost Smiers, that we give up on copyright altogether and the suggestion that we keep expanding existing copyright regimes. Van Schijndel and Smiers propose a model of their own, the usufruct model, which they see as a civil law alternative to the Anglo-American notion of copyright as property: '[c]haracteristic of usufruct is that one does not have the ownership of an item; however, one is entitled to the usage of the fruits of the item . . . What we envision is that the creative work . . . exists only in the public domain, its ownership is shared amongst all, and thus belongs to the commons. Whoever enjoys the temporary usufruct of a certain artistic work has thus received it from the public domain'.[55]

As far as P. Bernt Hugenholtz and Christophe Geiger (who are Dutch and French-German, respectively) are concerned, one way of holding at bay Anglo-American property paradigms is to use a human rights framework. They are especially interested in freedom of speech and access to information, as these are mentioned in international human rights documents such as the Universal Declaration of Human Rights, the International Covenant on Economic, Social and Cultural Rights and the European Convention on Human Rights. We have already looked at Article 27 of the Universal Declaration and Article 15 of the Economic Covenant, and as for the European Convention, it promises, in Article 10, the right to freedom of expression, to hold opinions and to receive and impart information and ideas. An emphasis on human rights makes the protection of human dignity and the general common good central. And 'the reason why fundamental rights and human rights are an ideal basis from which to start is that they offer a synthesis of the bases of natural law and utilitarianism and represent the values from which intellectual property developed'.[56]

Writing, from a somewhat different perspective and in a different context, about the problems with trying to protect traditional cultural expressions by means of copyright, Andreas Rahmatian, an Austrian scholar currently based in England, reaches the conclusion that:

> The effect, perhaps ultimate motive, of a legal protection regime of traditional cultural expressions is the exercise of power in a neo-classical fashion that

---

[55] Marieke van Schijndel and Joost Smiers, 'Imagining a World without Copyright: the Market and Temporary Protection, a Better Alternative for Artists and the Public Domain', in Porsdam (ed.), supra n. 40, 156–157.

[56] Christophe Geiger, '"Constitutionalising" Intellectual Property Law? The Influence of Fundamental Rights on Intellectual Property in the European Union', 37 *International Review of Intellectual Property and Competition Law* (2006), 382. As for P. Bernt Hugenholtz, please see his 'Copyright and Freedom of Expression in Europe', available at www.ivir.nl/publications/hugenholtz/PBH-Engelberg.doc (last visited on 15 January 2009).

> preserves difference and potentially segregation between cultures in the form of a new kind of indirect rule . . . As far as the broader and vaguer protection of 'culture' is concerned, commercial and intellectual property laws are unsuitable measures altogether. The only appropriate framework would be that of constitutional law, and within that, of human rights, where the individual who perceives himself/herself as part of a certain cultural group can claim rights, and the interests of his/her community become crystallized and reflected in that individual and any other individual who perceives himself/herself part of that community.[57]

Then, Kim Treiger-Bar-Am, an American who recently did her Ph.D. at Oxford University, points to a strengthening of fair use/fair dealing defences as a way forward in the Anglo-American context. Treiger-Bar-Am is more optimistic when it comes to the interpretation by judges of copyright limitations than is Fiona Macmillan, as we saw above, and points to the expansion of fair use and to the interpretation of it as a First Amendment right as something which might turn out to be a hopeful new trend. 'Authors' rights arise from freedom of expression', she writes in a recent article, and 'while copyright and the freedom of expression often conflict, they also have close parallels'.[58] She argues that there already is an authors' rights tradition in place in the US and the UK, and proposes that both so-called primary or original creators and so-called secondary or re-mixing creators together be called 'authors' and protected as such. 'Once authors' rights are seen as a fundamental right of expression, and as present in the free speech principle and doctrine, the protection they offer will be strengthened.' Such a 'strengthening' of authors' rights may then aid 'authors in conflicts against copyright owners', just as 'the fair dealing exceptions under UK law and the fair use defence under both UK and US law' may 'be strengthened by bringing forward the conception of authors' rights'.[59]

Finally, Madhavi Sunder, in a highly interesting article on 'IP3', attempts to 'lay the foundation for a cultural analysis of intellectual property'.[60] The

---

57 Rahmatian, 'Universalist norms for a globalised diversity: on the protection of traditional cultural expressions', in Macmillan (ed.), supra n. 44, 229–230. Rahmatian is being critical, in this piece, of the sort of arguments made by Madhavi Sunder, outlined below. 'Traditional cultural expressions' (TCEs) include music, art, designs, names, signs and symbols, performances, architectural forms, handicrafts and narratives. Embodying local know-how and skills and transmitting core values and beliefs, they are viewed as being very important to the cultural and social identities of indigenous and regional communities. Their protection is often related to the promotion of creativity, enhanced cultural diversity and the preservation of cultural heritage.

58 Leslie Kim Treiger-Bar-Am, 'Authors' Rights as a Limit to Copyright Control', in Macmillan (ed.), supra n. 44, 359.

59 Ibid., 359, 361, 367.

60 Madhavi Sunder, 'IP3', 59 *Stanford Law Review* (2006), 258.

title is a metonym which refers to the rise toward the end of the 20th century of identity politics, the Internet Protocol and intellectual property rights, and Sunder suggests that 'the convergence of these "IPs" begins to explain the growth of intellectual property rights where traditional justifications for intellectual property do not. **IP3** reveals intellectual property's social effects and this law as a tool for crafting cultural relations'.[61]

With Sunder we move beyond a more or less strictly transatlantic dialogue to a transnational one. She does not see cultural rights as second-, but as third-generation rights which focus on communal development and distributive justice and link social justice to the attainment of greater cultural and social power. Identity politics are converging with intellectual property movements; new claims for intellectual property are voiced in terms of identity politics, cultural survival and human rights, and 'these new claims for intellectual property understand rights not just in the familiar terms of incentives-for-creation, but also as tools for both recognition and redistribution'.[62] The Internet and new digital technologies, or what Sunder calls the 'Internet Protocol', have made it possible for people all over the world not just passively to enjoy culture, but also actively to participate in making it themselves. In fact, what we are currently seeing, according to Sunder, is a New Enlightenment in which the levers of making cultural meaning are being disseminated much more widely than before: '[t]he New Enlightenment recognizes that liberty demands autonomy within culture, and simultaneously understands that equality requires the capability to participate equally in the social and economic processes of cultural creation. The freedom and equality battles of this new century will not only be about access to physical space, but also to discursive space'.[63]

The traditional intellectual-property-as-incentives approach does not take into account all the many different values that are involved in global cultural and intellectual production today. With her cultural approach, Sunder hopes to

---

61 Ibid.

62 Ibid., 273. When Sunder refers, here, to 'the familiar terms of incentives-for-creation' – and later also to 'the traditional intellectual-property-as-incentives approach' – she is thinking of the traditional theory of copyright according to which there would be insufficient incentives to invent, create and build commercial goodwill without intellectual property law. 'The Anglo-US copyright model is often framed as being about creating incentives for creative production', writes Kim Treiger-Bar-Am. 'The idea is that where creators and producers have the incentive of financial reward, they will continue to produce. The creation and communication of works will increase. Given such incentives to disseminate works, authors and media entrepreneurs are thought to be more likely to maximize the information available to society' (Treiger-Bar-Am, supra n. 58, 360).

63 Ibid., 320–321.

remedy this. It is interesting, however, that she does not wish to trash the traditional economic framework – 'in articulating a cultural approach I do not seek to displace the economic utilitarian analysis of intellectual property but rather to complement it'.[64] In fact, her way of complementing the utilitarian analysis is to look toward the so-called social relations approach to property. 'Despite laypersons' conceptions of property law as individualistic, economic, and absolute, in fact, real property law is today one of the most venerable, robust, and important mechanisms we have for organizing complex social life', she argues.[65]

Property rights have social effects – property law today is 'a rich and complex body of law, from nuisance law to antidiscrimination law to landlord/tenant law, which limits property rights to protect property interests (for example, the right to quiet enjoyment), personal interests in health and dignity, and the public interest (such as a clean environment)'.[66] Property law furthermore distributes rights in shared resources and recognizes unequal power relations, just as property rights balance incommensurable values, mediate relations between the individual and community and in general structure social relations. All in all, therefore, Sunder maintains:

> We need similar visions for intellectual property. Social movements have turned our attention to the cultural and material effects of intellectual property law. Theorists have alerted us to the potential benefits and dangers of the new technological architectures for facilitating personal and community flourishing. The conclusions are clear: improved social relations, measured by every individual's maximization of numerous moral values, from freedom to equality to health and efficiency, are not inevitable; they require the attention and active promotion of law. We must attentively design the legal and communications architecture in accordance with the kinds of social relations we want.[67]

In Chapter 5 we saw Daniel Whelan argue that today, if we wish to communicate with the most ardent critics of second-generation economic and social rights, we need to use a discourse that they understand and of which they approve – a market language or property discourse. For Sunder, it would seem, this argument is equally relevant when it comes to third-generation cultural rights. Both Whelan and Sunder are writing out of and against the background of an American context. It may not be quite so easy to persuade their European colleagues[68] – even though it is quite clear that most of the copyright scholars

64 Ibid., 322.
65 Ibid., 316.
66 Ibid., 317.
67 Ibid., 317–319.
68 See Pierre Bourdieu and his eloquent diatribe against neoliberalism in Bourdieu, supra n. 51, for example.

whose work we have looked at in this chapter prefer to stay within a property rights discourse. As the name implies, intellectual property rights have their origin in a property discourse, and even when European scholars look towards a human rights approach for ammunition against the worst effects of copyright overprotection, they do so not in order to discard but somehow to incorporate property rights. Christophe Geiger put it well, as we saw above: '[t]he reason why fundamental rights and human rights are an ideal basis from which to start is that they offer a synthesis of the bases of natural law and utilitarianism and represent the values from which intellectual property developed.'

It is worth recalling that the right to property is in fact itself a human right. Article 17 of the Universal Declaration states that:

> 1) Everyone has the right to own property alone as well as in association with others.
> 2) No one shall be arbitrarily deprived of his property.

In the European Convention, moreover, the clearest guarantee is in the first paragraph of Article 1 of the First Protocol:

> Every natural or legal person is entitled to the peaceful enjoyment of his possessions. No one shall be deprived of his possessions except in the public interest and subject to the conditions provided for by law and by the general principles of international law.

The famous British lawyer William Blackstone, whose work was to become extremely important in the American context, saw the right to property as 'that sole and despotic dominion which one man claims and exercises over the external things of the world, in total exclusion of the right of any other individual in the universe'. And he continued, 'one of the absolute rights inherent in every Englishman, is that of property, which consists in the free use, enjoyment, and disposal of all his acquisitions, without any control or diminution, save only by the laws of the land'.[69] The link between freedom and property has always been there, in other words – not least in connection with copyright and intellectual property in general: '[w]hile liberalism marks the birth of intellectual property . . ., it also establishes the freedom of commerce and industry, and its corollary the freedom of enterprise and the freedom of expression, tying the knot between property and liberty'.[70]

69 William Blackstone, quoted in Ali Riza Coban, *Protection of Property Rights Within the European Convention on Human Rights* (Aldershot and Burlington, VT: Ashgate Publishing, 2004), 14.

70 M. Vivant, quoted in Geiger, supra n. 35, 707.

A cautious conclusion to this chapter may therefore be that if somehow the discourse of property could be infused or enriched by a cultural discourse and a human rights discourse, sensitive to current claims of access to culture and of culture as empowerment, then maybe we have found a discourse that may be used in the attempt to improve transatlantic dialogues – and perhaps even beyond transatlantic dialogues also transnational dialogues. We need, as Lynn Hunt might phrase it, economic, social and cultural rights to become 'self-evident' – whatever that takes.

CONCLUDING REMARKS: CENSORSHIP BY MONEY[71]

American films account for no less than 70 per cent of the European television market. As regards the European cinema market, the situation is much the same; the figure may vary somewhat according to the latest box office hits, but the US again seems to account for around 70 per cent of the European market. By comparison, the market share accounted for by European films in the US is as low as 4 per cent. In the year 2000, Europe's balance of trade deficit with the US for audiovisual products was estimated at no less than 8.2 billion dollars![72]

How did the situation get to be like this? One important part of the answer has to do with copyright and the realities of cultural creativity. According to the US Constitution, the purpose of copyright is to provide an economic incentive for creative activity. One of the basic principles here is that copyright should belong to the party who bears the economic risk rather than to the creators of the work in question (the principle of property as a divestible or alienable right). Many Europeans see this differently. The European focus has traditionally been on the rights of the author or creator (moral rights or performers' rights). As some see it, this may well be changing, however. According to Reto M. Hilty, for example, with the EU Directive of 22 May 2001 on the harmonization of certain aspects of copyright and related rights in the information society,[73] European Member States have been committed to

---

[71] This is a phrase I have taken from Bourdieu, supra n. 51, 70.

[72] Reto M. Hilty, 'Copyright in a Digital Dilemma', *Max Planck Research, Science Magazine of the Max Planck Society*, Issue 3 (2003), 52. The following pages are taken from my article, 'From *Pax Americana* to *Lex Americana*: American Legal and Cultural Hegemony', in Fiona Macmillan (ed.), *New Directions in Copyright Law, Volume 1* (Cheltenham, UK and Northampton, MA, USA: Edward Elgar, 2005), 103–106.

[73] Directive 2001/29/EC of the European Parliament and of the Council of 22 May 2001 on the harmonisation of certain aspects of copyright and related rights in the information society.

implementing regulations that are not unlike those implemented in the US as a result of the 1998 Digital Millennium Copyright Act, which forms part of the amended US Copyright Act of 1976.

At issue here is the legal status given to technical means of protection and, as Hilty sees it, the problem is that decisions on granting access and enjoyment to third parties are being passed on to the investors in the cultural industry. Public coordination of the conflicting interests involved in copyright is losing ground to the more or less private order of the exploitation industry. The 'winners' in this whole process are the American entertainment industry and the American economy – and the 'loser' is the European consumer:

> The reality in the USA is equally real in Europe. The establishment of additional rights of exploitation is of little help to the creators of the works exploited, for whose benefit they are not really intended. The latest rights to be introduced – above all the legal enshrinement of technical measures – scarcely improve the creator's position, despite the innocence with which the object of the EU Directive [of 22 May 2001] is formulated . . . Rather, it is the case that these new rights are tools in the hands of the entertainment industry. And it is the – above all American – entertainment industry that primarily stands to profit in real terms.[74]

What we are witnessing, in other words, is a build-up of private power over cultural output. Fiona Macmillan describes what she calls 'copyright's commodification of culture'[75] in this way: '[t]he way in which the distribution rights attaching to copyright might be used by a multinational corporation to carve up the international market, is a small part of a much bigger story about the way in which commodification can lead to global domination of a market for cultural output'.[76] It is precisely this 'bigger story' about 'global domination of a market for cultural output' that interests me as a cultural historian. As Macmillan, Hilty, Geiger and others have shown, copyright has been one of the most essential tools in the orchestration of this global – and essentially American – domination.

It was in the 1970s, says Macmillan, that we saw the first horizontal and vertical mergers and acquisitions in the media and entertainment sector. One driving force behind these mergers was 'the desire to increase the level of corporate ownership over copyright interests'.[77] By reorganizing in such a way that their activities would now involve the integration of diversified lines of business such as the production and distribution of film and television, the

---

74 Hilty, supra n. 72, 52.

75 Fiona Macmillan, 'The Cruel ©: Copyright and Film', 24 *European Intellectual Property Review* (2002), 483.

76 Ibid., 485.

77 Ibid.

ownership of cinema chains and cable networks (both at home in the US and abroad) and the publication of books and music, media and entertainment corporations like Time Warner and Walt Disney became the owners of a substantial number of the world's copyright interests in cultural output – most importantly in this context, films.[78] The development continued throughout the 1980s and 1990s. At this later stage, corporations developed an interest in the production of the very content of this cultural output as well; owning the rights to the technology involved in the distribution of films and other cultural output was no longer enough.

Throughout this whole drive towards global domination of the market for cultural output, multinational conglomerates – and again, in this context especially the major US film studios – have been very adept at using copyright to further their own interests. In the area of film, unfortunately, copyright has helped further a kind of 'cultural homogenisation' – 'the more powerful the copyright owner the more dominant the cultural image, but the more likely that the copyright owner will seek to protect the cultural power of the image through copyright enforcement'.[79] The sad result is that 'cultural development is frozen not stimulated'.[80] Forget about diversity and alternative art, in other words – whether we are in Europe, the US, or Asia, we will be watching the same (American) blockbuster films and admiring the same (American) film stars.

It is this situation that Danish film maker Lars von Trier along with other European colleagues has been reacting against, as we shall see in Chapter 9.

---

78 Cf. also Bourdieu: '[t]he key point, however, is that commercial concerns, the pursuit of maximum short-term profit and the "aesthetic" that derives from that pursuit, are being ever more intensely and widely imposed on cultural production. The consequences of such a policy are exactly the same in the field of publishing, where high concentration of ownership is also found: in the United States at least, apart from two independent publishers, W.W. Norton and Houghton Mifflin, a few university presses that are themselves increasingly subjected to commercial constraints, and a handful of combative small publishers, the book trade is in the hands of eight giant media corporation. The great majority of publisher must assume an unequivocally commercial orientation and this has led, among other things, to an invasion of their lists by media stars and to censorship by money': supra n. 51, 69–70.

79 MacMillan, supra n. 73.

80 Ibid., 491.

8. Transatlantic dialogues on 'law and literature': from 'law and literature' to 'law and humanities'

'It's culture, stupid', to paraphrase a famous sentence by President Bill Clinton – or rather, it's law and culture. In this legalized day and age where we use a legal discourse to discuss major problems and where we present social, cultural and political claims in terms of rights, it could hardly be otherwise. In academic circles, since the late 1970s and early 1980s, we have seen this reflected in the 'law and literature' movement. Originally an American phenomenon – American culture and history being more thoroughly legalized than those of any other country – law and literature has gradually spread to European academic circles too. In this chapter, I shall argue that it makes sense to expand 'law and literature' into 'law and humanities'. This argument has been implicit in all the previous seven chapters; in fact, my theoretical and methodological approach throughout this book has been that of law and humanities. In this chapter, I want to reflect more openly on law and humanities as an academic field.

The most 'fundamental connection between law and literature', writes Kieran Dolin (2007), is that 'law is inevitably a matter of language. The law can only be articulated in words'.[1] This is no doubt one of the reasons why the law and literature movement from the very start has been focused on key fictional texts. In addition, the movement was started by lawyers and law professors who thought that law students (and lawyers in general) might benefit from reading great works of literature. For many 20th-century lawyers, the attempt to relate key legal writings to the canon of literature has been the most obvious way of connecting law and literature. Yet, as Dolin points out, this attempt 'depends on a particular understanding of literature, derived from a classical liberal education'[2] – an understanding which has over the last fifteen years or so come to be seriously questioned. To maintain simply that the study of literature can bring into the lives of lawyers beauty and empathy for the

[1] Kieran Dolin, *A Critical Introduction to Law and Literature* (Cambridge and New York: Cambridge University Press, 2007), 2.

[2] Ibid., 25.

situation of other people is to ask too little of law and literature, critics have maintained.

Canons of great writing, legal as well as literary, being 'critical constructs which serve the cultural interests of their proponents', literature should be valued, not for its capacity to preserve a particular cultural tradition, but rather for its capacity to challenge the status quo as it is expressed in and through law and for letting alternative voices be heard. At its best, the dialogue between law and literature may thereby reopen what seem like settled questions in the public domain and 'ethics and aesthetics become active partners with politics in creating the normative basis for a just society'.[3]

It is this move from what critics have called 'law in literature' to 'law as literature' and beyond that makes it possible to deal with texts or media other than the purely literary ones. In the European context, scholars pursuing law and literature have typically had a comparative literature or other literary (say, English) or linguistic background. For a variety of reasons, lawyers have been less interested in joining the ranks of those of us coming from the humanities. This is slowly changing, but it has meant that in the European context, as in the American, literary texts have been the focus of attention. As a cultural historian, I think the time has now come to use the move from 'law in literature' to 'law as literature' and beyond to allow law and humanities scholars also to engage with history, arts, philosophy, religion, popular culture, film, television, and music, for example. It is not only in literary works of fiction that law and order are constitutive of the dramatic action; non-literary works are also full of 'eternal' legal themes such as good, evil, duty, justice, criminality, punishment, and revenge. From the Internet to films, television and even journals – in our information or knowledge society, important negotiations concerning societal values are taking place in a variety of public spaces. And precisely because so many of these important discussions are carried out in a legalistic, rights-talk vernacular, scholars working within the field of law and humanities might actually be able to help explain to the general public, as well as to their fellow academics, what the underlying and really significant issues are.

My law and humanities case study, as it were, will be Danish film maker Lars von Trier and his so-called 'America trilogy'. Trier's work was mentioned briefly in Chapter 3 in connection with transatlantic dialogues, past and present. In the next and final chapter, the discussion of Trier's way of being anti-American in an all- or semi-American way will be continued and it will be argued that Trier touches, in his previous trilogies as well as in his current work, upon many of the 'big' themes that are of relevance in a law and humanities context.

3 Ibid., 27, 211.

Law and Literature: a Historical Overview

In *A Critical Introduction to Law and Literature*, Kieran Dolin includes a ten-page description of the field of copyright. 'Copyright is', he correctly explains, 'one of the clearest instances of the interrelation of legal and literary ideas, of literary concepts feeding into legal doctrine, and legal categories then shaping cultural practice. Not surprisingly, it is one of the focal points of Law and Literature studies.'[4] The pages on copyright occur in a chapter entitled 'Literature under law', the contents of which cover the ways in which law has regulated and controlled literature. 'The range of forbidden topics has varied according to the dominant ideologies of each society', he tells us, 'but religion, sexuality and political authority have traditionally been sensitive areas. Legal doctrines concerning blasphemy, obscenity and sedition have developed accordingly.'[5]

Dolin takes us through various instances in which writers and their texts have gone beyond what was perceived to be a socially accepted expression and have had to suffer, as a consequence, the force of the law. The criminalizing of indecent performances, the common-law term for which is 'libel' (obscene libel, blasphemous libel and seditious libel), makes for interesting and often amusing stories, but we should not forget, says Dolin, that 'a dialectical relationship has . . . existed between literary expression and social authority. Many texts now canonized as literature were written within and against legal restrictions . . .'[6] He sees 'law's assumption of its right to regulate literature' as one of two fundamental relations between the two fields of law and literature. The second fundamental relation is 'literature's insistence that law is inescapably a matter of language'[7] – an insistence which has led scholars to focus, at different times and for different reasons, on areas such as rhetoric and law, linguistic studies of law, and narrative jurisprudence.

A short historical overview may be in order.[8] 'Much of contemporary legal scholarship', wrote R. Richard Banks in 1997, 'expresses a narrative impulse. Eschewing the traditional norms and forms of legal scholarship, many professors have turned to storytelling to capture issues not easily elucidated through more conventional approaches.'[9] The narrative approach that Banks was talking

---

4 Ibid., 62–63.

5 Ibid., 43.

6 Ibid., 44.

7 Ibid., 15.

8 I will be drawing in what follows on my introduction to *Folkways and Law Ways: Law in American Studies*, which I edited for Odense University Press in 2001.

9 R. Richard Banks, 'The Political Economy of Racial Discourse', 9 *Yale Journal of Law and the Humanities* (1997), 217.

about had been gaining prominence through the writings of Critical Legal Feminist and Critical Race Theory (CRT) scholars who had produced a significant amount of 'different', non-traditional and often very personal writing about gender, race and law. This writing, which included personal essays, memoirs and full autobiographies, was often written for a broader audience than that of traditional legal scholarship. In Chapter 2, we looked at Patricia Williams' *The Alchemy of Race and Rights* of 1991 – a text which was later to be considered one of the founding CRT texts.

In using storytelling as a way of alerting lawyers and non-lawyers alike to the fact that, as Robin West put it, 'laws have a profound impact upon the subjectivity of people, children, slaves, women, and other living things who either might or might not participate in their textural production, interpretation, or critique', CRT scholars built on and further developed concerns which had been present in the law and literature movement from its tentative beginnings in the late 1970s.[10] A project defined somewhat modestly, in a 1996 article by Bruce L. Rockwood, as 'a process of reading and comparing literary and legal texts for the insight each provides into the other, and whose combined force illuminates our understanding of ourselves and our society', the law and literature movement originally consisted of two somewhat different enterprises or concerns: 'law-in-literature' and 'law-as-literature'. This distinction was introduced by Robert Weisberg in an influential and much-quoted article, which was published in the very first issue of the new *Yale Journal of Law and the Humanities* in 1988. As Weisberg himself pointed out, the distinction was most useful in terms of sorting out existing scholarship in the field. In practice, 'the best works on the two sides of the line tend to converge, because they constitute the work that captures the best insights about the relationship between the aesthetic and the political-ethical visions and forces in society'.[11]

Law-in-literature scholars pursued the detailed study of specific authors and texts for the light these might shed on legal issues and their impact on our lives. Underlying – and partly shaping – such study were two basic assumptions: first, that law and legal thinking have always been or are increasingly becoming too rigid, technical and abstract, and, second, that precisely because the law is a generalizing and abstracting mechanism, it may at times be necessary to supplement its professionally detached and rational voice with a more human and passionate one. This is where literature came in. In *Law and Literature: A Misunderstood Relation* (1988), Richard Posner, a one-time law

---

10 Robin West, 'Communities, Texts, and Law: Reflections on the Law and Literature Movement', 1 *Yale Journal of Law and the Humanities* (1988), 155.

11 Robert Weisberg, 'The Law-Literature Enterprise', 1 *Yale Journal of Law and the Humanities* (1988), 5.

professor turned judge and a key player in the law-in-literature debate, cited a number of important connections between law and literature: the issue of interpretation is central to both; legal texts resemble literary texts in being highly rhetorical; literature is subject to legal regulation under such rubrics as defamation, obscenity and copyright; and judicial opinions often employ literary devices. Finally, the legal process has a significant theatrical dimension to it, which is attractive to writers of literature.[12]

What chiefly interested Posner was what lawyers may learn from literature and literary theory. Expressing a 'warm though qualified enthusiasm for the field of law and literature', he pointed to the way in which literary works can teach lawyers empathy and give them insights into the concerns and problems of other people.[13] In a legalized society such as the American where people trained in law occupy powerful positions, the educational patterns of the country's law school become important way beyond the legal community itself. When it came to some of the larger and more ambitious claims made on behalf of law and literature by post-structuralist critics, though, Posner's attitude was less positive. Here, other participants in the law in literature enterprise saw greater potential in the new, interdisciplinary field.

James Boyd White, Richard Weisberg and Robert Weisberg did not limit their interest to literary texts and literary theory that might clarify the place of law in society, but were willing to confront some of the more (politically) controversial consequences of bringing together two different fields of inquiry. In his 1995 survey, *Law and Literature: Possibilities and Perspectives*, Ian Ward sees James Boyd White as a kind of transitional figure, whose interests spanned both parts of the law-literature enterprise.[14] As for the law-as-literature part of this enterprise, which is the more elusive and hard-to-define part, Ward suggests that its essence is 'the suggestion that the techniques and methods of literary theory and analysis are appropriate to legal scholarship'.[15] The belief in the usefulness of literary scholarship to legal scholarship has led law-as-literature scholars to pursue different areas of inquiry – chief among these hermeneutics and rhetoric. As some scholars have seen it, questions relating to the interpretation of legal texts are the most pressing; for others, a focus on how legal arguments attempt to persuade is more relevant. Among the former may be mentioned Stanley Fish and Ronald Dworkin who, in their work, have stressed that legal practice is legal interpretation and that legal scholars and

---

[12] Richard A. Posner, *Law and Literature: A Misunderstood Relation* (Cambridge, MA: Harvard University Press, 1988), 8–9.

[13] Ibid., 353.

[14] See Ian Ward, *Law and Literature: Possibilities and Perspectives* (Cambridge and New York: Cambridge University Press, 1995), Chapter 1.

[15] Ibid., 16.

judges may learn a thing or two from their colleagues in the humanities who are engaged in literary analysis and interpretation.

For legal scholars such as Gerald Frug and James Boyd White, it became increasingly important to look at how legal writers read and write texts – to look at the rhetorical contents of legal arguments. A thematic or textual approach, or both, to law may distract us from the politics of law, these writers felt. Neither approach quite catches the way in which a text, in assuming to speak for everyone, may instead obscure important differences between speakers of different genders, races or classes. Legal writing is as open to the uses and misuses of power as any other kind of writing, and it is only by emphasizing the dimension of figurative description of style that we may successfully expose legal writing as a vehicle for the distribution and use of power. Indeed, for Robin West, the true promise of law and literature lay in its ability to educate about the politics of law. The analogy between law and literature should therefore not be carried too far, she cautioned; adjudication may be interpretive in form, but in substance it is an exercise of naked power in a way that literary interpretation is not.[16]

The need to listen to what West called 'the textually excluded – those robbed of subjectivity and speech',[17] led to that narrative impulse in legal scholarship that R. Richard Banks talked about, as we saw, and to what has since been called, by Dolin and others, narrative jurisprudence or legal storytelling. But other scholars such as Peter Brooks, Brook Thomas and James Boyd White have also pointed to the centrality of narrative in law, to the importance for trial lawyers of constructing and telling a convincing story as well as to certain more existential issues related to narrative.

Finally, before I end this mini-survey of the law and literature movement, I want to mention one additional development or offshoot: law and popular culture. This is a development which is especially relevant to my case study, in Chapter 9, of Lars von Trier and his 'America trilogy'. Much like law and literature scholars, practitioners of law and popular culture are interested in legal storytelling – in what kinds of legal stories are being told and how these are being constructed, and in what ways the people who consume them are affected by them. Most people learn about their legal system only indirectly, from crime novels, newspapers, films and television. If we want to know anything about popular beliefs concerning law and justice, therefore, these are the media that we should look at.

Legal storytelling in popular culture merits our attention for several reasons. First of all, what people consider necessary, acceptable or just may

---

16 See Robin West, 'Adjudication Is Not Interpretation', in R. West, *Narrative, Authority, and Law* (Ann Arbor, MI: University of Michigan Press, 1993).

17 West, supra n. 10, 143.

form the basis for their support of the legal system. If we concentrate our efforts at understanding the role of law in society and culture around the reading of specific legal texts and the operation of the legal system, we miss out on what may actually be viewed as one important source of law: the popular imagination. Second, the popular myths, images and storytelling conventions which help shape the popular imagination remind us that we are surrounded by many different legal meanings. For professional lawyers and law professors, legal ideas and symbols are bound to have a different meaning from the one they hold for lay persons. And various groups in a nation or culture may experience and therefore think very differently about the law and its practitioners.

For Richard Sherwin, the worlds of law, film and television increasingly overlap, and this calls for a careful examination of the images and stories appearing in popular culture – 'law in our time has entered the age of images. Legal reality can no longer be properly understood, or assessed, apart from what appears on the screen', as he writes in his Preface to *When Law Goes Pop: The Vanishing Line Between Law and Popular Culture* of 2000.[18] David Ray Papke's research reflects a 'concern with the dominant American culture's most basic law-related faith, institutions, motifs and disbelievers'.[19] It is, he argues, in the attention to cultural configurations and conventions such as courtroom trials, lawyer novels and films that the analysis of law and popular culture must begin. And John Denvir has concentrated his scholarly efforts on Hollywood films. Unapologetic products of mass culture, Hollywood films may turn out to provide a comparative advantage over more 'serious' narrative texts, he has argued, in that they 'draw upon a broader variety of communicative tools than novels in their attempt to engage our emotional response'.[20]

How are law and lawyers presented to the public – as heroes or villains? Is the legal system portrayed as a well-functioning part of democracy or as a part which can no longer be trusted to work fairly and impartially? What role do various groups and segments of the population play in the day-to-day operation of the legal system, and how are these reflected in popular culture and the media? As law and popular culture scholars see it, representations in popular culture of law and lawyers are a cultural barometer of sorts that can provide useful information about current norms and values as well as about alternative normative possibilities and ways of thinking.

---

18 Richard K. Sherwin, *When Law Goes Pop: The Vanishing Line Between Law and Popular Culture* (Chicago, IL: University of Chicago Press, 2000), p. ix.

19 David Ray Papke, 'Law in American Culture: An Overview', 15(1) *Journal of American Culture* (1992), 4.

20 John Denvir, 'Legal Reelism: The Hollywood Film As Legal Text', 15 *Legal Studies Forum* (1991), 196.

LAW AND HUMANITIES IN A CIVIL-LAW CONTEXT

Drawing on the work of Gillian Beer, Kieran Dolin argues that interdisciplinary activity promotes not closure, but instead change and transformation. Literature can challenge law by letting alternative voices be heard; at the same time, literature and culture in general also draw from the law:

> . . . it is not the role of literature to introduce love into an aridly rationalist law. Rather, that suggestively open phrase, 'the laws of love' [the title of a poem by the Irish poet Eavan Boland dedicated to Mary Robinson, the former President of Ireland and United Nations Human Rights Commissioner], encompasses some important discourses of law, such as the tradition of equity, the construction of a general duty of care, and the development of human rights law, as well as ethical insights that emerge from literature, philosophy and other disciplines.[21]

For Julie Stone Peters, on the other hand, the interdisciplinarity involved in law and literature is less promising. It is one, she writes in a much-quoted article in 2005 on 'Law, Literature, and the Vanishing Real: On the Future of an Interdisciplinary Illusion', not so much of 'the shared content of law and literature, as its shared longing'.[22] Peters starts her article by telling a little story about a meeting between a group of law professors and a group of literature professors – a made-up story or caricature in which anyone who has been involved in law and literature for a while will nonetheless recognize a kernel of truth. As the professors talk about what they see as the potential of law and literature, each group is surprised, and in the end disappointed, at what they perceive as certain naïve attitudes on the part of their colleagues toward the other group's profession. The law professors find that their literary colleagues, in their wish to use law to create a better world, have a reductive view of law, just as the literature professors, for their part, find the need on the part of their legal colleagues to work with and through literature in order to gain access to a previously inaccessible reality embarrassing and impossible. To the law professors it is clear in the end that 'the literature professors needed to go to law school', and to the literature professors it is just as clear that 'the law professors needed to go to grad school'.[23]

Peters uses this little story to argue that the interdisciplinarity of law and literature has been marred by the wish on the part of its practitioners to find in the other discipline a cure for everything perceived to be wrong with their own discipline. Law and literature, she writes,

---

21 Dolin, supra n. 1, 212.

22 Julie Stone Peters, 'Law, Literature, and the Vanishing Real: On the Future of an Interdisciplinary Illusion', 120.2 *PMLA* (2005), 448.

23 Ibid., 443.

> might be seen as having symptomatized each discipline's secret interior wound: literature's wounded sense of insignificance, its inability to achieve some ever-imagined but ever-receding praxis; law's wounded sense of estrangement from a kind of critical humanism that might stand up to the bureaucratic state apparatus, its fear that to do law is always already to be complicit in alienation from alienation itself. Each in some way fantasized its union with the other: law would give literature praxis; literature would give law humanity and critical edge.[24]

What does this mean for the future of law and literature? Well, argues Peters, unless the literature part of law and literature is widened so as to open up towards cultural studies and the humanities in general, all that will remain is the 'interdisciplinary illusion' referred to in the title of her article. Law and literature should leave behind its 'narrow dual disciplinary signifiers' and instead transform itself into 'something bigger and necessarily more amorphous':

> Like literature itself as a discipline, embarrassed by too narrow an association with the strictly literary, law and literature is beginning to shed its second term and to meld into 'law, culture, and the humanities' (the title of the scholarly organization that seems now to serve as home for the discipline-formerly-known-as-law-and-literature), erasing 'literature' with a new lexicon ('culture', 'the humanities') that raises a new set of anxieties for a (still) new millennium.[25]

I second Peters' suggestion of expanding law and literature into law and humanities; this is, I also think, where the future of the discipline lies. As a European, I would like to suggest a second expansion, moreover: an expansion into European civil-law territory. As most scholarly commentary on law and literature has its origin in the English-speaking world, the common law has always formed a strong background. Kieran Dolin's book, *A Critical Introduction to Law and Literature*, from which we have already quoted several passages, is a good case in point. Dolin is not only (and perhaps not even primarily) interested in 'law and literature', but also in the intersection of law and literature in general – the way in which, despite their apparent separation, law and literature have been closely linked fields throughout history. This is reflected in the structure of his book. Part One, 'Eminent domains: the text of the law and the law of the text', contains two chapters, whereas Part Two, which is about 'Law and literature in history' starts, in Chapter 3, with Francis Bacon and 'Renaissance humanism and the new culture of contract' in order to end with a chapter on 'Law and literature in post-colonial society' (Chapter 7) and a final chapter on 'Race and representation in contemporary

---

24 Ibid., 448.
25 Ibid., 451.

America'. By far the major part of the book, that is, concerns the history of the shifting relations between the two fields of law and literature in the English-speaking part of the world, and the common law – in both its original, British version and its post-colonial version – is central to Dolin's argument throughout. It could hardly be otherwise, the object of his analysis being law and literature in the English-speaking part of the world only.

Since the first books were published on 'Law and Literature' in the US in the 1970s and 1980s, also, a canon of sorts has developed of both primary and secondary sources. This canon is primarily – though not exclusively – formed around Anglo-American texts, and it is often the same core texts which are discussed. And when in the past texts have been allowed into the 'law and literature' canon which were not originally written in English, they would typically come from larger European countries such as France and Germany.

To someone from a (small) civil-law country, this makes one wonder what 'law and literature' looks like in a civil-law context. What happens when the texts discussed are Scandinavian, Spanish, Dutch or Polish, and what happens when these texts interact, not with the common law, but with the civil law? Briefly and put simply, the civil law, which characterizes the legal systems of mainland Europe, has its roots in Roman law and is based on codes of law, which set out the main principles that guide the law. The most famous examples of such codes are the French Civil Code of 1804 and the German *Bürgerliches Gesetzbuch* of 1900. Whereas legislation is seen as the primary source of law in civil-law countries, cases are the primary source of law in common-law countries such as Great Britain and its former colonies, the United States, Canada and Australia. This makes for different methodological approaches. In civil-law countries, courts reason against the background of general rules and principles and base their judgments in particular cases on the provisions of codes and analogies from statutory provisions. Civil law starts with certain abstract rules, that is, which judges must then apply to concrete cases.

By contrast, in common-law countries, statutes are interpreted more narrowly and abstract rules are drawn from concrete cases. Focusing on specific cases and emphasizing the practical wisdom of judges, the common law furthermore understands law to have a moral dimension and perceives law to spread upward from the bottom and not merely downward from the top. Much of, say, American common law has by now actually been codified, but American lawyers still conceive of the common law as a way of arguing legally which operates as much in constitutional cases as in areas like torts and contracts. Common law is also often called judge-made law since, historically, it was judges who actually made or pronounced the law of the land. These are interesting differences – differences which could, one might think, lead to different ways of looking at law, literature, culture and history.

In their introduction to a special issue of the *European Journal of English Studies* of 2007, Greta Olson and Martin A. Kayman argue that European approaches and perspectives might offer some much-needed breadth, if not vitality, to law and literature. One example is provided by an essay in the special issue, written by María Ángeles Orts Llopis, on the translation of contract law from American English into European Spanish. Orts Llopis's essay demonstrates, Olson and Kayman write, how:

> technical difficulties in translating specific lexical items . . . open out onto larger issues in the legal cultures and the socio-economic relations the relevant terms of art regulate. These differences relate to the differing traditions of jurisprudence that inform Spanish and American law. By approaching the topic from the necessarily comparativist position of the translator, Orts Llopis's contribution engages a self-consciousness about local languages, juridical paradigms and practices which recontextualises the continuing relevance of questions of language, law, text and justice. Such work is increasingly necessary as globalization, conducted over-whelmingly through the medium of English, establishes contracts between various linguistic and legal cultures.[26]

Within the past few years, a couple of European law-and-literature research networks have seen the light of day. Professor of English at the University of Giessen, Germany, Greta Olson is co-founder with Jeanne Gaakeer, Judge and Professor at the Erasmus University Rotterdam, of the 'European Network for Law and Literature'. This network aims, as it says on the network's website, 'to embrace the variety of disciplines and languages its participants work in as potential sources of scholarly richness and innovation. It is our belief that work on Law and Literature in Europe can develop a profile that more clearly reflects and articulates the cultural identities and legal backgrounds of its participants.'[27]

In Italy, a group of scholars from both the field of English literature and the field of comparative law have formed around Professor Daniela Carpi, University of Verona, to work on 'Equity, Law and Literature'.[28] It is the concept of equity in English law and literature, starting from the 16th century up to today which is of interest, and the goal of the four sub-groups is 'to produce an understanding of the different meanings and outcomes of equity in Anglo-Saxon culture, to evaluate its advantages and drawbacks, analyse its

---

26 Greta Olson and Martin A. Kayman, 'Introduction: From "Law-and-Literature" to '"Law, Literature, and Language": A Comparative Approach' 11(1) *European Journal of English Studies* (2007), 1–2.

27 This is quoted from http://www.eurnll.org/ where more information on the 'European Network for Law and Literature' can be found.

28 More information can be found about the project on 'Equity, Law and Literature' at http://equity.lawliterature.eu/.

typologies and incidence, different in time and space, and to question its possible forms and usefulness. The four teams set out to highlight the notion of equity from an international perspective, that is by studying the application of equitable principles in the context of international law.'[29] In June 2008, together with Professor Monateri of the University of Torino Law School, Daniela Carpi founded a new cultural association for the study of law and literature, the Italian Association of Law and Literature (Associazione Italiana di Diritto e Letteratura AIDEL).[30]

Finally, there is the Nordic Network for Law and Literature, of which I am a member.[31] Within this network, various interesting alternative ways of working with law and literature have surfaced. How viable these ultimately will turn out to be is anyone's guess, but they may give us an idea of possible European responses to 'law and literature', American-style. For the so-called 'Bergen School of Law and Justice and Literature' – which consists of Arild Linneberg, Professor of Comparative Literature at the University of Bergen, Norway, and Bjørn Christer Ekeland and Johan Dragvoll, two Research Fellows at the University of Bergen – a deconstructivist reading of and approach to law is the way to go. In his latest book, *Twelve and a Half Speeches on Literature and Law and Justice* of 2007, Linneberg argues, for example, that:

> law is full of stories. Without stories, no legal action. Prosecutor, defense attorney, witnesses, the accused, plaintiff and defendant, experts, judges – everyone has his or her own version of what happened, when and also why. Law is literature. To reach a verdict the judge must tell a story, compose: construct the most plausible version of the sequence of events. Judges are often bad poets, they are often wrong. To read verdicts that have ended in a miscarriage of justice is to read appallingly unconvincing stories with mistakes which any serious writer would be ashamed to make.[32]

---

29 Quoted from http://equity.lawliterature.eu/project/the-project/#more-41 (last visited on 15 January 2009).

30 More information on the Italian Association of Law and Literature can be found at http://equity.lawliterature.eu/2008/06/28/aidel-italian-association-of-law-and-literature/#more-139 (last visited on 15 January 2009).

31 For more information about the Nordic Network for Law and Literature, please see: http://littrett.uib.no/index.php?ID=Nyheter&lang=Eng (last visited on 15 January 2009).

32 Arild Linneberg, *Tolv og en halv tale om litteratur og lov og rett* (Twelve and a Half Speeches on Literature and Law and Justice) (Oslo: Gyldendal Norsk Forlag AS, 2007), 23 – my translation from the Norwegian. The following quotations from Linneberg's book are also my own translations.

The phrase 'miscarriage of justice' is important. For Linneberg, Dragvoll and Ekelund, a deconstructive way of reading texts – texts of both fiction and non-fiction such as legal verdicts – can lead to an unmasking of the power games played by judges, courts and politicians. Dragvoll has been working on a well-known Norwegian case involving a poet called Fredrik Fasting Torgersen, who has been asserting, for close on the past fifty years, his innocence of the murder of a young girl. There have been a number of attempts over the years to have the case reopened, but so far the Norwegian courts have been unwilling to comply. By means of a deconstructive and rhetorical reading of the documents relating to the Torgersen case, Dragvoll has succeeded in pointing out a number of inconsistencies and mistakes.

This focus on the miscarriage of justice has led to an interest in 'the discussion of the new natural law-inspired international law concerning questions of war and peace' – a discussion which 'according to the Bergen School of Law and Justice and Literature is the most inflammable theme today within Literature-and-Law studies'.[33] By offering a deconstructive reading of the Icelandic sagas as well as of Norwegian writers such as Ludvig Holberg and Henrik Ibsen, moreover, Linneberg shows how, in much Nordic literature from the sagas on, 'right and wrong, guilt and innocence, crime and punishment, atonement and reconciliation [have] turned into moral-philosophical questions'.[34]

For another participant in the Nordic Network, Senior Lecturer/Professor of International Law (ad interim) Jarna Petman at the University of Helsinki, Finland, a possible way out of our current international problems with 'inflammable themes' such as terrorism and war is 'extreme legal positivism'. One of the founders of *No Foundations: Journal of Extreme Legal Positivism* – 'an open-access journal issued only in the internet . . . established and run by the Extreme Legal Positivism group, a team of researchers working under the auspices of the Chair of Jurisprudence at the University of Helsinki'[35] – Petman is very critical of present beliefs in (international) law to cure all evils. There is no higher law; law is made in parliaments by politicians and any attempt to appeal to higher principles of natural law – for instance in discussions concerning human rights – is misguided:

> Being a formalistic culture, law (justice) is the promise of anti-imperialist universalism. Since there are rules that govern interaction with both friends and enemies, this means that there is a solid basis for international relations even where values

---

33 Ibid., 24.

34 Ibid., 49.

35 For more information on *No Foundations*, please see http://www.helsinki.fi/nofo/ (last visited on 15 January 2009).

> and aims may be different. The rules create principles, a vocabulary and a context for ongoing debate on the good and bad aspects of the international system.
>
> There is no law that stands outside politics. The moment we forget this, international law is reduced to a false universalism. International law can stay true to its own ideals only as long as it remains a project aware of its own transparency and of its own political nature.[36]

For the Extreme Legal Positivism group to which Petman belongs, moreover,

> the positivist concept has serious implications for law's relation to politics and ethics. Law, being a human-made social institution, is susceptible to any change within the infinite scope of human will. In consequence, there is no moral obligation to obey the law *per se*, as the law is not intrinsically just, but always potentially evil. The justness of law must be considered in separation. Any attempt to justify acts of cruelty in the name of law-abidingness shows a deep misconception about the nature of law. Civil disobedience, the breaking of the law for political reasons, is the litmus test for a democratic society. In brief, people are responsible for their law. Thus, although the ethical and political resources of society are external to law, the positivist construct still relies heavily on them.[37]

Petman is currently finalizing her Ph.D. under the supervision of Professor Martti Koskenniemi. We looked at his work in Chapter 4 in connection with the question whether or not taking legal action may necessarily always be the best way to proceed. As successful as the two European courts may be said to be, other ways of fighting – especially political ways – are also called for in Koskenniemi's opinion. Another influence on Petman and her fellow extreme legal positivists is the jurisprudential movement known as Scandinavian Legal Realism – a movement which was founded by Swedish philosopher Axel Hägerström and Danish law professor Alf Ross. As Hägerström and Ross saw it, certain bad and distorting metaphysical influences on law had to be countered, and they set about working toward providing a solid philosophical foundation for a scientific knowledge of law.

As one of the Swedish participants in the network, Associate Professor and Director of Studies at the School of Computer Science and Communication, the Royal Institute of Technology in Stockholm, Leif Dahlberg, sees it, law should be investigated as social and cultural practice more broadly. In a new

---

36 Jarna Petman, 'On Teaching International Law', January 2007, available at the University of Helsinki homepage: http://www.helsinki.fi/inbrief/column/07_january.html (last visited on 15 January 2009). See also Petman's university homepage for information about her research and publications: (http://www.helsinki.fi/eci/Staff/Petman.htm).

37 Quoted from the Research Plan for the Project on Legal Constructions of Reality, led by Kaarlo Tuori, graciously sent to me by Jarna Petman.

project, tentatively entitled 'Legal spaces: The construction and representation of legal spaces in law, literature and political philosophy', Dahlberg intends to look at law not only as 'an institution for resolving conflicts, regulating social behaviour and maintaining social stability in society', but also as a social and rhetorical space

> that may have any of the following functions: to delimit (territorial) jurisdictions; to internally separate one legal domain from another (e.g. civil law, family law, labour law); the conceptual and textual organization of legislation and legal statutes; to organize the material and ideological structures of social space(s) in order to constitute a balance of political powers (executive, juridical, legislative); or to designate the concrete physical locations of and places where legal transactions take place and conflicts (hopefully) are resolved.[38]

One focus of this project will be the crucial importance of the relation between law, popular culture and media, how they affect and regulate each other – a topic which Dahlberg has worked on for a few years.[39] Finally, the work of another Norwegian participant in the network, Bjarne Markussen, should briefly be mentioned. Markussen, an Associate Professor of Nordic Studies and Media at the University of Agder, Norway, is also interested in that interdisciplinary space between literature, film and law and has recently published a book on family life as it has been represented by authors and film makers. The book also shows how such legal narratives have had an impact on law makers and legislation from the beginning of the 19th century until the present day, and most of the texts used are Norwegian (e.g. *A Doll's House* by Henrik Ibsen).[40]

---

38 Leif Dahlberg, 'Legal Spaces. The construction and representation of legal spaces in law, literature and political philosophy', a project description graciously shared with me by Dahlberg.

39 Among Dahlberg's recent publications in English may be mentioned 'The Menace of Venice. Reading and Performing the Law in/of The Merchant of Venice', *The Staging of Law* (Copenhagen: Museum Tusculanum Press, forthcoming); 'Achilles' Foot and the Law: Legal Space(s), Striated and Smooth', in D. Carpi (ed.), *Practising Equity, Addressing Law: Equity in Law and Literature* (Heidelberg: Carl Winter, forthcoming); 'Unforgotten, Unforgiven. On the Representation of Pain and Suffering in Marguerite Duras' La Douleur', *Polemos* (2008) 2; 'Legal Fictions in Contemporary Law', in L.-Å. Skalin (ed.), *Fact and Fiction in Narrative* (Örebro: Örebro University, 2005), 179–210.

40 Bjarne Markussen, *Rettshistorier: Barn og foreldre i litteratur, film og lovgivning* (Legal Stories: Children and parents in literature, film and legislation) (Oslo: Unipub, 2008).

CONCLUDING REMARKS

When we add to the work of my colleagues from Norway, Finland and Sweden my own research, as presented in this book, on the importance in the European context of human rights talk and my argument in favour of expanding law and literature into law and humanities, it becomes quite clear that there is not one, but several, 'Nordic' approaches to law and humanities. What Linneberg, Petman and I do seem to have in common, however, is a belief in the importance of human rights and of international law. Though deconstructing the language of power, Linneberg does voice a need for international law, and though Petman reminds us that it is politicians who make law and not law that makes politics, she still talks about the 'principles', 'vocabulary' and 'values' of international law and human rights. Each in our own way, it would thus seem, we do confirm the kind of European approach to international law and human rights on which I reflected in Chapter 6. And what Dahlberg, Markussen and I share is an interest in popular culture and media – an interest, more broadly speaking, in a law and humanities which moves beyond the purely literary.

This tentative link to a possibly European way of looking at these things notwithstanding, it is difficult, at this early point – the Nordic network having only officially started in 2005[41] and the two other European networks around the same time or later – to come up with any conclusive statements about what happens in a European civil-law context when non-English texts are used. Were I to hazard a guess as to what the future may bring, however, I would say that we will be seeing more research on legal positivism and its possible effects on culture (and vice versa) coming out of European law and humanities circles. The strong affinity for parliamentary democracy and accompanying doubts about moving toward 'government with judges' and about putting too much faith in law, felt and expressed by European scholars and intellectuals such as Conor Gearty and Martti Koskenniemi (see Chapter 4), for example, are likely, in my opinion, to make themselves felt.

It is not that the belief in the possibilities of human rights and international law to help create a better and more just world is any weaker among such European scholars. On the contrary, as I have argued throughout this book, human rights are viewed as an ever stronger instrument in the European context. This is true both for the European believers in law's empowerment and for European scholars of the type for whom 'the law is not intrinsically

[41] The members of the steering committee of the Nordic Network had met for the first time in December 2002, but it was only in 2005 that the network officially started.

just, but always potentially evil', (cf. the Research Plan for the Project on Legal Constructions of Reality, quoted above). For the latter, though, human rights ought to be seen as a political and not just as a legal project. Such scholars, who are reacting, in some ways, to their colleagues who have let themselves be persuaded by the belief in law's empowerment, American-style, are more willing to deconstruct or de-mask the law itself and not just the way in which it is being interpreted and used by legal professionals than their American colleagues are.

Although Americans may well be less enthusiastic now after having experienced first-hand the misuse of law by the George W. Bush administration in the name of the war against terrorism, it still makes sense, in the American context, I think, to talk about law as a civic religion of sorts. It is this belief in law as natural law, as something above or higher than politics that is missing among European practitioners and intellectuals of the law-is-always-potentially-evil sort. They do realize that in a parliamentary democracy there is a risk that minority views will drown in the will of the majority, and that this may lead to an emphasis, in an increasingly multiethnic European setting, on judicial review and judicial activism, but they still wish the fight for human rights to be anchored in and legitimized through politics.

There are also European scholars – and we have encountered some of them in the previous chapters – who have been inspired by their American colleagues to see in law the possibility for making the fight for a better world more effective. Their number may well grow – especially if the two European courts continue to be as successful as they have been in the past few years – in which case the legal positivist camp may step up its fight against beliefs in natural law. It would be my guess that one forum in which we will see this fight between legal naturalists and legal positivists being fought out will be law and humanities. Whoever 'wins' and whatever consequences this may have for European literary and cultural life, new and interesting research is going on in the European context on law and humanities – research which may open up new themes and help make 'law and literature', American-style more many-faceted.

9. Transatlantic dialogues on film: the case of Lars von Trier

In March 1995, participating in a conference in Paris on the future of film(s), Lars von Trier presented some new ideas that he had just developed together with a younger colleague, Thomas Vinterberg. These ideas were presented in the shape of a manifesto by the name of *DOGME 95. DOGME 95*, Trier said in his presentation of the manifesto, represented a collective of film directors, founded in Copenhagen in the spring of 1995, who were of the opinion that 'a rescue operation' was needed in order to counter 'certain tendencies' in the cinema of today – tendencies embodied most of all in the films made in Hollywood.

With this manifesto, Dogme-film was born. What at first seemed like a happening and an ironic comment on the first one hundred years of film – after having read aloud his and Vinterberg's manifesto, Trier threw a handful of red leaflets with the text of the manifesto printed on them at his audience and then left – quickly became something much more serious. The quasi-religious set of rules, presented as a 'Vow of Chastity', came to be taken quite seriously as an exciting attempt at renewing filmic method and technology.

What the first one hundred years of film have brought us, Trier and Vinterberg say in their manifesto, is 'illusions via which emotions can be communicated . . .' And they continue:

> Predictability (dramaturgy) has become the golden calf around which we dance. Having the characters' inner lives justify the plot is too complicated, and not 'high art.' As never before, the superficial action and the superficial movie are receiving all the praise.
> The result is barren. An illusion of pathos and an illusion of love.
> To DOGME 95 the movie is not illusion!
> Today a technological storm is raging of which the result is the elevation of cosmetics to God. By using new technology anyone at any time can wash the last grains of truth away in the deadly embrace of sensation. The illusions are everything the movie can hide behind.
> DOGME 95 counters the film of illusion by the presentation of an indisputable set of rules known as THE VOW OF CHASTITY.[1]

1 DOGME 95 can be found at http://www.geocities.com/lars_von_trier2000/dogme_95.html (last visited on 16 January 2009).

Among the rules drawn up and confirmed by DOGME 95 are the following: shooting must be done on location (rule no. 1), the camera must be handheld (rule no. 3), the film must not contain superficial action (weapons are not allowed and murders must not occur, for example) (rule no. 6), and the director must not be credited (rule no. 10). The first two DOGME films were *The Celebration* and *The Idiots*, directed by Thomas Vinterberg and Lars von Trier, respectively – or so rumours have it. True to Chastity Vow no. 10, the films do not specifically say so. Other Dogme films have since followed. Even outside Denmark, the concept of Dogme seems to have caught on.

Why is this, one might ask – what has made DOGME 95 so popular? After all, others have written and/or performed film manifestos before – the so-called Oberhausen manifesto of 1962 comes to mind, for example, which later came to play quite a role for German directors such as Rainer Werner Fassbinder, Werner Herzog and Wim Wenders. Likewise, there is nothing new about the ten rules – low budget movies are hardly a new and revolutionary concept. The answer, as the foremost expert of von Trier and his movies in Denmark, Professor Peter Schepelern, points out, clearly lies elsewhere:

> The main thing is to find artistic salvation in filmic/film-technological asceticism as a counterweight to the love of genre clichés and special effects in especially American movies, their ceaseless worshiping of the golden calf . . .There are international articles and conferences about the topic – perhaps because Dogme – with its suggestion of a path for the art of film to take in opposition to Hollywood's expensive machinery – has become an optimistic role model for film directors in smaller countries, stimulating especially for younger artists.[2]

It is Trier's presentation of his work as an attempt to 'counter the film of illusion' – that is, Hollywood movies – which is of special interest in this connection. A curious mixture of high- and low-brow, Trier's films are not blockbusters. His first films were exercises in (European) existential pain; it is only with the America trilogy that they have become more political, commentaries on what is currently happening on the world scene. And it is in this more political phase that Trier has become relevant to a discussion concerning transatlantic themes.

After taking a brief look at some of the early films, I will concentrate on three of Trier's later films – *Dancer in the Dark*, *Dogville* and *Manderlay* – as these are set in the United States and, at least to a certain extent, feature American themes and concepts. What interests me is the way in which Trier, in these later movies, succeeds in being critical of the US while simultaneously making much

---

2 Peter Schepelern, *Lars von Triers film. Tvang og befrielse* (Lars von Trier's Films: Obsession and Liberation) Copenhagen: Rosinante, 2000), 224, 227. This and later translations from Schepelern's book are my own.

use of American phenomena and themes. With his love-hate relationship with the US Trier joins the ranks of European critics and commentators from Crèvecoeur and de Tocqueville to Zygmunt Bauman and Ulrich Beck for whom 'America' is much more than just a nation or a place.

LARS VON TRIER'S TRILOGIES

From quite early on, Lars von Trier has liked to group his films into trilogies. His first trilogy was his 'Europe trilogy', consisting of *The Element of Crime* (1984), *Epidemic* (1987) and *Europe* (1991). As the name implies, it is *Europe* that is in focus here. All three films comment on fateful moments in European history – especially as these relate to Germany. 'Nazism and the Second World War were very important cultural events', Trier said during his work with the Europe trilogy. 'I'm obsessed with Germany . . . My movies show my obsession with the universe of war. The ultimate stage for films and dreams.'[3] This fascination is quite explicit in *Europe* (as well as in some of the work he did while still a student at the Film School in Copenhagen). It is furthermore implicit in *The Element of Crime,* which is set in a Germany faced with ruin, as well as in the television production and later film, *The Kingdom* of 1994, the Danish title (*Riget*) of which is a nickname for the Danish national hospital (Rigshospitalet) in Copenhagen where the action takes place, but also happens to be the direct Danish translation of the German word 'Reich'.

To a certain extent, Germany simply equals Europe in Trier's mythology. 'For me . . .Germany is very important, because when we [Danes] look toward Europe, we see Germany. Somehow, I especially relate Europe to Germany – Europe being at one and the same time a threat and an almost enchanted place.'[4] In what he called a 'press book' of the late 1980s, Trier explained that what the three films making up the Europe trilogy have in common is a particular theme: '[a]n idealistic person comes to a place that he cannot control. For me, the three films mark an attempt to draft a big painting of Europe which will say a lot about this continent.'[5] This is a theme to which he would repeatedly return later; in his 'America trilogy', as we shall see, the irony of the idealist who wishes to do good but ends up doing just the opposite becomes even more palpable. At this point, furthermore, the theme is used not only about a particular person, but also about that person's country: the United

3 Von Trier, quoted in ibid., 124.
4 Quoted in ibid., 127.
5 Quoted in ibid., 126.

States. In the early films, it is presented against the background of a Europe which is crushed – an old and tired continent full of brutality and crime.[6]

Trier's next trilogy of films consists of *Breaking the Waves* (1996 – his international breakthrough), *The Idiots* (1998 – his first Dogme film) and *Dancer in the Dark* (2000). This trilogy is sometimes referred to as the 'Golden Heart trilogy', because all three films – prominently featuring female characters who sacrifice themselves for others – are inspired by the children's book, *Golden Heart.* The book is a picture book which tells 'the fairytale of the girl who became a princess', one of Trier's favourite books as a child. The story seems to have originated with the Brothers Grimm and their story, *Die Sterntaler,* about an orphaned and poor little girl without a name – another German influence on Trier's work.[7]

In stark contrast to the war-torn, decadent and rather masculine universe of the Europe trilogy, the Golden Heart trilogy is populated by women who are much too saintly for their own good. They 'suffer' from a goodness bordering on stupidity – a goodness, which in Bess' (*Breaking*) and Selma's (*Dancer*) cases leads directly to martyrdom. Both Bess and Selma sacrifice themselves for the people they love – Bess for her dying husband, and Selma for her son who will go blind like Selma herself if she does not find the money to pay for an eye operation. This is goodness purified by physical suffering, even humiliation – goodness which is victorious only in death.[8]

Selma's physical humiliation is taken one step further than Bess'. While Bess has to debase herself by sleeping with strangers ('sleeping her way to Paradise', as one of Trier's co-workers puts it),[9] Selma becomes the victim of the ultimate physical humiliation: She is tied to a piece of wood and then hanged! The religious overtones that are very clear in *Breaking the Waves* – Bess is sent to Heaven while the church bells are ringing – are only implicitly there in *Dancer.* What is very explicitly there, though, is a (European) criticism of the (American) death penalty. Over and over again, as we saw in Chapter 6, the American wish to hold on to the death penalty has been an obstacle to the US signing international human rights documents. As in the later films, *Dogville* and *Manderlay,* Trier's critical commentary on the one remaining superpower in the world takes the form of a (human) rights discourse. If, in *Dancer,* the climax is Selma's death by hanging, in *Dogville,* one of the most interesting scenes is the final conversation between Grace and her gangster father, conducted as a veritable trial between good and evil, just as the practical and philosophical framework of *Manderlay* is the curious

6 Ibid., 128.
7 Ibid., 212–213.
8 Ibid., 250.
9 Ibid., 207.

'Mam's Law' and the issue at stake is the ultimate abuse of civil and political rights, slavery.

Dancer was Trier's sixth movie in Cannes. Beginning with *The Element of Crime*, all his major movies have premiered in Cannes. *The Element of Crime* received the Jury's technical prize. *Europe* and *Breaking* both received prizes too, but it was only in 2000, with *Dancer*, that Trier won the coveted Palme d'Or. Not all critics approved of the Jury's choice. Especially the American critics were sceptical of the way in which the European art film seemed to be taking over classical American film genres. They took Trier to task for making a movie on the US – a movie which was set in the US and the plot of which revolves around a criticism of the American justice system – without having ever been to the US himself.

In an interview conducted around the time of the release of *Dogville*, Trier tells us that there were two things that inspired him to write *Dogville*:

> First of all, I went to Cannes with *Dancer in the Dark* and I was criticized by some American journalists for making a film about the USA without ever having been there. This provoked me because, as far as I can recall, they never went to Casablanca when they made Casablanca. I thought that was unfair so I decided then and there that I would make more films that take place in America. That was one thing.

The other thing that inspired him, he claims, was listening to 'Pirate Jenny', the song by Bertolt Brecht from *The Threepenny Opera*. 'It's a very powerful song and it has a revenge theme that I liked very much.'[10] On the theme of how and why a European observer of the US can take it upon himself to deal with that country without having first visited it, Trier again waxed eloquent in an interview with Danish TV from Cannes on 23 May 2003. This was right after *Dogville* had premiered. The treatment the movie had received in the American press was no more favourable than that *Dancer* had received. Reviewing the film, Todd McCarthy wrote, for example:

> There is no escaping the fact that the entire point of *Dogville* is that von Trier has judged America, found it wanting and therefore deserving of immediate annihilation. This is, in short, his '*J'accuse*!' directed toward an entire nation. . . .
>
> The identification with *Dogville* and the United States is total and unambiguous, even without the emphatically vulgar use of pointedly grim and grisly photographs of Depression-era have-nots and crime victims under the end credits, accompanied, as if it were needed, by David Bowie's 'Young Americans.' Through his contrived tale of one mistreated woman, who is devious herself, von Trier indicts as being unfit to

10 Interview with Lars von Trier, available at http://thecia.com.au/reviews/d/dogville.shtml (last visited on 15 January 2009).

inhabit the earth a country that has surely attracted, and given opportunity to, more people onto its shores than any other in the history of the world. Go figure.[11]

To this sort of criticism from his American audience, Trier responded that Americans might actually benefit from a movie such as his. It might give them an impression about how their country is perceived from the outside. When asked by the journalist from Danish TV interviewing him at Cannes in 2003, what he knew about the US, he answered:

> I know insanely much about America . . . partly because of television channels such as your own, about eighty percent of what I get into my head is American. This is too much – unreasonably much. To enter a foreign country with troops and occupy it is nothing by comparison to the way in which we have let ourselves be occupied all these years. It standardizes the cultural picture in a deeply idiotic way.

Americans ought to be able to take a little criticism, he continued. To complain as much as some had was a sign of weakness; besides, 'the moment you have great strength, you also have a moral obligation to use it in the right way'.[12]

Dogville is supposed to be the U in USA – the first in a trilogy the topic of which is America. It is set in a small city (on a hill) in the Rocky Mountains. In *Manderlay*, the second film in the trilogy, which premiered in 2005, Grace continues her exploration of American society and ends up on a plantation in the South where slavery still exists. And the third film, which has not yet been produced and perhaps never will be, is then supposed to be set in Washington, DC. Instead of going West, Trier is moving East. It is worth mentioning in this connection also that Trier wrote the manuscript for Thomas Vinterberg's movie, *Dear Wendy*, which was also released in 2005. The plot of *Dear Wendy* involves 'a young boy in a nameless, timeless American town [who] establishes a gang of youthful misfits united in their love of guns and their code of honor'.[13]

Starting with *Dancer*, it would thus seem, Trier has embarked upon an American phase. His commentary on the US is unmistakably that of a European and, like his earlier films, his 'American' films are still films about

---

11 Todd McCarthy, reviewing *Dogville* for the magazine *Variety*, quoted in Bo Fibiger, 'A Dog Not Yet Buried – Or *Dogville* as a Political Manifesto', P.O.V. No.16 – FILM & POLITICS. Fibiger's essay can be read at http://pov.imv.au.dk/Issue_16/section_1/artc7A.html (last visited on 15 January 2009).

12 Lars von Trier, Interview with Danish Television, Cannes, 23 May 2003, available on the second CD ('Added Value') which comes with the *Dogville* DVD. My translation from the Danish.

13 Plot summary from the Internet Movie Database, available at http://www.imdb.com/title/tt0342272/ (last visited on 16 January 2009).

films – 'the claim', as Peter Schepelern puts it, 'that one quickly "forgets" the strong "*Verfremdungseffekt*" posed by the white lines drawn on the floor, is somewhat rash, to put it mildly'.[14] But Trier's interest in the US (whether provoked by the angry commentary of American critics after *Dancer* or not) seems to have made him more involved in what goes on in the world of today. He is moving – at least somewhat – away from the spiritual, religious and purely aesthetic toward the more political. 'Of course one has to be political', he said in the interview with Danish TV mentioned above, 'it's much easier not to be, and it's probably also much more dangerous to be political – and it has to be dangerous, otherwise it's no fun. But political it must be.'

And in this more political phase, much of his commentary is carried out in a legal discourse or against a legal background.

Dogville

Dogville is normally 'read' as an allegory – or as a parable. The didactic or parable-like quality of the movie is underscored, first of all by the stylized universe which never lets us forget that we are watching a representation of something (as already mentioned), but also by the role of the narrator who constantly comments on what is going on, and by the fact that the movie does not take place in the present, but instead during the Depression. The film itself 'knows' that it is an allegory or an 'illustration', as one of the main characters, Tom, mentions several times.

Choosing to 'illustrate' can lead to certain problems. The result can seem too constructed and puppet-like. At the same time, though, it can signal artistic skill and an aspiration to aim at something 'higher'.[15] Both are the sorts of things that European critics love Trier for – his allegories are open to a whole range of different interpretations – but that American critics hate him for. Waving the flag of 'high art' and criticizing the US in the process (without ever having set foot in the country), Trier stirs up all the American disdain for Europe that we talked about in Chapter 3 in connection with transatlantic dialogues, past and present.

I 'read' *Dogville* as an allegory of morality – human or personal, but also national morality. As the narrator informs us at the very beginning, the people of Dogville are basically good and decent people. When Grace (played by Nicole Kidmann) arrives on their doorstep, however, she brings with her the outside world and its problems. Running away from a team of gangsters –

---

14 Peter Schepelern, 'Lidelse i allegorisk univers' (Suffering in an allegorical universe) 20 *Ekko* (2003), 26–30. My translation from the Danish.

15 Ibid., 4.

headed, as it turns out, by her own father (played by James Caan) – Grace needs shelter. With some encouragement from Tom (played by Paul Bettany), the self-appointed town philosopher and spokesman, the little community agrees to hide her and, in return, Grace agrees to work for them. But then, when a police search for Grace sets in, the people of Dogville want to get more out of harbouring poor Grace. They make her do all kinds of chores for them – chores which even include being raped by several of the men – and Grace learns the hard way that in this town goodness is only skin-deep. When moral choices have to be made – when the townspeople decide what to do with Grace, and when Grace herself gets the chance to revenge herself at the very end – the choices made are not happy ones. The townspeople eventually turn Grace in to the gangsters, and Grace decides to have her revenge over them – in a big way.

In one of the most interesting scenes toward the end of the movie, we follow a conversation between Grace and her gangster father concerning the nature of human beings. Grace finds it hard to cope with her father's strong conviction that human beings are petty and evil when they get the chance, and for a while it looks as if she is about to follow in the footsteps of Bess and Selma in her willingness to forgive and endure all. However, after having gone for a walk, she changes her mind, and the film ends in an orgy of shooting and killing which clearly shows that this is not – at least not fully – a Dogme film (according to rule number 6).

A sort of trial between good and evil is taking place right there in the car as Grace and her father (relatively calmly) discuss the issue of human nature. At the beginning of her stay, Grace herself was the object of a people's court of sorts. Before a jury – not of twelve, but of fifteen, and not of her peers, as it turns out – it was decided that she could stay in Dogville. Trier is playing upon one of the most well-known of American genres, the courtroom drama. He is doing so even more explicitly in *Dancer*, of course – where we get one of the most interesting courtroom scenes ever presented in film. Law literally goes pop here (I am referring to Richard K. Sherwin's *When Law Goes Pop: The Vanishing Line Between Law and Popular Culture*, mentioned in Chapter 8), as Trier is using one of the most American of genres, the musical, to criticize the American legal system and the death penalty. Why? – because he knows very well – if only from watching all the courtroom dramas that are shown on Danish television – that the American is a highly legalized culture, and that, in fact, if you want to get to the deepest layers of the American creed, you need only look to the national preoccupation with the rule of law.

The original outline of *The Element of Crime* talked about a 'futuristic crime story with religious undertones',[16] just as the inspiration for *The*

[16] Thomas Alling, 'Sightseeing with the Holy Ghost', in Jan Lumholdt (ed.), *Lars von Trier Interviews* (Jackson: University Press of Mississippi, 2003), 25.

Kingdom was American crime series such as *N.Y.P.D. Blue* and Barry Levinson's *Homicide.*[17] In a number of interviews, Trier has made it clear, moreover, that the major frame of reference for his creative work are other films rather than works of literature. When asked by Bo Green Jensen about the importance for *Dogville* of works such as Thornton Wilder's *Our Town* (1938) and Sherwood Andersen's *Winesburg, Ohio* (1919), for example, Trier answered, 'OK, I am not that well-read. I have read some Steinbeck which I found very amusing. And then I have seen a few plays, *A Streetcar Named Desire* . . . Oh yes, and then I have also read some Mark Twain . . .'[18]

While there are exceptions – the revenge theme of *Dogville* being inspired by Brecht's *Threepenny Opera*, as we saw above, and the two different portrayals of Grace in *Dogville* and *Manderlay*, respectively, owing a lot to both the Marquis de Sade and *The Story of O* by Pauline Réage – Trier's world is primarily the world of pictures, the visual world of film and television. As he said to the journalist from Danish TV, about 80 per cent of those pictures originate in the US and a good many of those pictures from which he feels that he knows 'insanely much about the U.S.' are pictures which have some connection with law and legal themes – those pictures that interest law and popular culture scholars.

Dogville is more than an allegory of human morality. Trier is also commenting on national American morality here. To the rest of the world, America presents itself as more moral than other nations, and hence as more deserving of power. It has earned the right to be hegemonic and must never yield its sovereignty, or its overwhelming military and economic power. We know from countless surveys – Ziauddin Sardar and Merryl Wyn Davies' international bestseller, *Why Do People Hate America?* of 2002 being one example[19] – that nothing galls non-Americans more than American moral hypocricy. Saying one thing and doing something completely different, playing morally better than everyone else is something which non-Americans find it very hard to stomach. And this is the sort of moral hypocricy which Trier also criticizes. In the interview with Danish TV, in which he commented that 'the moment you have great strength, you also have a moral obligation to use it in the right way', he continues:

> [Americans] are given choices to make like the rest of us. These choices may run counter to common sense or ethics. And they do. It's not their fault, and not at all

[17] Schepelern, supra n. 2, 174.

[18] Bo Green Jensen, interview with Lars von Trier in *Euroman*, April 2003. My translation from the Danish.

[19] Ziauddin Sardar and Merryl Wyn Davies, *Why Do People Hate America?* (Cambridge: Icon Books, 2002).

the fault of their nationality. But there might be something in that country's policies that means that it's easier for them to be put in such a scrape.

Manderlay

Interestingly enough, *Manderlay* did not draw as much negative American commentary when it was released as *Dogville* had done. As Trier himself sees it, this may have something to do with the fact that the action in *Manderlay* revolves around the issue of race:

> I think it is because [American journalists and critics] are so enormously afraid of that race conflict that they simply shut up. It was funny because at that press conference [at Cannes], not a single critical question was asked. It was the easiest, most peaceful press conference that I have ever been to. I am completely sure that that is the reason why. They were just so pacified by Danny Glover's presence, but also by the whole problematic. You cannot criticize it without getting in too deep.[20]

Even more so than the 'first' Grace in *Dogville*, Grace in *Manderlay* (played by Bryce Dallas Howard, replacing Nicole Kidman) is the personification of the 'idealistic person [who] comes to a place that [s]he cannot control', mentioned in the so-called press book of the late 1980s. Though well-meaning, she both is ill-informed and acts without thinking. And this time, the criticism being more precise in its use of race relations in the US as a framework, Trier's comment on American wishes 'to make the world safe for democracy' is more effective. He hits where it hurts the most and where the moral hypocrisy is the most palpable.

With *Manderlay* Trier continues the saga of Grace begun in *Dogville*. The year is 1933. Having left the Rocky Mountains behind, Grace is now travelling through the South with her gangster father (played by Willem Dafoe, replacing James Caan). In Alabama, they happen upon the plantation of Manderlay at which, some seventy years after it was abolished in the rest of the country, slavery still exists. The black people at Manderlay are in servitude, governed by an odd set of rules known as 'Mam's Law'. Grace is shocked – having recently herself been held in something resembling enslavement – and she decides to stay on at Manderlay together with some of her father's gangsters whom he has graciously allowed her to 'keep'. With their help, when Mam dies, she takes over. One of her first acts is to abolish Mam's Law, though she holds on to it instead of burning it as Mam had asked her to do on her deathbed. Then, one of the gangsters being the lawyer Joseph who knows a lot about contracts, she has a contract set up which makes the former slaves shareholders in

20 Bo Green Jensen, 'Den anden Grace' (The other Grace), *Weekendavisen*, 3 June 2005. My translation from the Danish.

Manderlay. Grace had specifically asked for Joseph to stay on at Manderlay with her, apparently intending her dreams of introducing democracy to Manderlay and its inhabitants to have a solid foundation in contract law. She soon learns, though, that bringing important change like that is neither as easy nor as obvious as it at first seems.

Grace's attempts to help the former slaves reach freedom and democracy meet with one obstacle after another. Wilhelm, the house slave (played by Danny Glover), repeatedly tells her that the slaves are simply not yet ready to live in freedom – and that even if they were, the rest of American society is not ready to receive them. Events at Manderlay sometimes seem to prove Wilhelm right, but just as often it is Grace's own lack of knowledge and unwillingness to listen and learn that lead to problems. One crucial moment occurs when Grace tells the former slaves to cut down some of the trees in Mam's garden (the 'Old Lady's Garden', as they call it) in order to get wood for the repair of their run-down houses. As it turns out, these trees performed a very important task; they acted as a windbreak to prevent dust storms from damaging the crops and the houses at Manderlay. When the next dust storm arrives, Grace learns the hard way that her way of doing things, well-intentioned as it was, has brought only misery on everyone at Manderlay.

This is where the parallels to the current situation in Iraq as well as to certain other less successful foreign policy decisions in America's past are most obvious, but throughout we sense a more generalized critique of imperialism. Grace here becomes a modern-day version of Graham Greene's quiet American, Alden Pyle.[21] Trier also treats us to a satirical comment on democracy, American style, when he has Grace institute a system of town-hall meetings where ballots are taken on everything from less important issues, such as when a person can tell a joke, to a much more important issue, such as the death penalty. Grace literally gets away with murder, as she kills old Wilma who has stolen the food of a dying child – because it has been decided at one of the communal meetings that Wilma must be punished. 'You said so many times that we're entitled to it', as the father of the dead child whose food was taken by Wilma puts it; he is referring to Grace's numerous 'lessons' to Manderlay's inhabitants on justice. Another of these lessons was about the importance of unleashing one's anger.

And through it all run a number of loaded racial aspects. Like Mam and her family, Grace is white, and by taking over from Mam, she perpetuates exactly the kind of racial relationship that had been the dominant one in slave states. In the end, of course, Wilhelm and the other blacks want to force her to

[21] See Graham Greene, *The Quiet American* (New York: Random House, 1992), which was written in 1955.

become a new Mam – a final meeting having been held and a final ballot having been cast concerning the need for a new Mam. In this ballot, Grace 'won', her teaching about the importance of ballots and consensus once more coming back to haunt her. And in another ironic racial twist, when Grace feels the need to penalize Mam's family members for not having learned enough about race, their faces are painted brown just like those of the white actors playing blacks in the old minstrel shows. In addition, there are Grace's sexual fantasies about and intercourse with Timothy, who turns out not to belong to the category of the proud 'nigger' (category I in Mam's Law) after all, but instead to category VII – the pleasing 'nigger', the chameleon-type 'nigger' who will do anything to please those around him. As it turns out, it is Timothy who has gambled away the money made on the cotton harvest. His fellow inhabitants at Manderlay decide that he must be punished, and in one of the last scenes of the film he is ready to be flogged. When he calls out to Grace, 'aren't you forgetting something: You made us', she vents her sexual frustration and anger at him for not being the proud, Category I 'nigger' whom she first took him to be by doing that flogging herself, thus effectively going back on every one of her former principles. It is at this moment she realizes that 'Manderlay too was a place the world would be better off without'.

We are only about six minutes into the film when Mam's Law is first introduced. This happens in the scene where Mam lies dying and asks Grace to burn it. Grace tells her that she will not do so as everything must now come out into the open. 'The Constitution can be found in any courthouse', she says, thus making an interesting comparison between the two legal documents. As things start to go wrong, Grace finds herself drawn to Mam's Law. She consults it and finds that it contains rules for running the plantation, but also 'something strangely familiar', a table with descriptions of categories of blacks ('niggers'). She does not read it quite carefully enough, though; if she had, she would have been forewarned about Timothy's true nature. Next to his name, Mam – or, as it turns out, Wilhelm – had written: '[c]aution, diabolically clever'.

As Grace learns toward the very end of the film, it is indeed Wilhelm, and not Mam, who wrote Mam's Law – a fact that Wilhem explains by saying that 'we were not quite ready yet . . . I wrote that law for the good of everyone.' The new anti-slavery statutes 'terrified us', he continues, and so he and Mam decided that the prolongation of slavery was the lesser evil. Mam's Law 'allowed slaves to complain about their masters', for example, to blame their masters rather than to have to take responsibility themselves for whatever went wrong at the plantation.

Trier's criticism of American race relations and of the death penalty (making us think back to *Dancer*) is furthermore highlighted by the photographs shown after the film ends. Accompanied by David Bowie's

'Young Americans', these photographs of white violence against blacks and black poverty are a very effective and highly critical comment on the US civil rights era. And when, in between the many photographs which show the appalling conditions under which blacks used to live in the US, we come across photographs which point not only to the activities of the Ku Klux Klan, to the practice of lynching and of the death penalty, but also to the American involvement in Vietnam, the message is clear: if the US cannot keep its own house in order, it has no business presenting itself as a moral force for good in the world. Among the final photographs are one of Abraham Lincoln – the president who issued the Emancipation Proclamation in 1863 and promoted the passage of the Thirteenth Amendment to the Constitution, officially abolishing slavery – and another of George W. Bush, praying. Again, the implication is clear: the Constitution's promise of equal rights and respect for everyone has to this day not been realized; in fact, under (the praying) George W. Bush, the US may even have regressed.

As was the case with the photographs shown at the end of *Dogville*, several of the photographs shown in *Manderlay* are taken from 'American Pictures' by Trier's fellow Dane, Jakob Holdt.[22] For years, Holdt has travelled the world with his pictures and accompanying lectures on the United States. With their exposure of the social problems in the US, 'American Pictures' somewhat resemble those of another Dane, the muckraker Jacob Riis. His work on *How the Other Half Lives* (1890) is viewed as one of the most influential works on social reform in the US and is mandatory reading in any American studies course on the period it covers and exposes. What Trier takes from both is the moral indignation toward poverty – or, to put it in human rights terms, toward the lack of economic, social and cultural rights in American society. In terms of second generation rights, no less than in terms of first generation rights, in the opinion of these Europeans, the US ought to be ashamed of itself.

Trier does not directly use such human rights rhetoric. The inspiration for *Manderlay* comes from Jean Paulhan's epilogue to the erotic novel, *The Story of O*, published in 1954, which tells the story of a group of freed slaves in 1838 in Barbados, who return to their former master and ask him to take them back as slaves. When he refuses, they kill him and his family, move back into the plantation and start living as slaves again. The film's name is a reference to the mansion in the old Hitchcock film, *Rebecca* (1940), which is based on the novel by British author Daphne du Maurier. Trier thus plays many intertextual games with us in this film, as he did in his previous films. At the same time, however, he succeeds, by using Mam's Law as a frame of reference from

[22] More information on Jakob Holdt's 'American Pictures' can be found at http://www.american-pictures.com/dansk/index.htm (last visited on 16 January 2009).

beginning to end as well as by literally framing his story by photographs which expose some of the worst problems of poverty and violence, especially as these relate to race, in modern America, in producing an artistic and visual commentary which 'reads', in some ways, like a human rights document.

CONCLUDING REMARKS

So, is Trier anti-American – are his American critics right to be mad at him? In some ways he is. And yet, with *Dancer in the Dark*, *Dogville* and *Manderlay*, he has stepped into the footsteps of countless other European intellectuals, writers and artists who have tried to make sense of America, and who have found that they are, to use Dan Turèll's expression (Chapter 3), 'American-Europeans'.

In Chapter 3, we discussed whether anti-Americanism in Europe is a cultural phenomenon mostly or whether it has by now also taken on a political quality. The sort of anti-Americanism that Trier exhibits in his films is first and foremost a cultural criticism – a criticism which is founded in his irritation as an artist at the sort of cultural monopoly the world's remaining superpower is and has for the past many years been exerting. Culture being the money maker that it is, and cultural matters being as politicized as they currently are, Trier's cultural criticism inevitably also becomes a political statement. He cannot vote in the US, as he once said in an interview, but what he can do is to comment artistically and critically on the country which has become a cultural and political hegemon.

His Dogme project was, in part, a reaction against the power of Hollywood to produce lavishly expensive films that become commercial successes and in the process also succeed in setting a particular cultural agenda. It was a purification project or getting-back-to-basics project that would hopefully bring about a new attitude toward film making. It is really only one of his films, *The Idiots*, which is, strictly speaking, a Dogme-film. But the Dogme rules have played a part in most of the films which followed. Both *Dogville* and *Manderlay* have a strictness or theatrical quality about them. With their white lines drawn on the floor and their stylized universe, which never lets us forget that we are watching a representation of something, they recall several of the Dogme rules.

Trier's founding in 1992 of the film company Zentropa together with Peter Aalbæk Jensen was another conscious reaction against the sort of growing monopolistic control over the use of artistic representations by market dominating producers and distributors such as American film companies. As we saw in Chapter 8, as a result of certain developments in copyright and intellectual property law as a whole, these companies today enjoy a substantial power over our cultural consumption – they effectively decide what we do or do not read, watch or hear. Trier and Jensen each own 25 per cent of Zentropa. Yet another 25 per cent is owned by employees and others closely associated with the company, and the last 50 per cent was bought by Nordisk Film (the Nordic Film Company) in February 2008. In its own words and opinion, the company differs 'from the major competitors in the market by having established a decentralized autonomous organisation structure which creates space for new ideas and alternative methods of productions'.[23]

In February 2008, Trier and Zentropa established a new foundation, the 'Brilleabe Fonden' (roughly, 'The Four-eyes Foundation') which aims to help young Danish film makers get started in the increasingly competitive film market. The press release announcing the existence of this new foundation explicitly said that:

> in order to help the survival, in this world of more and more result-oriented and audience-seeking television stations and film institutes, of the elitist film and in order to stem the tide of these tendencies, Zentropa has decided to set up the FOUR-EYES FOUNDATION . . . The foundation's money will be distributed by film instructor Lars von Trier personally, who will assess the films in question. Financial support will be given to films which to a considerable degree explore the language and/or contents of films.[24]

Though playing, in *Breaking* and *Dancer*, with the genre of melodrama and certain kitsch elements and enjoying the fact that, at last, his films seemed to win the approval not just of film critics, but also of a wider audience, Trier now seems back at his old game: creating – and supporting – films that are not made for general consumption. Whether or not his own elitist films to come will be European commentaries on the US we cannot know. Rumours have it that he does not intend, at this point, to finish his American trilogy, but has instead moved on to other film turf.

In addition to a critical commentary on and wish to counter certain tendencies within international film, Dogme 95 and its 'vow of chastity', which reads, in the words of an American critic, 'like a cross between Moses' Ten Commandments and a naughty anarchist pamphlet',[25] was also an attempt to come to terms with control. Having control, being controlled and/or losing

---

23 More information about the history of Zentropa can be found at http://www.zentropa.dk/about/historie (last visited on 16 January 2009).

24 More information about the 'Four-eyes Foundation' can be found at http://www.zentropa.dk/index.php?pageid=72&newsid=10 (last visited on 16 January 2009). My translation from the Danish.

25 Shari Roman, 'Lars von Trier: The Man Who Would Be Dogme', in Lumholdt, supra n. 16, 135.

control – the concept of 'control' runs like a red thread through all of Trier's work. In an interview for a Danish weekly in 1998, appropriately entitled 'The Man Who Would Give Up Control', Trier said about Dogme:

> At one level the Dogme rules emerged from a desire to submit to the authority and the rules I was never given during my humanistic, cultural-leftist upbringing. At another level they express the desire to make something quite simple. In a normal film production you are hampered by having to make decisions about and control an infinite number of things such as filters and colors. The Dogme 95 rules basically say that you mustn't do any of that.[26]

In 1995, Trier continues, he simply telephoned Thomas Vinterberg and asked him 'if he wanted to come along and create a new wave'. Vinterberg said that 'he'd be delighted' to do so.

> The Dogme rules are – just like in a religion – impossible to abide by, but they provide some guidelines, and I needed some of that at the time. I needed to lose control, and in that way I was very egotistical in inventing these Dogme rules. Yes it's true, they're pretty tough to abide by, but that makes it a scream to make the film . . .[27]

On the one hand, what interests Trier is what happens when some person or some nation gets a lot of power and control. Choices have to be made, and in Trier's universe the choices made are rarely happy ones. On the other hand, we also meet in his films people who do not want to have control but wish, instead, to sacrifice themselves for others – like the women in the Golden Heart trilogy – or to avoid the possible anxiety of having too much freedom – like the slaves at Manderlay. For these, there is safety in rules, and just as Dogme gave Trier a necessary set of rules to abide by at a time when he needed such rules, so Mam's Law provides easy-to-follow guidelines. The problem is, of course, that for most of us – including Trier himself – there is a tension between the wish/need to follow and to break rules, to give up and to seek autonomy. At various times in our lives and for a variety of reasons, we may even alternate between the need to seek reassurance in a group or a larger community and the need to assert our individuality and opposition to such a group or a community and its values.

In exploring in his films this tension from a variety of angles, several of them legal, Trier touches upon many of the 'eternal' or 'big' issues which great works of literature also explore, and this makes his films an obvious object of study for law and humanities scholars. For better or worse, films play a big

---

26 Peter Øvig Knudsen, 'The Man Who Would Give Up Control', in ibid., 118.
27 Ibid., 127.

role in shaping people's cultural vocabulary. Films are increasingly becoming a common frame of reference in what Richard Sherwin and others have referred to, as we saw in Chapter 8, as the age of images: legal reality can no longer be properly understood, or assessed, apart from what appears on the screen. If law is indeed going pop, as Sherwin has argued, then it is more important than ever for law and humanities scholars to make films an object of serious scholarly inquiry.

In Chapter 1, we saw Wim Wenders also talking about the age of images. Today, no other realm of culture displays as much power as does the image. Europeans therefore have to make their own movies and give their European audiences European alternatives to Hollywood productions. Europeans have let slip away one of the most effective ways of broadcasting dreams and values, and what Europe needs are European film makers who can create films which discuss these dreams and values, according to Wenders. Trier is one such European film maker who has been broadcasting dreams and values. He has not had as large an audience for his films as Wenders himself has had. And now, after having succeeded in making films for a somewhat larger audience, he may be on his way back to making more elitist, inaccessible films. In some ways, this is too bad. Yet, a soul for Europe may be created in more ways than one.

Conclusion

There are times, Professor Mark Gibney remarked to me recently, when he wonders whether what the European Court of Human Rights does is really human rights. Instead, what it seems to be doing is a Europeanized version of international law – and these two cannot truly be equated. This could most clearly be seen, he went on, in the Court's Bancovic decision from 2001, which suggested that there are limits to Europe's love affair with human rights.[1]

In his book, *International Human Rights Law: Returning to Universal Principles* (2008), Gibney offers a detailed analysis of *Bancovic v. Belgium*.[2] The case was brought by six citizens of the Federal Republic of Yugoslavia and concerned a NATO bombing mission during the Kosovo crisis in April 1999. Sixteen people were killed and another sixteen were seriously injured. The citizens bringing the case, who were either family members of the deceased or had themselves been injured, complained that the NATO bombing violated not only Article 2 (right to life), but also Article 10 of the European Convention on Human Rights (freedom of expression). The Court dismissed the case because the claimants were not within the jurisdiction of any of the European states, Yugoslavia not itself being a state party to the European Convention and the Convention not being designed for application throughout the world, even when the conduct of the member states was at stake.

As Gibney sees it, a 'true' human rights court would have heard this case. European states were being accused of human rights violations; yet, by holding that the human rights protections of the European Convention did not generally apply to individuals outside of 'Europe', the EctHR used 'territorial considerations … as a way of demarcating, but really eliminating altogether, the protection of human rights'.[3] The Bancovic decision is part of a sad trend in the West – Europe as well as the US – to hide behind notions of sovereignty. This means that,

[1] Professor Mark Gibney, personal communication with the author, August 2008.

[2] Mark Gibney, *International Human Rights Law: Returning to Universal Principles* (Lanham, MD, Boulder, CO, New York, Toronto, Plymouth, UK: Rowman & Littlefield Publishers, Inc., 2008), 65–78.

[3] Ibid., 65.

> human rights has evolved into something that it was never intended to become. Rather than being based firmly on universal principles and values, 'human rights' has instead become parochial, territorial, and ultimately self-serving. Much worse, and in large part as a result of this approach, 'human rights' has offered almost none of the protection that it promises or that its framers intended.[4]

The international human rights system that has been instituted since World War Two simply 'has not worked' and Gibney concludes his book by maintaining that 'we can, we should, and we must do better than we have'.[5]

One of the arguments of this book having concerned the difference in opinion toward international law on the part of Americans and Europeans, it is interesting – and indeed somewhat depressing – to hear an expert of international law complain that the European Court of Human Rights has been as guilty lately of interpreting international law in purely domestic terms as has the US Supreme Court. What Gibney draws our attention to, however, is important – namely that even though the European system seems to be working toward covering a greater range of rights for citizens of the EU, solidarity should not stop at Europe's own borders. Europe should not become a fortress and human rights in Europe not just another Euro-centric and exclusionary project. It was in the European context that the assault on sovereignty launched by René Cassin and others – the wish to 'desacralize' claims of state sovereignty, as Cassin put it, to create something *beyond* the nation state – was first institutionalized. But in order for human rights to become the truly universal system originally intended by the framers of the Universal Declaration of Human Rights, Europeans must not rest on their laurels but keep pushing for the rights of those living outside their own borders.

Is the Glass Half Full or Half Empty?

Born in the Enlightenment of the eighteenth century, the language of universalism is, Jay Winter reminds us, in and of itself 'deeply problematic'. So is the discourse of human rights: 'In some forms, to speak of human rights is to bypass politics entirely; it is a vague invocation of neo-liberal notions of rational individuals and rational markets'. In many ways, therefore, 'the shift from social class and nation to civil society and human rights is not a change from worse to better, but from one set of historical problems to another'. But this does not make those minor utopian visions of men and women who dared to

---

4 Ibid., 2.
5 Ibid., 143.

think and act in different ways – 'to break with convention, to speculate about the unlikely in the search for a better way' – any less worth remembering.[6]

For those who tend to think that the glass is half full rather than half empty, the minor utopian twentieth century vision of human rights and its institutionalization in the European regional human rights system is a hopeful one. Things are by no means perfect, but the EU is a start. 'Domestic' in the European context increasingly means all of the EU member states combined, after all; it no longer refers only to Germany, Great Britain, France or any other individual European nation-state. And if, furthermore, that minor utopian vision could be made to include a transatlantic co-operation, it might lead to the establishment of a positive discourse and course of action building on the commonalities of Western values concerning democracy, the rule of law and the belief in human rights. If we in the West could agree to such a common discourse and course of action, then perhaps we might better be able to do something constructive about the globalized problems we are currently facing. Recent surveys show that the populations on both sides of the Atlantic, though sceptical of current transatlantic dialogues – or the lack thereof – actually do wish a stronger transatlantic co-operation on key issues such as the environment and the fight against terrorism.

The strong American rights tradition and the current attempts in the European context to further human rights make an obvious starting point. One of the arguments of this book has been that European narratives are currently being constructed which centre around human rights. It has furthermore been argued that what seems to be developing in the European context around writers and artists such as Danish film maker Lars von Trier, whose work has been used as a case study of sorts, is a version of the American law and literature/humanities movement: a human rights law and humanities. While the kinds of (human) rights focused on by European writers and artists are somewhat broader than those of American writers, the emphasis on a rights discourse remains. It is this emphasis that carries hope for the future of the transatlantic dialogue.

The narratives constructed in the European context show a certain similarity to American dreams of the right to have rights. Only, unlike their American colleagues, European intellectuals, policy professionals, writers and artists tend to focus on the whole spectrum of human rights and not only on civil and political rights. For Lars von Trier, for example, whose 'America trilogy' has a distinctly transatlantic thematic focus, the critical commentary on the US takes the form of an artistic and visual attack on what Trier sees as a fatal lack

---

6 Jay Winter, *Dreams of Peace and Freedom: Utopian Moments in the 20th* Century (New Haven & London: Yale University Press, 2006), 207–8.

in the US not only of first generation, but also of second generation rights. As 'interpreted' by Trier, who has never set foot in the US and whose knowledge about the country therefore comes from his heavy consumption of American popular culture and from watching the news, the US makes itself guilty of not caring for its poor and destitute who are simply told that they only have themselves to blame for their plight. In addition, the US has a tendency to preach one thing abroad and to do something else at home and this constitutes unworthy behaviour on the part of the world's only remaining super power, according to Trier.

Like most other European fellow-consumers of American film and popular culture, Trier knows the importance in the US of rights talk. What he may not be aware of, though, is that President Franklin Delano Roosevelt actually made an attempt to solve some of the worst problems in the wake of World War Two by introducing a Second Bill of Rights. In his State of the Union Address on 11 January 1944, Roosevelt stated that having economic rights would guarantee American security, and that America's place in the world depended upon how far these and similar rights had been carried into practice. Nothing much came of Roosevelt's proposal for a Second Bill of Rights at the time, but parts of it went directly into the United Nations International Declaration of Human Rights, which mentions the whole spectrum of human rights. It was Roosevelt's widow, Eleanor Roosevelt, who was the chair person of the committee put in charge by the UN of drafting such a Declaration, and she succeeded in passing on some of her husband's ideas. Though foreign to the thinking of many Americans today – and perhaps especially to those of a neo-conservative temper – the idea of human rights as indivisible does figure, in other words, in the American tradition.

In addition to American preferences for first generation over second generation human rights, Americans and Europeans have also had differences of opinion when it comes to the role of international law and legal institutions, as already mentioned. Within the past few years, 9/11 and the ensuing so-called war on terror has been one of the most serious challenges to international human rights and to transatlantic relations within the area of human rights. While agreeing that terrorism must be stopped, the Europeans do not always see eye to eye with the Bush administration on how this must be achieved. This has increasingly become clear in European responses to the refugee crisis at Guantánamo, for example. The Bush administration explicitly chose Guantánamo Bay in Cuba, the oldest US base overseas, to hold foreign nationals suspected of being involved in terrorism. These were called 'enemy combatants' and on the basis of the Detainee Treatment Act of 2005 and the Military Commissions Act of 2006, a system was developed which allows only a very limited judicial review of military determinations concerning the status of these foreign nationals.

As far as the Europeans are concerned, Guantánamo detainees ought to have the right to habeas corpus, that is, to challenge the lawfulness of their detention in an independent and impartial court. Europeans have accordingly reacted to the refugee crisis at Guantánamo by calls for Guantánamo to be closed and for the US government to either release the men at Guantánamo or provide them with fair trials. They have furthermore maintained that the US must respect the rights guaranteed by the international human rights treaties it has itself ratified – within, but also outside its own territorial borders. To this, the Bush administration responded that if the Europeans are so anxious to see the detainees leave Guantánamo, the least they can do is to allow the resettlement of those detainees from 'high risk countries' into EU countries.

In December 2007, the European Parliament did actually pass a resolution which calls on the EU to resettle Guantánamo detainees who fear torture in their countries of origin. 'European Union member States have repeatedly called the United States to shut down Guantánamo. Now they should go beyond the naming and shaming, and open their doors to Guantánamo's refugees who can't be sent to their home countries for fear of torture', commented the President of the International Federation for Human Rights, Souhayr Belhassen.[7] In many European countries, the idea of receiving former Guantánamo detainees is not all that popular, though. This is where matters currently stand, Europeans making themselves vulnerable, for once, to American accusations of being hypocritical when it comes to making good on the promise of international human rights.

Copyright, the West and the Rethinking of Values

As Europe seems to have become less important to American ways of thinking, the US has become a constant subtext to European discussions about the future. What used to be called, around the time of the American writer Henry James, somewhat Euro-centrically the 'international theme' is still alive and well, though. Apart from the area of human rights and the area of law and humanities, it has furthermore been argued in this book, there are transatlantic dialogues going on within the field of copyright. Where copyright concerns meet human rights concerns, something very interesting and increasingly relevant in our so-called knowledge society happens. Sometimes, European responses to copyright as property rights, Anglo-American style, take the form of a plea for a human rights-orientation in the direction of freedom of speech or access to knowledge. However critically European copyright scholars are of

7 Souhayr Belhassen, quoted on the International Federation for Human Rights website: http://www.fidh.org/spip.php?article5008 – last visited on 16 January 2009.

the expansion of the property rights paradigm of copyright, with one or two exceptions, they do prefer to honour the intellectual roots of copyright, though. Copyright is an intellectual property right and as such has its roots in property ways of thinking and arguing. And it may well be that using a property rights discourse may be the way to go in terms of furthering a transatlantic dialogue on this issue, some of these scholars suggest.

Perhaps what is really going on in the various transatlantic dialogues discussed in this book is a negotiation of what the 'true' West is and should become in the future. As other parts of the world are becoming political and economic players to be reckoned with, and as the values and norms of a West that has been guilty of unspeakable human rights crimes in the past have been questioned, this West has been forced to rethink its values. What seems to have been the result on the European side of the Atlantic is a renewed and somewhat chastened commitment to democracy, the rule of law and human rights. And while there may be differences in the way in which these values are expressed at this point in time in Europe and the US, there is a common core upon which future transatlantic dialogues may be built.

I hazarded a guess, in Chapter Eight, that future research in the European context concerning law and humanities might revolve around legally positivist criticisms of natural law. The American belief in law's empowerment and in law trumping politics, so to speak, is coming our way in Europe. The two European courts – the European Court of Justice and the European Court of Human Rights – are both becoming more activist; in fact, several scholars have remarked upon their resemblance to the US Supreme Court in this respect. It is this European development toward 'government with judges' – this turn from politics to law, parliamentary democracy to constitutional democracy – that adherents of European legal positivism or legal realism may increasingly, as they become aware of it and as they see it crop up in certain human rights discourses, feel the need to object to. An emphasis on law as politics, pure and simple, and as embedded in a concrete political and cultural context, could lead to a distrust of the kind of universal principles and values behind human rights that for Mark Gibney, as we saw, is the very essence of international law.[8]

It may be overstating the case to argue that the sort of 'domestic' approach to human rights by the European Court of Justice, criticized by Gibney, stems from a more relativistic or positivistic way of looking at and arguing about law. But can it be completely ruled out that, consisting as it does of judges trained for the most part in civil law and legal positivism, the Court has a tendency to see law as rooted in and reflecting European political systems

---

8 I thank Sebastian Porsdam Mann for raising this issue with me.

only?[9] This would admittedly not explain why the US Supreme Court has also been guilty of the same sort of 'domestic' approach. In the American context, though, as we have seen, other reasons beyond the concern for sovereignty such as federalism and fears that international law suffers from a democratic deficit also play a part. This is one of the issues of a more ideological kind that will no doubt have to be discussed in future transatlantic dialogues. There will be others, of course, and it is my hope that the sort of cultural-historical and history-of-ideas-based law-and-humanities approach taken in this book may help clarify the underlying issues involved in such dialogues.

---

9 I am aware that this does not apply to English judges who have, of course, been trained in a common-law system. However, as we saw in Chapter Four, Irish/English legal scholars such as Conor Gearty are among some of the fiercest critics of law-as-empowerment ways of thinking, American-style.

Epilogue

On 31 March 2009 the Obama administration announced its intention to seek election as one of the 47 members of the United Nations Human Rights Council. While well-received by most Western countries, this decision was derided by John Bolton, who served as ambassador to the UN during the Bush administration, for giving credibility to an institution that neither had nor deserved any such credibility.

The Human Rights Council, which was established in 2006, constitutes an attempt to correct the worst flaws of its predecessor, the Human Rights Commission. On this Commission sat representatives of some of the worst dictatorships in the world, and John Bolton and other Bush administration hawks greeted the new Council with much scepticism. They were not sure whether it would mean an improvement and so far, their scepticism has turned out to be warranted. The Council has focused much of its energy on Israel and with the resolution on 'religious defamation' adopted on 26 March 2009, it has set itself on a collision course with Western ideas about free speech. Supported mostly by Islamic countries, the resolution was passed in spite of strong appeals from a number of secular as well as Christian, Muslim and Jewish groups who, in a joint statement, had argued that by denouncing the 'defamation' of faith the Council would risk supporting regimes that set out to 'silence and intimidate human-rights activists, religious dissenters and other independent voices.'[1]

It is probably no coincidence that the decision on the part of the Obama administration to re-engage with the Human Rights Council came only 5 days after the Council passed the 'religious defamation' resolution. Barack Obama used to teach constitutional law and has shown a keen interest in human rights issues. For human rights activists everywhere, this American willingness to re-join discussions about free speech and the nature of religious freedom is a hopeful sign and one that is bound to boost America's image in many quarters around the world.

In April 2009, moreover, Barack Obama attended two important meetings in Europe: the G-20 Leaders' Summit on Financial Markets and the World

[1] 'Diplomacy, faith and freedom: America rejoins the argument over which human rights are sacred', *The Economist*, 4 April 2009, 53.

Economy, held in London, and the NATO Summit meetings of Heads of State and Government, held in Kehl, Germany and Strasbourg, France. This European visit was the first foreign visit Obama made as the 44th president of the United States, and Europeans cannot help asking themselves whether the mere fact that Obama's first foreign visit was paid to Europe is significant, and whether his reassuring comments about the importance of transatlantic cooperation made during this visit signify that European opinions still matter – for instance when it comes to human rights?

For the most part, the European mass media have given President Obama a royal treatment, reflecting the highly positive attitudes among the European peoples towards him. Yet, we should probably be careful to separate wishful thinking from *realpolitik*. The thorny issue of accepting former Guantanamo prisoners into Europe still remains, for example, and so does the need for stronger European support in Afghanistan. The Americans may no longer wish to talk about 'the war against terror', but they still want Europeans to send more troops to Afghanistan – something most European countries are anything but keen to do.

Reading the press coverage of Obama's European trip and of these issues, I was reminded of one of the last times that I met former United States Congressman Tom Lantos. When Lantos, who unfortunately died in January 2008, participated in a panel discussion on the 2006 midterm elections at the University of Southern Denmark in Odense, he surprised his audience by giving a passionate and stirring talk on the 'vicious' and 'totally unacceptable' anti-Americanism currently at play in Europe. Congressman Lantos, who visited Odense to see his daughter, Katrina Swett, defend her Ph.D. dissertation on Friday, 1 December 2006, was the new chairman of the International Relations Committee in the US House of Representatives. His party, the Democratic Party, had won the midterm elections and from now on, when President Bush needed or wished to consult with the legislative branch of the American government on foreign policy issues, it was Congressman Lantos and then-Senator Joseph R. Biden Jr. – the chairman of the US Senate Committee on Foreign Relations – whom he needed to approach. When Lantos spoke about the transatlantic relationship, therefore, we knew we had better listen.

What we had looked forward to hearing on that December day in Odense was something very different. We had hoped that Lantos would tell us that now, finally, the US would think less unilaterally and would listen to its allies (especially those in Europe). Lantos' message to us that day in Odense was, however, a simple one: if Europeans expect the United States to stop acting unilaterally, and if Europeans want to have some influence on the global scene, they will have to share with the United States the burden of responsibility. A Hungarian survivor of the Holocaust, Lantos felt that he could say things to an audience of fellow-Europeans that perhaps it would be harder for other members of Congress to get across. Europeans are of course, he told us, perfectly welcome to criticize American foreign policy, but when European politicians start whipping up anti-American feelings in the general public for short-term political gain (as did Gerhard Schröder in the German national election of 2005), the transatlantic dialogue greatly suffers as a consequence. Only if Europe works *with* the US – and not *against* it – do we have a chance of solving the immense problems currently facing us all.

As high as European hopes currently are for improved relations with the Obama administration, that is, we should be careful not to expect too much, too soon. On the other hand, nothing at all will happen unless one believes that it matters to fight for something better – and belief in something better is what the 44th president of the United States is giving us right now.

Bibliography

Abdelgawad, Elisabeth Lambert (2008), *The Execution of Judgments of the European Court of Human Rights* (Human rights files, No. 19, Strasbourg: Council of Europe Publishing, 2nd edition)

Alling, Thomas (2003), 'Sightseeing with the Holy Ghost', in Jan Lumholdt (ed.), *Lars von Trier Interviews* (Jackson: University Press of Mississippi)

Alston, Philip (ed.) (1999), *The EU and Human Rights* (Oxford: Oxford University Press)

Alston, Philip and J.H.H. Weiler (1999), 'An "Ever Closer Union" in Need of a Human Rights Policy: The European Union and Human Rights', in Philip Alston (ed.), *The EU and Human Rights* (Oxford: Oxford University Press)

Anderson, Perry (2007), 'European Hypocrisies', in 30 *London Review of Books* 20 September

Árnason, Ágúst Thór (2001), 'Constitutionalism: Popular Legitimacy of the State?', in Martin Scheinin (ed.), *Welfare State and Constitutionalism – Nordic Perspectives* (Copenhagen: Nordic Council of Ministers)

Ash, Timothy Garton (2004), *Free World: America, Europe, and the Surprising Future of the West* (New York: Vintage Books)

Auerbach, Jerold S. (1983), *Justice Without Law? Resolving Disputes Without Lawyers* (New York and Oxford: Oxford University Press)

Balabar, Etienne (2004), *We, the People of Europe? Reflections on Transnational Citizenship* (Princeton, NJ, and Oxford: Princeton University Press)

Banks, R. Richard (1997), 'The Political Economy of Racial Discourse', 9 *Yale Journal of Law and the Humanities*, 217

Bauman, Zygmunt (2004), *Europe: An Unfinished Adventure* (Cambridge: Polity Press)

Bech-Petersen, Ole (2000), *Encounters: Danish Literary Travel in the United States* (unpublished dissertation, the University of Southern Denmark)

Beck, Ulrich and Edgar Grande (2002), *Macht und Gegenmacht im globalen Zeitalter* (Frankfurt am Main: Suhrkamp)

Beck, Ulrich and Edgar Grande (2004), *Der kosmopolitische Blick* (Frankfurt am Main: Suhrkamp)

Beck, Ulrich and Edgar Grande (2004), *Das kosmopolitische Europa. Gesellschaft und Politik in der Zweiten Moderne* (Frankfurt am Main: Suhrkamp)

Bell, Derrick (1995), 'Who's Afraid of Critical Race Theory?' 4 *University of Illinois Law Review* 893

Berman, Russell A. (2004), *Anti-Americanism in Europe: A Cultural Problem* (Stanford, CA: Hoover Institution Press)

Bernitz, Ulf and Hedvig Lokrantz Bernitz (2005), 'Human Rights and European Identity: The Debate about European Citizenship', in Gráinne de Búrca (ed.), *EU Law and the Welfare State: In Search of Solidarity* (Oxford: Oxford University Press)

Bourdieu, Pierre (2003), *Firing Back: Against the Tyranny of the Market* (New York and London: The New Press)

Boyle, Kevin (2007), 'Transatlantic Human Rights Dialogue', in Rikke Frank Jørgensen and Klaus Slavensky (eds.), *Implementing Human Rights: Essays in Honour of Morten Kjærum* (Copenhagen: The Danish Institute for Human Rights)

Bradley, Kieran St C. (1999), 'Reflections on the Human Rights Role of the European Parliament', in Philip Alston (ed.), *The EU and Human Rights* (Oxford: Oxford University Press)

Buitenweg, Rob (2007), *Human Rights, Human Plights in a Global Village* (Atlanta, GA: Clarity Press, Inc.)

Búrca, Gráinne de (ed.) (2005), *EU Law and the Welfare State: In Search of Solidarity* (Oxford: Oxford University Press)

Búrca, Gráinne de (2005), 'Towards European Welfare?', in Gráinne de Búrca (ed.), *EU Law and the Welfare State: In Search of Solidarity* (Oxford: Oxford University Press)

Byers, Michael and Georg Nolte (eds.) (2003), *United States Hegemony and the Foundations of International Law* (Cambridge: Cambridge University Press)

Böss, Michael (2001), 'American Links to Legal Reform in Ireland, 1937–1997: A Study in the International Impact of American Constitutional Law', in Helle Porsdam (ed.), *Folkways and Law Ways: Law in American Studies* (Odense: Odense University Press)

Coban, Ali Riza (2004), *Protection of Property Rights Within the European Convention on Human Rights* (Aldershot and Burlington, VT: Ashgate Publishing)

Collignon, Stefan (2006), 'Introduction', in Guy Verhofstadt, *The United States of Europe: Manifesto for a New Europe* (London: Federal Trust for Education and Research)

Council of Europe (2007), *State of Human Rights and Democracy in Europe* (Strasbourg: Council of Europe Publishing)

Council of Europe, Committee of Ministers (2008), *Supervision of the execution of judgments of the European Court of Human Rights*, 1st annual report, 2007 (Strasbourg: Council of Europe)

Cronin, Anne M. (2002), 'Consumer Rights/Cultural Rights: A New Politics of European belonging', 5(3) *European Journal of Cultural Studies* 307

Dahlberg, Leif (2005), 'Legal Fictions in Contemporary Law', in L.-Å. Skalin (ed.), *Fact and Fiction in Narrative* (Örebro: Örebro University), 179

Dahlberg, Leif (2006), 'Images of European Injustice. A Reading of Eyvind Johnson's *Drömmar om rosor och eld*', in S. H. Rossel et al. (eds.), *Der Norden im Ausland - das Ausland im Norden. Formung und Transformation von Konzepten und Bildern des Anderen vom Mittelalter bis heute*, Wiener Studien zur Skandinavistik, Bd 15 (Vienna, Verlag Praesens), 220

Dahlberg, Leif (2006), 'On the Open and Closed Space of Public Discourse', 27(2) *Nordicom Review* 35

Denvir, John (1991), 'Legal Reelism: The Hollywood Film As Legal Text', *Legal Studies Forum*, 15

Dolin, Kieran (2007), *A Critical Introduction to Law and Literature* (Cambridge and New York: Cambridge University Press)

Dreyfuss, Rochelle Cooper, Harry First and Diane Leenheer Zimmerman (eds.) (2000), *Innovation Policy in an Information Age* (Oxford: Oxford University Press)

European Commission, External Relations (2007), *The European Union: Furthering Human Rights and Democracy Across the Globe* (Luxembourg: Office for Official Publications of the European Communities)

The European Task Force on Culture and Development (1997), *In from the margins: A contribution to the debate on Culture and Development in Europe* (Strasbourg: Council of Europe)

Ferrera, Maurizio (2005), 'Towards an "Open" Social Citizenship? The New Boundaries of Welfare in the European Union', in Gráinne de Búrca (ed.), *EU Law and the Welfare State: In Search of Solidarity* (Oxford: Oxford University Press)

Fibiger, Bo (2003), 'A Dog Not Yet Buried – Or *Dogville* as a Political Manifesto', P.O.V. No.16, *Film & Politics*. Available at http://pov.imv.au.dk/Issue_16/section_1/artc7A.html

Fish, Stanley (1994), *There's No Such Thing as Free Speech: And It's a Good Thing Too* (New York: Oxford University Press)

Fluck, Winfried (2004), 'The Americanization of German Culture? The Strange, Paradoxical Ways of Modernity', in Agnes C. Mueller (ed.), *German Pop Culture: How 'American' Is It?* (Ann Arbor, MI: University of Michigan Press)

Fukuyama, Francis (1992), *The End of History and the Last Man* (London and New York: Penguin Books)

Gaines, Jane M. (1992), *Contested Culture: The Image, the Voice, and the Law* (London: The British Film Institute)

Gearty, Conor (2006), *Can Human Rights Survive?* (The Hamlyn Lectures 2005, Cambridge: Cambridge University Press)

Geiger, Christophe (2006), ' "Constitutionalising" Intellectual Property Law? The Influence of Fundamental Rights on Intellectual Property in the European Union', 37 *International Review of Intellectual Property and Competition Law* 371

Geiger, Christophe (2007), 'Copyright and the Freedom to Create – A Fragile Balance', 38 *International Review of Intellectual Property and Competition Law* (IIC) 371

Geiger, Christophe (2008), 'Flexibilising Copyright – Remedies to the Privatisation of Information to Copyright Law', 39 *International Review of Intellectual Property and Competition Law* (IIC) 178

Gibney, Mark (2008), *International Human Rights Law: Returning to Universal Principles* (Lanham, MD: Rowman & Littlefield Publishers, Inc.)

Giddens, Anthony (2007), *Europe in the Global Age* (Cambridge: Polity Press)

Ginsburg, Jane C. (1994), 'A Tale of Two Copyrights: Literary Property in Revolutionary France and America', in Brad Sherman and Alain Strowel (eds.), *Of Authors and Origins: Essays on Copyright* (Oxford: Clarendon Press)

Gitlin, Todd (2003), 'Europe? Frankly, America doesn't give a damn . . .', *The Guardian*, 3 February 2003 – available at http://www.guardian.co.uk/world/2003/feb/03/usa.comment1

Glendon, Mary Ann (1991), *Rights Talk: The Impoverishment of Political Discourse* (New York: Free Press)

Goldhaber, Michael D. (2007), *A People's History of the European Court of Human Rights* (New Brunswick, NJ, and London: Rutgers University Press)

Gorman, Robert A. and Jane C. Ginsburg (eds.) (1993), *Copyright for the Nineties: Cases and Materials* (Charlottesville, VA: The Michie Company, 4th edition)

Gutman, Amy (ed.) (2001), *Human Rights as Politics and Idolatry* (Princeton, NJ: Princeton University Press)

Habermas, Jürgen (2001), *The Postnational Constellation: Political Essays* (Cambridge, MA: MIT Press)

Hall, Kermit L., Paul Finkelman and James W. Ely, Jr. (eds.) (2005), *American Legal History: Cases and Materials* (New York and Oxford: Oxford University Press, 3rd edition)

Haseler, Stephen (2004), *Super-State: The New Europe and Its Challenge to America* (London and New York: I.B. Tauris & Co. Ltd)

Held, David (2004), *Global Covenant: The Social Democratic Alternative to the Washington Consensus* (Cambridge: Polity Press)

Hilty, Reto M. (2003), 'Copyright in a Digital Dilemma', *Max Planck Research, Science Magazine of the Max Planck Society*, Issue 3, 48

Holderness, Mike (1995), 'Copyright and Authors' Rights' – availablc at http://media.gn.apc.org/c-rights.html#proper

Honig, Bonnie (2003), *Democracy and the Foreigner* (Princeton, NJ, and Oxford: Princeton University Press)

Hugenholtz, P. Bernt (2000), 'Copyright and Freedom of Expression in Europe', in Rochelle Cooper Dreyfuss, Harry First and Diane Leenheer Zimmerman (eds.), *Innovation Policy in an Information Age* (Oxford: Oxford University Press) – also available at www.ivir.nl/publications/hugenholtz/PBH-Engelberg.doc

Hunt, Lynn (2007), *Inventing Human Rights: A History* (New York and London: W.W. Norton & Co.)

Huntington, Samuel (2002), *The Clash of Civilizations* (New York: Free Press)

Ignatieff, Michael (2001), 'Human Rights as Politics', in Amy Gutman (ed.), *Human Rights as Politics and Idolatry* (Princeton, NJ: Princeton University Press)

Ignatieff, Michael (ed.) (2005), *American Exceptionalism and Human Rights* (Princeton, NJ, and Oxford: Princeton University Press)

Ignatieff, Michael (2005), 'Introduction: American Exceptionalism and Human Rights', in Michael Ignatieff (ed.), *American Exceptionalism and Human Rights* (Princeton, NJ, and Oxford: Princeton University Press)

Isa, Felipe Gómez and Koen de Feyter (eds.) (1997), *International Protection of Human Rights: Achievements and Challenges* (Bilbao: University of Deusto)

James, Henry (1983), *Autobiography* (Princeton, NJ: Princeton University Press)

Joffe, Josef (2006), 'Dissecting Anti-isms', *The American Interest Online*, Summernote – available at http://www.the-american-interest.com/ai2/article.cfm?Id=83&MId=4

Jørgensen, Rikke Frank and Klaus Slavensky (eds.) (2007), *Implementing Human Rights: Essays in Honour of Morten Kjærum* (Copenhagen: The Danish Institute for Human Rights)

Kagan, Robert (2003), *Of Paradise and Power: America and Europe in the New World Order* (New York: Knopf)

Karst, Kenneth L. (1993), *Law's Promise, Law's Expression: Visions of Power in the Politics of Race, Gender, and Religion* (New Haven, CT, and London: Yale University Press)

Katzenstein, Peter J. and Robert O. Keohane (eds.) (2007), *Anti-Americanisms in World Politics* (Ithaca, NY, and London: Cornell University Press)

Keller, Ursula and Ilma Rakusa (eds.) (2003), *Europa schreibt. Was ist das europäische an den Literaturen Europas?* (Hamburg: edition Körber-Stiftung)

Kilbourne, Susan (2000), 'Placing the Convention on the Rights of the Child in an American Context', in Henry J. Steiner and Philip Alston (eds.), *International Human Rights in Context: Law, Politics, Morals* (Oxford: Oxford University Press, 2nd edition)

Knudsen, Peter Øvig (2003), 'The Man Who Would Give Up Control', in Jan Lumholdt (ed.), *Lars von Trier Interviews* (Jackson, MS: University Press of Mississippi)

Koch, Ida Elisabeth (2006), 'Economic, Social and Cultural Rights as Components in Civil and Political Rights: A Hermeneutic Perspective', 10 *The International Journal of Human Rights*, 405–30

Koskenniemi, Martti (1999), 'The Effect of Rights on Political Culture', in Philip Alston (ed.), *The EU and Human Rights* (Oxford: Oxford University Press)

Kroes, Rob (2000), *Them and Us: Questions of Citizenship in a Globalizing World* (Urbana and Chicago, IL: University of Illinois Press)

Krugman, Paul (2007), *The Conscience of a Liberal* (New York and London: W.W. Norton & Co.)

Leonhard, Mark (2005), *Why Europe Will Run the 21st Century* (London: Fourth Estate)

Lessig, Lawrence (2006), '(Re)creativity: How Creativity Lives', in Helle Porsdam (ed.), *Copyright and Other Fairy Tales: Hans Christian Andersen and the Commodification of Creativity* (Cheltenham, UK and Northampton, MA, USA: Edward Elgar)

Linneberg, Arild (2007), *Tolv og en halv tale om litteratur og lov og rett* (Twelve and a Half Speeches on Literature and Law and Justice) (Oslo: Gyldendal Norsk Forlag AS)

Lumholdt, Jan (ed.) (2003), *Lars von Trier Interviews* (Jackson, MS: University Press of Mississippi)

Lundestad, Geir (2003), *The United States and Western Europe since 1945: From 'Empire' by Invitation to Transatlantic Drift* (Oxford: Oxford University Press)

Macmillan, Fiona (2002), 'The Cruel ©: Copyright and Film', 24 *European Intellectual Property Review*, 483

Macmillan, Fiona (ed.) (2005), *New Directions in Copyright Law, Volume 1*, (Cheltenham, UK and Northampton, MA, USA: Edward Elgar)

Macmillan, Fiona (2006), 'What might Hans Christian Andersen Say about Copyright Today?', in Helle Porsdam (ed.), *Copyright and Other Fairy Tales* (Cheltenham, UK and Northampton, MA, USA: Edward Elgar)

Macmillan, Fiona (ed.) (2007), *New Directions in Copyright Law, Volume 6* (Cheltenham, UK and Northampton, MA, USA: Edward Elgar)

Maduro, Miguel Poiares (1999), 'Striking the Elusive Balance Between Economic Freedom and Social Rights in the EU', in Philip Alston (ed.), *The EU and Human Rights* (Oxford: Oxford University Press)

Maduro, Miguel Poiares and Loïs Azoulai (eds.) (2009, forthcoming), *The Future of European Law: Revisiting the Classics in the 50th Anniversary of the Rome Treaty* (Oxford: Hart Publishing)

Markovits, Andrei S. (2007), *Uncouth Nation: Why Europe Dislikes America* (Princeton, NJ, and Oxford: Princeton University Press)

Markussen, Bjarne (2008), *Rettshistorier: Barn og foreldre i litteratur, film og lovgivning* (Legal Stories: Children and parents in literature, film and legislation) (Oslo: Unipub)

Marshall, T.H. (1977), *Citizenship and Social Development* (London and Chicago, IL: University of Chicago Press)

Marsling, Jeppe (2005), 'On the Human Rights Hymn' (Copenhagen: Institute for Human Rights)

Martinsen, Dorte Sindbjerg (2005), 'Social Security Regulation in the EU: The De-territorialization of Welfare?', in Gráinne de Búrca (ed.), *EU Law and the Welfare State: In Search of Solidarity* (Oxford: Oxford University Press)

Menon, Anand (2008), *Europe: The State of the Union* (London: Atlantic Books)

Moravcsik, Andrew (2005), 'The Paradox of US Human Rights Policy', in Michael Ignatieff (ed.), *American Exceptionalism and Human Rights* (Princeton, NJ, and Oxford: Princeton University Press)

Mueller, Agnes C. (ed.) (2004), *German Pop Culture: How 'American' Is It?* (Ann Arbor, MI: University of Michigan Press)

Murphy, John F. (2004/2005), *The United States and the Rule of Law in International Affairs* (Cambridge: Cambridge University Press)

O'Leary, Síofra (2005), 'Solidarity and Citizenship Rights in the Charter of Fundamental Rights of the European Union', in Gráinne de Búrca (ed.), *EU Law and the Welfare State: In Search of Solidarity* (Oxford: Oxford University Press)

Olson, Greta and Martin A. Kayman (2007), 'Introduction: From "Law-and-Literature" to "Law, Literature, and Language": A Comparative Approach', 11(1) *European Journal of English Studies*, 1

Ostendorf, Berndt (2002), 'Why is American Popular Culture so Popular? A View from Europe', 34 *American Studies in Scandinavia* 1

Ostrovsky, Aaron A. (2005), 'What's So Funny About Peace, Love, and Understanding? How the Margin of Appreciation Doctrine Preserves Core Human Rights within Cultural Diversity and Legitimises International Human Rights Tribunals', 1 *Hanse Law Review* – also available at SSRN: http://ssrn.com/abstract=716242

Pagden, Anthony (ed.) (2002), *The Idea of Europe: From Antiquity to the European Union* (Washington, DC: Woodrow Wilson Center & Cambridge University Press)

Pagden, Anthony (2002), 'Europe: Conceptualizing a Continent', in Anthony Pagden (ed.), *The Idea of Europe: From Antiquity to the European Union* (Washington, DC: Woodrow Wilson Center & Cambridge University Press)

Papke, David Ray (1992), 'Law in American Culture: An Overview', 15(1) *Journal of American Culture* 3

Passerini, Luisa (2002), 'From the Ironies of Identity to the Identities of Irony', in Anthony Pagden (ed.), *The Idea of Europe: From Antiquity to the European Union* (Washington, DC: Woodrow Wilson Center & Cambridge University Press)

Paulus, Andreas (2003), 'The Influence of the United States on the Concept of the "International Community" ', in Michael Byers and Georg Nolte (eds.), *United States Hegemony and the Foundations of International Law* (Cambridge: Cambridge University Press)

Peters, Julie Stone (2005), 'Law, Literature, and the Vanishing Real: On the Future of an Interdisciplinary Illusion', 120 PMLA: Publications of the Modern Language Assoc., 442

Porsdam, Helle (1999), *Legally Speaking: Contemporary American Culture and the Law* (Amherst, MA: University of Massachusetts Press)

Porsdam, Helle (ed.) (2001), *Folkways and Law Ways: Law in American Studies* (Odense: Odense University Press)

Porsdam, Helle (2005), 'From *Pax Americana* to *Lex Americana*: American Legal and Cultural Hegemony', in Fiona Macmillan (ed.), *New Directions in Copyright Law, Volume 1* (Cheltenham, UK and Northampton, MA, USA: Edward Elgar)

Porsdam, Helle (ed.) (2006), *Copyright and Other Fairy Tales: Hans Christian Andersen and the Commodification of Creativity* (Cheltenham, UK and Northampton, MA, USA: Edward Elgar)

Porsdam, Helle (2007), 'On European Narratives of Human Rights and Their Possible Implications for Copyright', in Fiona Macmillan (ed.), *New Directions in Copyright Law, Volume 6* (Cheltenham, UK and Northampton, MA, USA: Edward Elgar)

Posner, Richard A. (1988), *Law and Literature: A Misunderstood Relation* (Cambridge, MA: Harvard University Press)

Power, Samantha and Graham Allison (eds.) (2000), *Realizing Human Rights: Moving from Inspiration to Impact* (New York: St. Martin's Press)

Rabkin, Jeremy (2005), *Law Without Nations? Why Constitutional Government Requires Sovereign States* (Princeton, NJ, and Oxford: Princeton University Press)

Rahmatian, Andreas (2007), 'Universalist Norms for a Globalised Diversity: On the Protection of Traditional Cultural Expressions', in Fiona Macmillan (ed.), *New Directions in Copyright Law, Volume 6* (Cheltenham, UK and Northampton, MA, USA: Edward Elgar)

Rasmussen, Morten (2009, forthcoming), 'From Costa v. ENEL to the Treaties of Rome – A Brief History of a Legal Revolution', in Miguel Poiares Maduro and Loïs Azoulai (eds.), *The Future of European Law: Revisiting the Classics in the 50th Anniversary of the Rome Treaty* (Oxford: Hart Publishing)

Reid, T.R. (2004), *The United States of Europe: The New Superpower and the End of American Supremacy* (New York: Penguin Books)

Rifkin, Jeremy (2004), *The European Dream: How Europe's Vision of the Future is Quietly Eclipsing the American Dream* (Cambridge: Polity Press)

Robins, Kevin (2006), *The Challenge of Transcultural Diversities: Transversal Study on the Theme of Cultural Policy and Cultural Diversity*, Final report (Strasbourg: Council of Europe Publishing)

Roman, Shari (2003), 'Lars von Trier: The Man Who Would Be Dogme', in Jan Lumholdt (ed.), *Lars von Trier Interviews* (Jackson, MS: University Press of Mississippi)

Rosenmeier, Morten (2001), *Værkslæren i ophavsretten* (The Concept of 'Work' in Copyright Law) (Copenhagen: Jurist- og Økonomforbundets Forlag)

Ruttley, Philip (2002), 'The Long Road to Unity: The Contribution of Law to the Process of European Integration since 1945', in Anthony Pagden (ed.), *The Idea of Europe: From Antiquity to the European Union* (Washington, DC: Woodrow Wilson Center & Cambridge University Press)

Rytter, Jens Elo (2001), 'Judicial Review of Legislation – a Sustainable Strategy on the Enforcement of Basic Rights', in Martin Scheinin (ed.), *Welfare State and Constitutionalism – Nordic Perspectives* (Copenhagen: Nordic Council of Ministers)

Sardar, Ziauddin and Merryl Wyn Davies (2002), *Why Do People Hate America?* (Cambridge: Icon Books)

Scheinin, Martin (ed.) (2001), *Welfare State and Constitutionalism – Nordic Perspectives* (Copenhagen: Nordic Council of Ministers)

Sherman, Brad and Alain Strowel (eds.) (1994), *Of Authors and Origins: Essays on Copyright* (Oxford: Clarendon Press)

Schepelern, Peter (2000), *Lars von Triers film. Tvang og befrielse* (Lars von Trier's Films: Obsession and Liberation) (Copenhagen: Rosinante)

Schepelern, Peter (2003), 'Lidelse i allegorisk univers' (Suffering in an allegorical universe) *Ekko*, no. 20, 26

Sherwin, Richard K. (2000), *When Law Goes Pop: The Vanishing Line Between Law and Popular Culture* (Chicago, IL: University of Chicago Press)

Shore, Chris (2000), *Building Europe: The Cultural Politics of European Integration* (London: Routledge)

Slaughter, Anne-Marie (2005), 'A Brave New Judicial World', in Michael

Ignatieff (ed.), *American Exceptionalism and Human Rights* (Princeton, NJ, and Oxford: Princeton University Press)
Spielman, Dean (1999), 'Human Rights Case Law in the Strasbourg and Luxembourg Courts: Conflicts, Inconsistencies, and Complementarities', in Philip Alston (ed.), *The EU and Human Rights* (Oxford: Oxford University Press)
Stanley, Dick (2006), *Recondita Armonia – A Reflection on the Function of Culture in Building Citizenship Capacity*, A study prepared for the Council of Europe in the framework of the European Year of Citizenship, Policy Note No. 10 (Strasbourg: Council of Europe Publishing)
Steiner, Henry J. and Philip Alston (eds.) (2000), *International Human Rights in Context: Law, Politics, Morals* (Oxford: Oxford University Press, 2nd edition)
Stolleis, Michael (2009), *The Eye of the Law: Two Essays on Legal History* (Abingdon, UK: Birkbeck Law Press)
Sunder, Madhavi (2006), 'IP3', 59 *Stanford Law Review* 257
Sunstein, Cass R. (2004), *The Second Bill of Rights: FDR's Unfinished Revolution and Why We Need It More Than Ever* (New York: Basic Books)
Sunstein, Cass R. (2005), 'Why Does the American Constitution Lack Social and Economic Guarantees?', in Michael Ignatieff (ed.), *American Exceptionalism and Human Rights* (Princeton, NJ, and Oxford: Princeton University Press)
Symonides, Janusz (1998), 'Cultural Rights: A Neglected Category of Human Rights', 158 *International Social Science Journal*, Dec. 1998 – also available at http://www.iupui.edu/%7Eanthkb/a104/humanrights/ cultrights.htm
Tibi, Bassam (2002), *The Challenge of Fundamentalism: Political Islam and the New World Disorder* (Berkeley, CA: University of California Press)
Tibi, Bassam (2004), *Europa ohne Identität? Leitkultur oder Wertebeliebigkeit* (Munich: Siedler)
Tindall, George Brown and David E. Shi (1996), *America: A Narrative History* (New York and London: W.W. Norton & Co., 4th Edition), Vol. II
Tocqueville, Alexis de (1969), 'Author's Introduction', in A. de Tocqueville, *Democracy in America* (trans George Lawrence and ed J. P. Mayer (New York: Anchor Books)
Torremans, Paul L.C. (ed.) (2008), *Intellectual Property and Human Rights*, Enhanced Edition of *Copyright and Human Rights* (Alphen aan den Reijn: Kluwer Law International)
Treiger-Bar-Am, Leslie Kim (2007), 'Authors' Rights as a Limit to Copyright Control', in Fiona Macmillan (ed.), *New Directions in Copyright, Volume 6* (Cheltenham, UK and Northampton, MA, USA: Edward Elgar)
Vagts, Detlev N. (2001), 'Hegemonic International Law', 95 *American Journal of International Law* 843

Verhofstadt, Guy (2006), *The United States of Europe: Manifesto for a New Europe* (London: Federal Trust for Education and Research)

Verschueren, Herwig (2007), 'European (Internal) Migration Law as an Instrument for Defining the Boundaries of National Solidarity Systems', 9 *European Journal of Migration and Law*, 307–46

Ward, Ian (1995), *Law and Literature: Possibilities and Perspectives* (Cambridge and New York: Cambridge University Press)

Weisberg, Robert (1988), 'The Law-Literature Enterprise', 1(1) *Yale Journal of Law and the Humanities* 1

Wenders, Wim (2006), 'Giving Europe a Soul?', speech delivered on 18 November 2006 in Berlin at the conference entitled 'A Soul for Europe' – available at http://www.signandsight.com/features/1098.html

West, Robin (1988), 'Communities, Texts, and Law: Reflections on the Law and Literature Movement', 1(1) *Yale Journal of Law and the Humanities* 129

West, Robin (1993), *Narrative, Authority, and Law* (Ann Arbor, MI: University of Michigan Press)

Whelan, Daniel J. (2005), 'The United States and Economic and Social Rights: Past, Present . . . and Future?', Human Rights & Human Welfare, Working Paper No. 26 – available at http://www.du.edu/korbel/hrhw/working/ 2005/26-whelan-2005.pdf

Williams, Patricia J. (1991), *The Alchemy of Race and Rights: Diary of a Law Professor* (Cambridge, MA: Harvard University Press)

Williams, Shirley (2000), 'Human Rights in Europe', in Samantha Power and Graham Allison (eds.), *Realizing Human Rights: Moving from Inspiration to Impact* (New York: St. Martin's Press)

Winter, Jay (2006), *Dreams of Peace and Freedom: Utopian Moments in the 20th Century* (New Haven, CT and London: Yale University Press)

Index